Truth Matters

Truth Matters

Realism, anti-realism and response-dependence

Christopher Norris

Edinburgh University Press

For Carol and Daniele, Anselmo and Tomaso

Edinburgh University Press Ltd
22 George Square, Edinburgh

Typeset in 10 on 12 point Linotype Sabon
by Hewer Text Limited, Edinburgh, and
printed and bound in Great Britain by
MPG Books Ltd, Bodmin, Cornwall

Published in hardback by Edinburgh
University Press in 2002

A CIP Record for this title is available
from the British Library

ISBN 0 7486 1598 9 (paperback)

Contents

Contents

Acknowledgements

I should like to thank various colleagues and friends for encouraging my interest in the topics here discussed and for helping me to bring this work to completion over the past two years. Alex Miller and Duncan McFarland (in the Philosophy Section at Cardiff) have an expert knowledge of the Response-Dependence literature which has often pointed me in new directions and saved me from ignoring some important contribution that either forced me to re-think certain claims or provided welcome argumentative support. Robin Attfield, through his published work and many conversations, helped to focus my mind on the relevant issues in moral philosophy and meta-ethics while Alessandra Tanesini set me thinking again about Wittgenstein, Kripke and the rule-following considerations. That neither she nor Alex has managed to convince me that this debate amounts to more than a large red herring is probably my fault rather than theirs. Michael Durrant's long-awaited book *Sortals and the Subject-Predicate Distinction* appeared shortly after his retirement from Cardiff and too late for discussion here although it is hard to know just how deeply my ideas have been influenced by his philosophic counsel and authoritative knowledge of debates within the analytic tradition. Andrew Belsey, Pat Clark, Andrew Edgar, Stephen Moller, Kathryn Plant, Peter Sedgwick, and (especially) Barry Wilkins have each of them helped to provide a friendly, supportive, and above all non-competitive working environment. Such conditions are all too rare in a context of ceaseless research 'productivity' monitoring, bureaucratic interference and quality-control mechanisms which offer something like an object lesson in how to damage intellectual morale and suppress the freedom of academic enquiry.

On a happier note, let me also thank my postgraduate students in Cardiff – among them Jason Barker, Gideon Calder, Ed Dain, Paul Gorton, Paul Hampson, Carol Jones, Keith McDonald, Laurence Peddle, Daniele Procida, and Sotos Shiakides – for their good companionship and sheer dedication to the work in hand, often despite severe financial hardship and a whole range of adverse circumstances. As is usually the case (though more so than usual in my own recent experience) the flow of ideas at this level is very much a two-way thing and often leaves the supervisor wondering who should be paying those sometimes exorbitant fees. Anyway I am grateful to them and other recently-completed Ph.D. students (including Christa Knellwolf, Marianna Papastephanou, and David Roden) for no end of stimulating talk and constructive critical feedback. It is a long while now since I thought seriously about leaving Cardiff for a university post elsewhere but decided that itchy feet and the vague notion of pastures new were no good reason for making such a move. There was even a time – the mid-1980s – when I might have followed a large company of British academics on their westward trek and fetched up in a country that has now witnessed the 'election' (or the corporately managed and judicially connived-at levering into office) of President George W. Bush. If such musings seem remote from the topic of this book then readers might wish to keep them in mind when considering what I have to say in Chapters 4 and 5 about response-dependence theory and its bearing on issues of ethics, legality, and constitutional warrant. Most big decisions take on an appearance of inevitability in retrospect but the decision to stay in Cardiff is one that I have never had cause to regret.

Cardiff, July 2001

Note: Slightly different versions of Chapters 1, 4 and 5 have previously appeared in the journals *Frame*, *Metaphilosophy*, and *Philosophy and Social Criticism*. I am grateful to the editors and publishers concerned for their permission to reprint this material.

Introduction

I

In this book I discuss various issues that have come to preoccupy many philosophers working in the broadly 'analytic' tradition whose chief concerns are with epistemology and philosophy of language and logic. Those issues have to do with the debate between realism and anti-realism, that is to say, the question whether truth in certain areas of discourse can be thought of as objective or 'verification-transcendent' or whether – as regards such areas – truth should be equated with 'best judgement' or the deliverance of optimised human epistemic grasp.[1] Thus it is centrally a matter of the truth-conditions (or the standards of assertoric warrant) which attach to statements that are well-formed and perfectly intelligible but for which – as yet – we possess no adequate means of proof or ascertainment. These would include a whole range of statements belonging to the so-called 'disputed class', among them unproven mathematical conjectures, scientific theories that exceed our powers of empirical verification, or historical statements that make some definite claim with respect to the course of past events but for which we possess neither eye-witness testimony nor any reliable evidence that would serve to settle the issue either way.[2] Should we take it – as the realist maintains – that such statements *must* be either true or false albeit unbeknownst to us, since their truth-value is fixed by the way things stand (or once stood) in mathematical, scientific, or historical reality?[3] Or should we take it rather – on the anti-realist's submission – that this claim simply cannot make sense since truth *just is*, so far as we can possibly know, restricted to the range of decidable statements that can be verified or falsified by application of the relevant criteria?[4]

Philosophical opinion is sharply divided along these lines. Realists count it a matter of sheer self-evidence that there have been, are, and will no doubt continue to be a great many truths that we just don't know yet which hold as a matter of objective fact quite apart from any merely contingent limits on our scope of knowledge or powers of epistemic grasp. To which anti-realists typically respond that if we don't know them – and hence cannot manifest a grasp of what it means to assert them with adequate warrant – then *ipso facto* we are in no position to advance such a strictly unintelligible claim. Thus the realist will say that in the case of a statement such as 'Goldbach's Conjecture is true' (i.e., 'every even number is the sum of two primes') the statement must be *either* true *or* false despite our possessing no formalised proof or means of checking its correctness throughout the non-denumerable range of even numbers. So likewise with well-formed but empirically unverifiable conjectures in the physical sciences and also with historical statements – such as 'Napoleon brushed his teeth twice on the eve of the Battle of Austerlitz' – concerning events which went unobserved or unrecorded at the time and are therefore incapable of ascertainment by any means at our disposal. Still, according to the realist, their truth-value is fixed by whatever is or was objectively the case and no matter what the limits of our present-best or even our future-best-attainable state of knowledge concerning them. To which the anti-realist standardly responds that if truth-values are indeed objective in this sense (i.e., 'epistemically unconstrained') then we are forever incapable of knowing anything since truth must be taken to transcend our utmost capacities of epistemic grasp. Moreover this would apply not only to statements of the 'disputed class' but also to that entire range of other statements for which we possess – or think that we possess – sufficient evidence or an adequate proof procedure. Hence the pyrrhic conclusion that 'nothing works' in philosophy of mathematics since we can *either* have objective truth as the realist wishes *or* a conception of mathematical knowledge that restricts the range of truth-apt statements to those which we are able to prove by application of this or that established procedure.[5] The problem is equally acute for philosophers of history or the physical sciences since here also, it is claimed, there is just no escaping the realist's dilemma, that is to say, the impossibility of our somehow having epistemic access to truths which are thought of as recognition-transcendent and hence (by very definition) as standing beyond our utmost epistemic reach. In which case the only way out of this dilemma is to endorse the anti-realist's proposal, exchange talk of objective 'truth' for talk of 'warranted assertibility', and thus make sure to close the gap – so easily exploited by the sceptic – between statements that we take to possess assertoric warrant and the conditions under which we can recognise such statements as holding good by our best means of proof or verification.

This whole line of reasoning will strike the realist as philosophically wrongheaded to the point of downright perversity. After all, she will counter, what can justify the adoption of a theory that flies so strongly in the face of our commonsense-realist intuitions and which does so, moreover, on highly contentious epistemological and logico-semantic grounds? Do we not have much better reason for accepting the massive self-evidence of progress in the physical sciences to date and the fact that such advances have most often come about through theories and conjectures that went beyond the existing observational data or means of empirical verification?[6] And in the case of mathematics is it not more rational to conclude that just as we now possess adequate methods of proof for theorems that were once unprovable (yet none the less valid for that), so likewise there must still be a whole vast range of well-formed but as-yet undecidable theorems whose objective truth-value is wholly unaffected by our present state of ignorance or indecision concerning it?[7] Any theory which argues to opposite effect, i.e., that truth simply *cannot* transcend our best capacities of proof or verification is one that puts the cart very firmly before the horse, or which derives far-reaching sceptical conclusions from a dubious basis in epistemology and philosophy of language. Thus the anti-realist holds that the issue about realism is a strictly metaphysical issue; that metaphysical issues are best engaged through a logico-semantic analysis of the truth-conditions for various orders of statement; that the truth-value of a given statement depends on its possessing such assignable truth-conditions; and hence that any utterance which fails to meet the criteria for warranted assertibility must for that reason be taken to fail the test for bivalent (true-or-false) status.[8] In which case – to repeat – it cannot make sense to postulate the existence of objective truth-values which apply to statements of the 'disputed class', such as 'Goldbach's Conjecture is true' (uttered so long as no proof is forthcoming) or 'the charge on every electron is negative' (uttered at any time before physicists had established that fact). For the realist, conversely, the truth-value of such statements is – and always was – objectively fixed according to whether or not they correspond with the way things stand in mathematical or physical reality. And again, the truth-value of 'Napoleon brushed his teeth twice on the eve of Austerlitz' is decided by his having or not having done so despite our present and (more than likely) our future lack of evidence by which to settle the issue. To suppose otherwise – that their truth-value must somehow depend on our best state of knowledge or evidential sources – is a premise that the anti-realist finds at least plausible while the realist will think it downright preposterous.

II

'Realism' is of course a term that has been differently applied in various historically-shifting contexts of debate. These have ranged all the way from scholastic philosophy – where it signalled a belief in the 'real' (as distinct from merely nominal) existence of universals and other such abstract entities – to the modern conception of scientific realism as entailing the physical or material reality of objects, properties, causal powers, microstructural attributes, and so forth.[9] Nowadays the issue is most often taken up between those who staunchly maintain this latter point of view and anti-realists (such as Michael Dummett) who argue that truth-claims cannot have any purchase beyond whatever we can prove or establish by the best means at our disposal.[10] For the anti-realist it is simply nonsensical to assert that there might (indeed must) be a great number of truths, whether in mathematics, the physical sciences, history, or other areas of discourse, which we cannot at present and indeed might never be capable of finding out. This follows from the basic anti-realist tenet that the meaning of a sentence is given by its truth-conditions and those conditions, in turn, through our capacity to recognise the kinds of situation in which it properly (correctly) applies. Thus, according to Dummett, there is just no way to make sense of the claim that some given sentence belonging to the disputed class must be either true or false – objectively so – despite our lack of any adequate criteria by which to adjudicate its truth or falsehood. For how should we then have acquired the capacity to utter that sentence with an adequate grasp of its truth-conditions or to recognise its usage by others as a usage apt for evaluation in bivalent (decidably true or false) terms? Rather we should treat it as non-bivalent and hence as making no reference to some further, unknown but veridical state of affairs that decides its truth-value independently of us and our limited means of ascertainment. To which the realist responds – once again – that this is to get the matter backwards and to count reality a world well lost for the sake of maintaining a dubious position in metaphysics, philosophical semantics, and philosophy of logic. Rather we should take it that the world exists (along with all its microstructural features, properties, physical constants, etc.) and continues to exert its causal powers unbeholden to us or whatever we may happen to think or believe concerning it.[11]

Such is the case for *ontological* realism as a thesis that precedes and alone makes sense of any claims we might advance with respect to our capacities for gaining knowledge of that ultimately knowledge-independent world. However most realists will wish to go further and assert an *epistemological* thesis, namely, that we are able to acquire such knowledge through certain well-tried procedures of empirical research, scientific theory-construction, and inference to the best (most rational or adequate) causal-explanatory account. Thus any argument – like Dummett's – which rejects this claim on metaphysical or logico-semantic grounds must find some alternative means of explaining why it is borne out by so much of our everyday experience, or again, why science has typically advanced by putting its various theories and predictions to the test of empirical confirmation or disconfirmation. As concerns mathematics the realist will hold that we *discover* the truth of certain theorems, conjectures, numerical hypotheses, etc., through a process that can best be thought of by analogy with the explorer who ventures into unknown terrain and learns to recognise geographical features which may perhaps remind her of previous expeditions into similar parts of the world or may resemble nothing that she has ever seen before. Thus some mathematical proofs are obtained by straightforward extrapolation from existing methods and techniques while others involve a more adventurous exercise of ground-breaking enquiry. However, in both cases what the mathematician discovers are objective truths about numbers, their properties and the logical relations between them which must be taken to hold for all time in all possible worlds and hence to have been capable of proof even when no such proof was forthcoming.

For the Dummettian anti-realist, conversely, we had much better think of mathematics by analogy with the process of artistic invention, or with the kinds of creative-exploratory thought which open up new realms of possibility for the working mathematician.[12] On this view there is no making sense of the idea that any statement 'x is true' where 'x' is an as-yet unproven theorem or conjecture might itself possess a definite truth-value (i.e., be objectively either true or false) despite our inability to prove or disprove it.[13] For it follows necessarily from Dummett's position that such a statement fails the test of warranted assertibility, that is to say, falls short of the criteria specified for statements that we are able to use and to recognise with an adequate grasp of their operative truth-conditions. And since those conditions are strictly a matter of epistemic warrant – of whatever we can prove or justifiably assert by the best means at our disposal – therefore we must take it that statements of this sort are non-bivalent (neither true nor false) pending the arrival of an adequate procedure for determining their truth-value. Such statements would include 'the square on the hypotenuse is equal to the sum of the squares on the two adjacent sides' uttered before Pythagoras produced his proof, or 'Goldbach's Conjecture is true' uttered as of today, 16 June 2001. They would also include a limitless range of well-formed yet undecidable statements in set-theory, philosophy of logic, theoretical physics, the life sciences, history, sociology, and every discipline where informed speculation may always run ahead of the methods and procedures for establishing the truth of any given claim. However – so the realist will argue – this leads to the surely absurd conclusion that mathematical truths are constructed rather than discovered, or that laws of physics (like Newton's inverse-square law of gravitational attraction) should somehow be thought of as having lacked a definite truth-value until such time as they fell within the compass of human intelligibility. To the realist this appears just a bad case of the old anthropomorphic delusion that 'man is the measure' or that truth extends just so far as human beings are able to grasp it on the basis of their given perceptual, cognitive, or epistemic capacities.

Such thinking finds a parallel in the so-called 'weak' anthropic principle advanced by some present-day philosophers of science and speculative cosmologists. This is the idea that unless certain fine-tuned physical constants had obtained (for instance, the ratio of gravitational and electromagnetic forces which allowed the sun to keep burning long enough to permit the evolution of carbon-based sentient life forms) then quite simply there could have been no observers around with the capacity to comprehend them.[14] It is important to distinguish this scientifically plausible version of the claim from the 'strong' providentialist version according to which the universe and all its constituent features came into being *just in order* that we (or other such sentient creatures) should evolve to the point of consciously grasping our place in the grand cosmic process. However – so the realist will argue – there is no support to be had from either version for the idea that any statement concerning those same laws or regularities has its truth-value fixed by the way things stand with our perceptual or conceptual capacities, rather than the way things stand in respect of micro- or macrophysical reality. Nor can it be thought – as in Dummett's logico-semantic rendition of the case – that the truth-value of our various statements (such as Newton's inverse-square law of gravitational attraction or Einstein's '$E = MC^2$') is dependent on our ability to acquire and to manifest a grasp of their operative truth-conditions. For this will strike the realist as just another variant on the Protagorean doctrine of man-as-the-measure, that is to say, an epistemic conception of truth as inherently restricted to the scope and limits of human understanding. Rather we should take it that the world exists and exerts its causal powers quite apart from the best conjectures of physical science and – even more – quite apart from those conjectures in metaphysics, epistemology, and philosophy of language that would purport to undermine the realist case on grounds that possess nothing like such a weight of accumulated scientific evidence.

So there is no reason, anti-realist prejudice aside, for adopting the idea that truth in such matters is epistemically constrained, or that we cannot make sense of any claim to the effect that certain strictly undecidable statements (e.g., 'Goldbach's Conjecture is true' or 'there exists a another solar system like ours in a radio-telescopically inaccessible region of the expanding universe') *must* be either true or false – objectively so – despite our lack of a proof-procedure or means of empirical verification.[15] What leads anti-realists to espouse this highly counter-intuitive view is their idea that truth-values apply only in the case of statements that are effectively decidable by the best techniques or through the best kinds of evidence to hand. After all, they ask, how can we possibly attach truth-values to sentences for which, *ex hypothesi*, we lack any means of determining their truth-conditions and hence any grasp of what would constitute evidence for their truth or falsehood? However we should then have to conclude that mathematicians working on a solution to Goldbach's Conjecture quite literally *have no idea* of what might count as an adequate formalised proof, or that astronomers quite literally *have no conception* of the state of affairs (i.e., the existence or non-existence of a duplicate solar system) that would serve to decide the truth-value of any statement concerning it. Indeed, there is more than a hint in Dummett's work that he subscribes to something like the strong anthropic principle when it comes to the issue of whether or not the conditions of our knowledge can be taken to determine what 'truly' occurred in the past or to affect the outcome of historical events through a kind of retroactive causal influence.[16] Moreover this impression is strongly reinforced by Dummett's argument that it can (in some cases) make logical sense to pray that events either should or should not have taken a certain course despite those events having 'already' occurred – and their upshot thus already been decided – according to our normal working conceptions of time, agency, and causal sequence.[17] At which point, again, the realist is likely to protest that we are straying into regions of abstruse metaphysical and theological doctrine which either find no legitimate support in Dummett's logico-semantic approach or should be seen as raising serious doubts as concerns the credibility of any such approach.

Perhaps this issue should be tactfully set aside as having to do more with certain aspects of Dummett's motivation in adopting such a stance, and less with the kinds of argument put forward by others (and himself) when defending the anti-realist case on purely philosophical grounds. Still there is the question as to whether anti-realism can claim to make adequate sense of our knowledge of the growth of scientific knowledge or our grasp of how the limits on human understanding at any given time may always be transcended by some crucial advance in the range of available proof-procedures or means of scientific hypothesis-testing. The same question arises with respect to Bas van Fraassen's 'constructive empiricist' approach to philosophy of science, one that programmatically restricts the range of statements construable in realist terms to those which concern objects visible to the naked eye.[18] More precisely, van Fraassen would include statements about objects discernible with the aid of 'simple' equipment like optical microscopes and telescopes, but not objects which show up only through the use of more sophisticated image-enhancing devices such as electron microscopes or radio telescopes. In the latter sorts of case, he insists, we should take the far wiser (less ontologically profligate) line and treat such statements as 'empirically adequate', that is to say, as borne out by our best observational evidence but laying no claim to literal truth as concerns the reality of those various postulated 'objects' that figure in our scientific discourse. Thus we are out on a limb – metaphysically over-committed – if we credit the existence of microscopic entities (such as molecules, atoms, and electrons) or of causal forces, laws of nature, and so forth which happen to elude our particular range of sensory-perceptual grasp.

In short van Fraassen's approach, like Dummett's, is one that involves both a high degree of scepticism with regard to the truth-content of our present best theories and – oddly conjoined with this – a strong inclination to treat human knowledge (its scope and limits) as deciding what shall count as a truth-apt statement. Where he differs from Dummett is in staking this position on an overtly anthropocentric appeal to the modalities of human perceptual or cognitive grasp rather than a logico-linguistic argument with its chief sources in Frege and Wittgenstein. It is here that his case is most likely to strike the realist as revealing an extraordinary lack of concern with the kinds of causal reasoning or inference to the best explanation that have characterised the history of scientific progress to date. Indeed it is hard to see how the physical sciences could ever have advanced beyond the stage of naive sense-certainty had they not been willing to overstep the bounds of direct empirical observation and work toward establishing the existence (not merely the instrumental yield) of just such elusive or recondite entities as can find no place in van Fraassen's drastically restrictive ontology.

III

I shall have more to say about these and related issues in the early part of this book. For the rest I shall be looking at one recent attempt to resolve what might otherwise appear an unresolvable conflict between two such deeply opposed conceptions of knowledge, rationality, and truth. Such is the 'response-dependence' (or 'response-dispositional') approach adopted in the main by philosophers of a qualified anti-realist persuasion who have nonetheless sought to meet the opposition on mutually acceptable terms. I should perhaps mention at this point that I find some of their arguments less than convincing and that my treatment will mix exposition and critique in roughly equal measure. However I shall keep these reservations in check for the next few pages of basic introduction to some complex and often wide-ranging topics of debate.

Response-dependence (RD) theory has emerged during the past decade-or-so as a focus of interest in various disciplines from epistemology and the philosophy of logic and mathematics to cognitive psychology, ethics, and political theory.[19] Its starting-point is Locke on the distinction between 'primary' and 'secondary' qualities', or those (like shape, extension and number) that are taken to exist independently of human response and those (like colour, texture or taste) which involve some normative reference to the nature and modalities of human sensory perception.[20] In the former case – so this argument goes – 'best opinion' can play no more than a *tracking* role since any statement about shape, number or extension has its truth-value fixed by the way things stand in reality as distinct from the way that they appear to human subjects who are suitably placed to perceive them aright. In the latter case, 'best opinion' plays a *determinant* (or constitutive) role since what counts as a correct judgement can only be decided with reference to those same perceptual powers and capacities.[21] Thus the truth-value of a statement such as 'this is a triangle' or 'this triangle encloses an area of 22.5 square inches' must be taken as objectively fixed quite aside from our geometrical perceptions or extent of mathematical knowledge, whereas the statement 'this triangle is red' cannot be assessed for its truth-value without taking stock of what qualifies as a normal human response under normal ambient conditions. Or again, more precisely: in the latter sorts of case best opinion fixes the reference of a judgement and thereby determines its truth-value rather than merely yielding an account of what we take to be the meaning of its various constituent terms.

On the other hand – as some would maintain – this doesn't prevent the deliverance of best opinion from *also* playing a truth-tracking role in so far as such judgements must refer to something (e.g., the wavelength-specifiable or reflectance-related properties of colour) which should figure in any adequate account. Hence the 'missing explanation argument' put forward by theorists of a qualified RD persuasion who wish to do more by way of meeting objections from the realist quarter.[22] On this view (briefly) any description of the criteria for correct judgement in the case of colours and other such physical qualities must allow for the existence of a causal link between perceiver and perceived as well as for the various RD-specified conditions that are taken to define what shall properly count as a normal or optimised response. For the most part – as theorists like Mark Johnston assume – this allowance can be made simply enough by building a 'because'-clause into the list of relevant criteria. Thus, according to Johnston, '[s]ubjects are able to sense a family of qualities had by a range of objects only if this empirical generalization holds of them: each of the subjects has a disposition which in standard conditions issues in the appearing of an object having some of the qualities (i) just when the object in fact has these qualities and (ii) partly because the object has these qualities.'[23] Or again, there is a crucial distinction to be drawn between the RD biconditional in its basic form ('*x* is red if and only if *x* is disposed to look red to standard subjects in standard conditions') and the modified version proposed by Johnston: '*x* is disposed to look red to standard subjects in standard conditions *because x* is red'.[24]

In the usual sort of case – this implies – the causal account will jibe with the response-dispositional account since both concern what it takes for a perception to meet the relevant (jointly specified) criteria. Indeed Johnston is at pains to insist that they *must* go together in *all* cases insofar as the causal relation concerned *just is* what evokes the appropriate response in a normal observer under normal ambient conditions. Thus: '[t]here is no conceivable situation in which these two dispositions – if they are genuinely two dispositions – come apart. The response-producing disposition is had by objects if and only if the corresponding response-issuing disposition is had by the relevant subjects'.[25] All the same the 'missing explanation' argument is one that seems to pose a problem for the standard RD position since it allows for their coming apart under certain (albeit untypical) conditions. That is to say, the possibility that even best opinion might get things wrong – perhaps through some humanity-wide restriction of our perceptual or conceptual powers – is one that the RD theorist had better acknowledge if he is not to endorse the relativist notion of 'truth' as whatever gains credence amongst some given community of human knowers or perceivers. In which case the realist might plausibly maintain that any modified version of the RD thesis which meets the missing-explanation challenge is bound to concede her cardinal point with regard to the standing possibility of error in our best perceptions or judgements.[26]

Still the chief claim of response-dependence theory is that it manages to bridge the conceptual divide between realists and anti-realists, or those who assert the existence of objective (recognition-transcendent) truth-values and those who profess to find such a notion strictly unintelligible. This is why the instance of Locke on colours has become such a *locus classicus* in the response-dependence literature. However the debate also takes in a wide range of philosophical topics, from Plato's conception of mathematical truth and his treatment of ethical issues in the *Euthyphro* to Kant's theory of judgement and Wittgenstein's paradox about rule-following as interpreted by Saul Kripke and others.[27] In each case it seeks a new answer to problems that have so far eluded any adequate solution on the terms laid down by traditional debate. Most importantly this theory claims to throw fresh light on certain long-standing issues in epistemology where philosophers have often tended to divide into realist *versus* anti-realist (or objectivist *versus* subjectivist) camps. Thus for some – Crispin Wright among them – it holds out the prospect of a sensibly pluralist or non-doctrinaire approach that would adopt the appropriate criteria of truth or warranted assertibility for each 'area of discourse', these latter ranging all the way from mathematics and the physical sciences to ethics, aesthetics, and comic response.[28] Where the RD conception exerts most appeal is through its claim to provide a good measure of objectivity by acknowledging the standard of 'best opinion' or optimised response while avoiding the kinds of problem that arise when truth is conceived in realist, objectivist or verification-transcendent terms.

Hence the idea that it offers a constructive way forward from Saul Kripke's so-called 'sceptical solution' to Wittgenstein's rule-following puzzle, i.e., his claim that communal warrant (or accordance with a certain shared arithmetical practice) is the furthest we can get by way of providing criteria of truth or correctness for statements like '68 + 57 = 125'.[29] From the RD standpoint such issues are best approached through a detailed specification of the extent to which, for any given area of discourse, best opinion is either truth-tracking or truth-determining. So, in principle at least, this approach leaves room for a realist conception of arithmetic discourse according to which the truth-conditions for any well-formed statement are a matter of objective warrant and in no way dependent on best opinion amongst some (no matter how expert) community of enquirers. However, I shall argue, this hope of providing an adequate answer to the sceptic or the anti-realist is often compromised by the strong inclination of RD theorists to downplay objectivist conceptions of truth in favour of a 'humanised' conception that yields crucial ground on the main issue as to whether truth can in principle transcend our present-best or even our utmost attainable scope of epistemic warrant.[30]

IV

In moral philosophy likewise the RD approach is often advanced as a means of splitting the difference between objectivist and subjectivist or cognitivist and noncognitivist theories. Thus debate turns mainly on the question whether – and just how far – moral values can be treated as analogous to Lockean 'secondary qualities' and thereby secure an adequate basis for ascriptions of right and wrong while also allowing due scope for the exercise of responsible judgement.[31] Here again it is a matter of finding some alternative to the realist view which takes moral values to obtain quite apart from any communal norms of best judgement and the opposite view which takes the appeal to best moral judgement as the furthest one can get by way of justificatory warrant. In Plato's dialogue – the source-text for much of this discussion – Socrates puts the realist case (pious acts are invariably those which the gods approve in virtue of their godlike ability to track moral truth) while Euthyphro adopts something more like the RD position (pious acts *just are* those which the gods approve since the gods' best judgement is itself constitutive of what counts as a pious act).[32] As we shall see there are large divergences of view among proponents, opponents and qualified advocates of the RD approach concerning the objective or response-dependent character of moral-evaluative discourse. However the tendency is chiefly to focus on what counts as an adequate moral response among subjects deemed competent to judge rather than on those salient properties of certain acts, practices, or social systems that render them intrinsically right or wrong by some standard such as their working to promote (or to hinder) the cause of greater human, animal, or environmental well-being. Thus, here as in the arithmetical case, there is a lingering anti-realist bias which often shows through despite the claim that an RD approach is able to accommodate the widest range of discourse-specific standards and criteria.

Nor is this at all surprising given the fact that Wright and others have adopted that approach very largely in response to various kinds of anti-realist argument whose force they continue to acknowledge while seeking to find some *via media* that would preserve more of our realist intuitions with regard to certain areas of discourse. That is to say, their thinking is still strongly marked by the influence of philosophers like Dummett who reject any version of the realist appeal to verification-transcendent truths, and again, by the argument of sceptics like Kripke who deny the existence of objective (practice-transcendent) standards that would fix the truth-conditions for correct rule-following quite apart from what counts as such among members of a like-minded community. There is a similar ambivalence about Wright's idea of 'superassertibility', defined as the set of criteria that have to be met by any statement that is (or that would be) readily endorsed by those in possession of all the relevant evidence, or by those optimally placed to judge under ideal perceptual, epistemic, or other such truth-conducive conditions.[33] This has the clear advantage of not tying truth to our present-best knowledge or means of verification, an argument that runs straight up against the problem of explaining how progress could ever come about in mathematics, the physical sciences, or any branch of enquiry. However it still goes along with a limit-point conception of best opinion – or idealised epistemic warrant – which leaves no room for truths that exceed the furthest scope of human perceptual or conceptual grasp.

In other words Wright's superassertibility-condition is one that makes truth ultimately dependent on the deliverance of those best qualified to judge rather than making the truth of their judgements dependent on the way things stand in reality. Thus it falls into line with other such attempts – by philosophers like Hilary Putnam – to defuse the issue between realists and anti-realists by adopting a long-run epistemic criterion (such as truth at the end of enquiry) that would supposedly meet all the realist's objections to a narrowly verificationist approach while also avoiding any troublesome commitment to the existence of objective truth-values that might lie beyond even our utmost powers of verification.[34] Yet this will scarcely satisfy the realist, holding as she does that the truth-value of any well-formed statement in a discourse apt for ascriptions of truth and falsehood is in no way dependent on the grounds we might have (or might eventually come to have) for asserting or denying that statement. To suppose otherwise is to manifest a confusion between *truth* and *certainty*, the former – she will argue – entirely unbeholden to our perceptual inputs, conceptual powers, epistemic placement, or whatever, while the latter has to do with just those conditions and the warrant they provide for our claiming to know the truth or falsehood of any given statement. It seems to me that this confusion very often crops up in the RD literature, especially as concerns mathematical truth and the status of hypotheses in the physical sciences.

Nor are these issues by any means confined to the more technical or specialised areas of present-day epistemology and philosophy of language. As I have said, they also have a crucial bearing on debates in moral philosophy, in particular the question whether 'best judgement' (i.e., the opinion of those presumptively best qualified to judge) must be taken as the last word regarding attributions of right and wrong. Moral realists like Peter Railton tend to be drawn toward an RD approach insofar as it offers (or appears to offer) a promising alternative to downright subjectivist or emotivist approaches even though they often raise doubts, understandably enough, concerning the idea that best opinion doesn't so much 'track' as itself *constitute* the proper (morally salient) standards or criteria by which such judgements are arrived at.[35] Thus there seems no room, on this account, for the realist view that certain practices – such as racial segregation, ethnic persecution, slavery, or the wanton infliction of cruelty on animals – are intrinsically wrong *even if* they enjoy widespread support among members of some given cultural community, including those whom the community regards as best qualified to judge. Of course there is always the fallback strategy of defining best opinion as that which would counterfactually prevail if those judges were fully apprised of the relevant facts and could also be relied upon to deliver the optimum (most rational and morally discriminate) verdict in this or that case. But then the argument becomes purely circular since best opinion is reduced to a tracking role (i.e., cannot fail to produce the right answer) and response-dependence theory is left with no genuine normative or justificatory work to do.

There is a similar problem when it comes to questions of legal, juridical, or constitutional warrant. Thus an RD approach would seem committed to the view that a body like the US Supreme Court is constitutionally the highest authority in the land on matters of, for example, electoral conduct or state legislature and that its verdicts are therefore *constitutive* of what counts as due process, democratic right, the fair conduct of elections, and so forth. However – as recent events have shown – this presumption is open to challenge should the Court be perceived to have acted unjustly or intervened in such a way as to compromise its own standing (and thereby abrogate that authority) through some biased, partisan, or politically motivated decision. Philip Pettit sees this as the main point at issue between those who adopt an outlook of 'contractualism proper' or 'constitutive contractualism' as their basis for a liberal polity and those who treat the contractualist theory in a more 'heuristic' spirit (i.e., as a useful method for addressing other, more fundamental questions of social and political justice). Thus the question arises: '[i]s a basic structure right or just because it is contractually eligible? Or is it contractually eligible because it is right or just: say, because it has a right-making property like fairness?'[36] Here again the disagreement can be seen as a secularised version of the issue in Plato's *Euthyphro* as to whether pious acts lay claim to that title just in virtue of the gods' approving them or whether they merit (and infallibly earn) the gods' approval just in virtue of their pious nature. In Pettit's words: '[t]he contractualist proper holds that it is right or just because it is eligible. He takes contractual eligibility to be of the essence of rightness. The theorist who uses the contractual method in a heuristic way holds that the structure chosen is contractually eligible because it is right or just. He thinks that if it would be chosen in appropriate circumstances, that is because it is fair or just'.[37] So in moral, social, and political terms a great deal depends on how the debate works out between Socrates and Euthyphro, or – as Pettit construes it – between those who espouse a substantive ('republican') conception of the common good and those of a present-day 'liberal' persuasion who place more emphasis on matters of contractual right and obligation. To this way of thinking 'the *Euthyphro* criterial test goes the wrong way' since, even if 'running the contractual argument may be a useful heuristic for picking out categorical, right-making properties', still 'contractual eligibility no longer serves as constitutive of rightness'.[38]

Moreover Pettit makes a point throughout his book of relating these moral and socio-political concerns to other topics that have figured centrally in RD debate, among them the Lockean issue with regard to secondary qualities, the problem of ascribing a determinate truth-content to beliefs or propositional attitudes, and the 'Kripkensteinian' paradox about rule-following. In each instance he takes due stock of the arguments for a response-dependent approach but enters important qualifications – most often from a realist perspective – at precisely the point where that approach leans over into a full-fledged case for the constitutive role of human perceptions or value-judgements. Thus he comes out strongly in favour of a non-Euthyphronist conception that would allow for an appeal beyond the standards of truth, moral value, or political justice that happen to define any merely *de facto* state of best opinion among those consensually deemed best qualified to judge. And this despite Pettit's equally strong determination to offer a theory of cognitive and evaluative judgement that keeps within the limits of a broadly naturalised epistemology and which yields no unnecessary hostages to sceptical fortune by decoupling the virtues (epistemic and moral) from the kinds of best practice that enable their realisation. Hence his preference for the republican tradition of thought in matters of moral and civic responsibility, that is to say, one that identifies those virtues in substantive or positive terms as opposed to the predominant liberal view (from Adam Smith to Isaiah Berlin) which equates freedom with the absence of state interference or encroachment on individual liberties. After all, '[w]hen we think about what makes for freedom in concrete settings, even what makes for negative freedom, we naturally look for the sort of protected status, the sort of objective and subjective assurance of non-interference, which requires a certain sort of law and a certain sort of culture'.[39] And this is to be had only from a conception of the virtues that accords full respect to the rational autonomy of individuals as thinking, willing, and judging agents while also acknowledging the extent of their dependence on reciprocal ideas of the common good or shared normative standards.

In which case, Pettit argues, we can also best address the problem about rule-following and other such epistemological issues from a standpoint informed by this jointly 'individualist' and 'holistic' approach, one that explains how the 'capacity for thought' requires 'the enjoyment of a certain kind of interaction', namely that 'the thinking subject must interact with other selves or, at the least, it must interact with its past selves'.[40] That is to say, the Kripkensteinian paradox results from supposing that the sole adequate ground of assurance in epistemological matters is the appeal to some privileged first-person state of knowledge either with respect to what *I* mean or intend by following some given rule, or with respect to whatever I can know about other, likewise solitary thinkers when they claim to be following the 'same' rule. However this Cartesian notion falls prey to all the standard sceptical rejoinders from Hume on down, along with the argument that Kripke develops from Wittgenstein, that is, that any such appeal to the supposed self-evidence of certain truths must involve the idea of a 'private language' that would somehow (impossibly) establish its own criteria of meaning and intelligibility.[41] Either that or we are faced with the problem that every first-order rule (like those of elementary arithmetic) will then require a higher-order rule for its own correct application, and that rule yet another higher-order rule, and so on to the point of an infinite (vicious) regress. Thus as Kripke sees it, there is simply no choice but to endorse his 'sceptical solution' to Wittgenstein's sceptical paradox, one that would entail our treating the truth of statements such as '68 + 57 = 125' as a matter of widespread agreement or correctness according to the verdict of communally sanctioned best opinion.

All the same this solution will appear nothing like so attractive if one rejects Kripke's way of setting up the debate and instead follows Pettit's suggestion for an alternative, non-sceptical approach to the rule-following problem. On his account, 'the purely solipsistic subject, the subject isolated from the society of past and present, would be incapable of thought'.[42] And again: '[o]nly by investing other subjects or selves with a certain authority on the reading of the rules it addresses, does it manage to target rules about which it may go wrong: does it manage to target rules that may represent an external constraint on the success of its enterprise'.[43] For there would otherwise be no escaping the Kripkensteinian dilemma, that is to say, the choice between a purely solipsistic (hence unworkable) theory of knowledge and a theory – the so-called sceptical solution – that equates truth with communal agreement and which thereby excludes the very possibility of error on the part of subjects who happen to endorse some community-wide consensus of best opinion.

V

So it is more than just a serendipitous play on words that connects the issue as to whether or not best opinion should be taken as 'constitutive' of truth in matters of perceptual or cognitive judgement with the issue as to whether – or just how far – constitutional warrant should be taken as the ultimate standard of moral, social, and political justice. A test-case here would be the instance of verdicts handed down by judges or courts in a legal system – like those which prevailed in Nazi Germany or apartheid South Africa – where the law has been corrupted in the interests of a brutal and oppressive political regime.[44] It is not at all clear how an RD theorist could find room for the appeal to a conception of natural justice or democratic right that claimed to transcend (and thus to invalidate) the kinds of verdict typically produced by the 'highest' constitutional authorities in any such wicked legal system. That is to say, their only option is once again to adopt an optimising strategy which says (in effect): 'we shall define "authority", "best judgement", or "constitutional warrant" as those terms *would* counterfactually be defined by any court or legislative body that fully respected the basic principles of justice, democracy, human rights, and equality before the law.' But then the legal realist (like the moral realist) will again be entitled to make her point that this leaves no room for substantive claims on behalf of a response-dependent account. For if there is always, in principle, an appeal open to some higher notion of constitutional authority – as opposed to its merely *de facto* embodiment in a given jurisdiction or legal system – then *true* best opinion must somehow be located outside or beyond the sphere of what presently constitutes 'best opinion'. In which case the RD theorist might as well concede that it is impossible to square any strong version of their claim with the argument for truth or justice as something more than a product of consensual wisdom among those duly authorised or deemed fit to opine.

My own view, in brief, is that RD approaches tend to promise rather more than they deliver, and that many of these problems remain firmly in place despite the sophisticated treatment accorded them in the recent literature. Most often the argument works out as a redefinition of 'realism' as applied to some given 'area of discourse', one that allows the maximum scope for judgement in its normative (whether epistemic or ethico-political) role. Hence, to repeat, one can perfectly well claim to be a Platonic realist with regard to numbers, sets, functions and other such mathematical entities just so long as one endorses a 'humanised' Platonism which allows for the part they play in our various knowledge-constitutive practices and which doesn't give way to the sublimated hankering after a realm of objective mathematical truths above and beyond those practices.[45] So likewise with the Wittgenstein-inspired debate about rule-following where RD theorists typically reject any straightforward appeal to the Kripkean sceptical (communitarian) 'solution' while offering no more by way of an alternative answer than the assurance that such-and-such just *is* the way that we standardly ('correctly') respond when set some arithmetical or other such rule-governed task to perform. Indeed this debate bears the marks of a strong Wittgensteinian influence whose effect has been mainly to slew it against any realist conception other than a kind of quasi-realism which meets the sceptic more than half-way by recasting these issues in discourse-relative or response-dispositional terms.

All the same it has provided a focus for some of the most interesting discussions in post-1980 epistemology and philosophy of mind. Thus RD theorists have been quick to register the challenge of anti-realism in various forms, of the Kripkean dilemma (or pseudo-dilemma) about rule-following, and – as I shall argue – the insufficiency of counter-arguments that rest on the Wittgensteinian appeal to communal warrant or customary practice. So this book has a twofold purpose: to lay out the issues along with something of the relevant background history and to offer a critique of response-dependence theory where it falls back to adopting implicitly an anti-realist or sceptical position. One distinctive feature of work in the broadly 'analytic' tradition is its tendency to treat philosophical issues as if they spring fully formed at each moment and can therefore be addressed with a minimum of reference to episodes in their own formative prehistory. It is for this reason that I have made a point of discussing not only the obvious source-texts (notably Plato and Locke) but also a number of other philosophers – from Kant to Hilary Putnam and John McDowell – who have played an important role in defining the RD agenda. It is a job worth doing, I think, since much of this debate has so far been conducted at a fairly technical level that is unlikely to engage the interest of non-specialist readers. I have therefore avoided any lengthy treatment of the finer doctrinal points while referring to them – in summary fashion – whenever this helps to clarify one of the larger philosophical issues. My hope is that the book will do joint service as a text accessible to undergraduates with some basic knowledge of the field and as a starting-point for more advanced discussion at postgraduate level.

References

1. For detailed reference to the burgeoning literature on realism, anti-realism, and response-dependence see Notes to subsequent chapters, especially pp. 93–4. Since this Introduction covers the same ground in summary style I have provided specific references only for canonical texts or those which relate to some particular point at issue.

2. See especially Michael Dummett, *Truth and Other Enigmas* (London: Duckworth, 1978).
3. See for instance William P. Alston, *A Realist Theory of Truth* (Ithaca, NY: Cornell University Press, 1996).
4. See Dummett, *Truth and Other Enigmas*; also Michael Luntley, *Language, Logic and Experience: the case for anti-realism* (London: Duckworth, 1988) and Neil Tennant, *Anti-Realism and Logic* (Oxford: Clarendon Press, 1987).
5. See for instance Paul Benacerraf, 'What Numbers could not be', in Benacerraf and Hilary Putnam (eds), *The Philosophy of Mathematics: selected essays*, 2nd edn (Cambridge: Cambridge University Press, 1983), pp. 272–94.
6. See Chapter 1, Notes 14 and 35 for a representative sampling of the recent literature.
7. For some strong recent arguments to this effect, see Jerrold J. Katz, *Realistic Rationalism* (Cambridge, MA: MIT Press, 1998) and Scott Soames, *Understanding Truth* (Oxford: Oxford University Press, 1999).
8. Dummett, *Truth and Other Enigmas*; also *The Logical Basis of Metaphysics* (London: Duckworth, 1991).
9. See for instance Michael Devitt, *Realism and Truth*, 2nd edn (Princeton, NJ: Princeton University Press, 1991).
10. See Notes 2, 4 and 8, above.
11. See especially Chapter 1, Notes 14, 35, 51 and 54.
12. Dummett, 'Truth' and 'Realism', in *Truth and Other Enigmas*, pp. 1–24 and 145–65.
13. See especially Dummett, *Elements of Intuitionism* (Oxford: Oxford University Press, 1977).
14. See for instance John Barrow and Frank J. Tipler, *The Anthropic Cosmological Principle* (Oxford: Oxford University Press, 1991).
15. I take the latter example from Soames, *Understanding Truth* (Note 7, above), where he argues for a realist conception of truth as always potentially transcending the limits of epistemic grasp or warranted assertibility. See also Alston, *A Realist Theory of Truth* and Katz, *Realistic Rationalism* (Notes 3 and 7, above).
16. See Dummett, 'Can an Effect Precede its Cause?', 'Bringing about the Past', and 'The Reality of the Past', in *Truth and Other Enigmas*, pp. 319–32, 333–50 and 358–74.
17. Dummett, 'Bringing About the Past', ibid.
18. Bas C. van Fraassen, *The Scientific Image* (Oxford: Clarendon Press, 1980) and *Laws and Symmetry* (Clarendon Press, 1989).
19. See Chapter 3, Note 1 and subsequent entries for detailed reference to the literature on response-dependence.
20. See especially Locke, *An Essay Concerning Human Understanding*, ed. A. S. Pringle-Pattison (Oxford: Oxford University Press, 1969), Bk II, Chapt. 8, Sect. 15, p. 69; also Crispin Wright, 'Moral Values, Projection, and Secondary Qualities', *Proceedings of the Aristotelian Society*, Suppl. Vol. 62 (1988), pp. 1–26.
21. See especially Crispin Wright, *Truth and Objectivity* (Cambridge, MA: Harvard University Press, 1992).
22. For a range of views on this topic, see Mark Johnston, 'How to Speak of the Colours', *Philosophical Studies*, Vol. 68 (1992), pp. 221–63 and 'Objectivity

Refigured: pragmatism without verificationism', in J. Haldane and C. Wright (eds), *Reality, Representation and Projection* (London: Oxford University Press, 1993); Philip Pettit, 'Terms, Things, and Response-Dependence', *European Review of Philosophy*, Vol. 3 (1998), pp. 55–66; Mark Powell, 'Realism or Response-Dependence?', ibid., pp. 1–13; Ralph Wedgwood, 'The Essence of Response-Dependence', ibid., pp. 31–54; Crispin Wright, 'Euthyphronism and the Physicality of Colour', ibid., pp. 15–30.

23. Mark Johnston, 'Are Manifest Qualities Response-Dependent?', *The Monist*, Vol. 81 (1998), pp. 3–43. See also P. Menzies and P. Pettit, 'Found: the Missing Explanation', *Analysis*, Vol. 53 (1993), pp. 100–9; Alex Miller, 'More Responses to the Missing-Explanation Argument', *Philosophia*, Vol. 25 (1997), pp. 331–49 and 'The Missing-Explanation Argument Revisited', *Analysis*, Vol. 61, No. 1 (January 2001), pp. 76–86.
24. See Miller, 'The Missing-Explanation Argument Revisited', ibid., p. 77.
25. Johnston, 'Are Manifest Qualities Response-Dependent?', p. 42, fn. 16 (Note 23, above).
26. See especially Peter Railton, 'Red, Bitter, Good', *European Review of Philosophy*, Vol. 3 (1998), pp. 67–84.
27. Ludwig Wittgenstein, *Philosophical Investigations*, trans. G. E. M. Anscombe (Oxford: Blackwell, 1953), Sects 201–92 *passim*; also Saul Kripke, *Wittgenstein on Rules and Private Language* (Blackwell, 1982); Bob Hale, 'Rule-Following, Objectivity, and Meaning', in Hale and Crispin Wright (eds), *A Companion to the Philosophy of Language* (Blackwell, 1997), pp. 369–96; Alexander Miller and Crispin Wright (eds), *Rule-Following and Meaning* (Teddington: Acumen, 2001).
28. Crispin Wright, *Truth and Objectivity* (Cambridge, MA: Harvard University Press, 1992).
29. See Note 27, above.
30. See for instance John Divers and Alexander Miller, 'Arithmetical Platonism: reliability and judgement-dependence', *Philosophical Studies*, Vol. 95 (1999), pp. 277–310 and Miller, 'Rule-Following, Response-Dependence, and McDowell's Debate with Anti-Realism', *European Review of Philosophy*, Vol. 3 (1998), pp. 175–97.
31. See especially Wright, 'Moral Values, Projection, and Secondary Qualities', *Proceedings of the Aristotelian Society*, Supplementary Vol. 62 (1988), pp. 1–26; also Mark Johnston, 'Dispositional Theories of Value', *Proceedings of the Aristotelian Society*, Vol. 63 (1989), pp. 139–74; Philip Pettit, *The Common Mind: an essay on psychology, society, and politics*, 2nd edn (Oxford: Oxford University Press, 1996); Peter Railton, 'Red, Bitter, Good', *European Review of Philosophy*, Vol. 3 (1998), pp. 67–84; Michael Smith, *The Moral Problem* (Oxford: Blackwell, 1994); and David Wiggins, *Needs, Values, Truth* (Oxford: Blackwell, 1987).
32. *Plato's Euthyphro, Apology of Socrates, and Crito*, ed. John Burnet (Oxford: Clarendon Press, 1977).
33. Wright, *Truth and Objectivity* (Note 28, above).
34. See for instance Hilary Putnam, *Reason, Truth and History* (Cambridge: Cambridge University Press, 1981), *The Many Faces of Realism* (La Salle, IL: Open Court, 1987), and *Realism with a Human Face* (Cambridge, MA: Harvard University Press, 1990).

35. Railton, 'Red, Bitter, Good' (Note 31, above).
36. Pettit, *The Common Mind*, p. 290.
37. Ibid., p. 290.
38. Ibid., p. 300.
39. Ibid., p. 317.
40. Ibid., p. 106.
41. See Note 27, above.
42. Pettit, *The Common Mind*, p. 106 (Note 31, above).
43. Ibid., p. 106.
44. See for instance David Dyzenhaus, *Hard Cases in Wicked Legal Systems: South African law in the perspective of legal philosophy* (Oxford: Clarendon Press, 1991) and *Judging the Judges, Judging Ourselves: truth, reconciliation and the apartheid order* (Oxford: Hart Publishing, 1998).
45. See Note 30, above.

Chapter One

Anti-realism, Scepticism, 'Constructive Empiricism'

I

Michael Dummett is a controversial thinker whose main interests are in philosophy of language, logic, and mathematics. Bas van Fraassen is a philosopher who has written about issues in logic, epistemology, and (most importantly) philosophy of science. My reason for yoking them together here is that they have both had a deep and widespread influence on the current anti-realist trend across a range of philosophical subject-areas. What I propose to do first is explain what 'anti-realism' amounts to in these various contexts, then distinguish their respective positions on the main points at issue, and lastly comment on the problems – as I see it – with this whole line of thought. I should say straight off that it is the kind of debate where intuitions are sharply divided and where philosophers of one or the other party very often can't see how anyone (or anyone capable of thinking straight) could possibly incline to the opposite persuasion. My own view is that anti-realism belongs to that class of philosophical doctrines – like scepticism about the 'external world' – which almost everyone knows to be false (including their advocates when off-duty) but which can none the less be made to look plausible by ingenious argumentation. However this is all the more reason to suspend judgement so far as possible and set out the issues with maximum clarity from both philosophical standpoints. Only then will we be in a position to assess their relative strengths and weaknesses.

Dummett is known chiefly for his anti-realist approach to issues of meaning and truth, an approach that grew out of his intensive study of the work of Gottlob Frege.[1] In this account the meaning of a statement is given by its truth-conditions, which in turn derive from our ability to manifest a knowledge of the kinds of situation to which it properly applies. That is to say, our only criterion of truth or falsehood is the capacity we have to verify or falsify the statement under review. So when

Frege holds that 'sense determines reference' Dummett takes this to entail that it is simply unintelligible to posit the existence of objective ('verification-transcendent') truths that somehow surpass or exceed the limits of our best-attainable knowledge.[2] In which case we cannot – or should not – make claims about truth or reality beyond whatever can be borne out by our proof-procedures, information sources, or practices of reasoning on the evidence to hand. Dummett's interpretation of Frege is also much influenced by his reading of the later Wittgenstein on the topic of 'language-games' or cultural-linguistic 'forms of life'.[3] Thus Wittgenstein's famous dictum 'Don't ask for the meaning, look at the use' is interpreted by Dummett as a sensible injunction to cease raising pointless issues about the nature of 'objective' reality and instead to examine the various ways that our talk makes sense in this or that context of enquiry. Indeed we should do well, he advises, to drop the very notion of 'truth', since it carries such a burden of unwanted metaphysical commitments, and replace it with the idea of 'warranted assertibility', or that which we can justifiably assert to the best of our knowledge. This was at any rate Dummett's position in his most influential and widely-discussed book *Truth and Other Enigmas*.[4] Since then he has adopted a somewhat more qualified anti-realist stance, one that makes room for the standing possibility of future advances in knowledge just so long as they lie within the limits of human perceptual, cognitive, or epistemic grasp.[5] In other words it is still a matter of 'warranted assertibility' but now with the express proviso that what counts as assertoric warrant is the prospect that we might be suitably placed to assert or deny the statement in question through some extension to the scope of our knowledge or powers of rational grasp. For Dummett this follows from the twofold requirement that such knowledge should be (1) capable of being *acquired* through understanding of the relevant language or discourse, and (2) capable of being *manifested* through our ability to talk in ways that bear witness to that same understanding. Thus it cannot make sense to suppose the existence of objective ('recognition-transcendent') truths that are thought of as somehow deciding the issue quite aside from our present-best or future best-possible powers of ascertainment.

It is well to be clear, by way of comparison, about just how far Dummett is willing to press with this line of argument. Some philosophers (van Fraassen among them) adopt an anti-realist stance with regard to certain subatomic particles, entities which play an explanatory role in the best current theories of physics, but which cannot as yet be detected or observed. On this view there is simply no need to take a stand on their existence as real-world, physical items just so long as the theory is empirically adequate, that is, well supported by other kinds of evidence or by the measure of straightforward predictive-observational success. Van Fraassen calls this outlook 'constructive empiricism' and has set forth its virtues in a series of brilliantly argued and (at times) sharply polemical books.[6] In effect it amounts to a somewhat more sophisticated version of the Logical Positivists' verification-principle according to which statements can be meaningful (i.e., have a definite truth-value) only so long as we possess some adequate proof-procedure or empirical means of checking them out.[7] On the realist account, as van Fraassen construes it, 'science aims to give us, in its theories, a literally true story of what the world is like; and acceptance of a scientific theory involves the belief that it is true'.[8] For the constructive empiricist, conversely, 'science aims to give us theories which are empirically adequate; and acceptance of a theory involves a belief only that it is empirically adequate'.[9] Van Fraassen thinks that we should be realists only about entities that fall within the range of unaided human perception, that is to say, which show up to the naked eye of a normally-endowed observer rather than requiring the use of electron microscopes, particle accelerators, or other such means of technologically-enhanced observation. With regard to the latter our best policy is to avoid any needless ontological commitments – such as those introduced by realist talk about the whole range of subatomic particles from electrons to quarks – and instead take a sensibly empiricist approach that conserves the observational data while keeping an open mind as concerns the reality 'beyond' or 'behind' phenomenal appearances.

Thus van Fraassen sees absolutely no virtue in the realist's willingness to yield extra hostages to fortune by supposing those particles to 'really' exist quite apart from the various complex technologies that provide our only means of observing or detecting them. After all, 'it is not an epistemological principle that one might as well hang for a sheep as for a lamb'.[10] In which case the realist is clearly backing a loser since (1) he is taking on excess 'metaphysical' commitments which by very definition go beyond the empirical evidence; (2) he is 'sticking his neck out' (a favourite phrase with van Fraassen) beyond the strict call of scientific-philosophical duty; and (3) any risks thus incurred are merely notional – not truly courageous – since he stands to lose no more than the constructivist empiricist in the event of some theory's turning out false under pressure from conflicting empirical evidence. The same goes for causal explanations which invoke 'laws of nature' or suchlike (in his view) occult powers in order to account for observed regularities in the course of experience or scientific investigation.[11] Here van Fraassen is broadly in agreement with a classical empiricist like Hume that nothing can justify a realist interpretation of our everyday ('commonsense') causal talk since, again, it goes beyond the empirical evidence which bears witness only to 'constant conjunction', or the way that certain types of event regularly succeed certain others. So realism with respect to 'laws of nature' is just a version of the *post hoc, propter hoc* fallacy, that is, the logical blunder of attributing causal necessity to what might – for all that we can possibly know – be merely random or contingent sequences of events. Where van Fraassen differs from Hume is in evincing far less anxiety on this score. Thus constructive empiricism requires 'a resolute rejection of the demand for an explanation of the regularities in the observable course of nature, by means of truths concerning a reality beyond what is actual and observable, as a demand which plays no role in the scientific enterprise'.[12] For here again (so he contends) the causal realist gains nothing – and risks nothing – by this wholly gratuitous display of courage not under fire.

Van Fraassen is the latest representative of a tradition in philosophy of science which goes back, *via* the Logical Positivists, to the great nineteenth-century physicist Ernst Mach and his refusal to credit the objective 'reality' of atoms despite their playing a crucial role in the most advanced scientific theories of his day.[13] What chiefly distinguishes van Fraassen's version of the argument is his steadfast – some would say perverse – insistence that realism *must* give way to 'constructive empiricism' at just that point where human observation comes up against its inbuilt perceptual-cognitive limits. After all, is there not something highly parochial (not to say grossly anthropocentric) about treating *human* powers and capacities as the measure of what 'really' exists, or what merits a place in our best current theories of subatomic particle physics? All the more so – his realist opponents would argue – since the greatest advances in natural science (from Galileo to Newton, Einstein and beyond) have most often involved a decisive break with 'naive', commonsense or everyday modes of perceptual grasp.[14] In short, there would seem no principled justification for the idea that science can best get along by imposing an arbitrary cut-off point which counts as 'real' all and only those objects that human beings are able to perceive in virtue of their own physical scale and powers of optical resolution. Thus van Fraassen's approach is open to the charge of erecting a wholesale methodological programme on some merely contingent facts about the way that we have evolved as creatures inhabiting a certain ecological niche and with certain distinctive – specialised though limited – perceptual capacities. Paul Churchland makes the point to witty effect when he asks us to imagine an 'arboreally rooted' philosopher (one Douglas van Firrsen) whose spatial perspective and range of observation would lead him to draw some very different conclusions as to where the line should properly be drawn between reality and empirical appearances.[15]

Dummett's anti-realism has a good deal in common with van Fraassen's constructive-empiricist doctrine though it also differs on some crucial points. Thus he agrees in rejecting any realist approach that would take on excess ontological baggage by assigning a truth-value to statements that involve the existence – or reality – of objects and events beyond those attested by our best available evidence.[16] He likewise agrees in counting it merely a form of 'metaphysical' extravagance to suppose that we could ever (in principle) be justified in asserting the objective truth or falsehood of statements whose meaning we are unable to specify in terms of their verification-conditions or what would count as decisive evidence either way. Where Dummett is less extreme than van Fraassen is in not tying his argument so closely to the radical-empiricist thesis which equates warranted assertibility with those restrictions imposed by the limits of unaided human perceptual grasp. On the other hand his programme is much wider in scope than van Fraassen's, involving as it does a verificationist approach which he takes to follow *by logical necessity* from certain aspects of our shared situation as language-using creatures whose knowledge simply *cannot* transcend the limits of linguistic communicability. In Crispin Wright's words: '[t]he anti-realist challenges the realist satisfactorily to explain how we could come by, and distinctively display, an idea of what it would be for a statement to be true independently of the existence of any means for our determining its truth'.[17] So Dummett's argument is one that puts tight – some would say absurdly restrictive – limits on the range of statements, theories, or hypotheses which can be taken as candidates for truth or falsehood, or even as making any kind of sense on this strict verificationist criterion. For if he is right then a great many others must be wrong in a great many basic beliefs, not least the commonsense-realist belief that there exist a great many objective (verification-transcendent) truths which we just don't know and which indeed we might never be able to find out by any means at our present or future-best epistemic disposal.

Dummett's anti-realism is therefore a thesis which potentially applies to every domain of human knowledge. Indeed he often presents it as a kind of ongoing research-programme unburdened with prior doctrinal commitments but designed more with a view to testing its applicability across various disciplines or subject-areas. Still it clearly figures as a default position or one that he thinks altogether more plausible – less ontologically extravagant – than the alternative (realist) option except in those relatively few cases where the latter can claim adequate epistemic warrant. However it is at just this point that the realist will want to challenge Dummett's argument by maintaining that truth is a matter of objective (verification-transcendent) fact rather than a matter of what we could know when all the evidence is in or under ideal epistemic conditions. Thus – according to the realist – the truth or falsehood of certain disputed statements may well be beyond our capacity to judge, or to offer some decisive evidence or proof which effectively decides the issue. After all, she will remark, there are many items of knowledge that we now accept as secure beyond reasonable doubt but which were once unknown or subject to doubt since we didn't (as yet) have the clinching evidence to hand or hadn't (as yet) hit upon an adequate proof-procedure. So surely we are entitled to extrapolate from this to the rational conjecture that there must still be a whole vast range of such to us unknown or maybe unknowable truths whose objective status is in no way affected by our merely not possessing the means or capacity to find them out. To suppose otherwise – so the realist maintains – is just a species of anthropomorphic delusion, that is, the kind of error that typically results from identifying truth with the scope and limits of human knowledge.[18]

II

There are three versions of this realist case which are worth distinguishing clearly since they carry a different argumentative force. One takes the form of a simple thought-experiment on basically inductive grounds. Thus: just as we can reasonably claim to know more than our scientific forebears about particle physics, molecular biology, the origins of the universe, etc., so likewise we can perfectly well conceive that our own knowledge will appear sharply limited in comparison with some future (humanly attainable) stage of scientific progress. The second has to do with our perceptual and cognitive limits, that is, the fact that we are physical creatures possessing a certain range of sensory inputs and a certain highly evolved but none the less restricted repertoire of data-processing capacities. Here again it is a matter of applying the inductive argument: just as we humans are better equipped for some kinds of knowledge-acquisition than other animal species, so likewise we can readily form the conception of creatures with different, more refined, cognitive powers whose science would far exceed anything attainable by us, even with the aid of electron microscopes, radio telescopes, and other such means of technologically-enhanced observation. Thus, for instance, they might be Martian microphysicists whose optical equipment and neural circuitry enabled them to register events at a subatomic level or, again, Martian mathematicians who could mentally check various proof-procedures whose complexity defeats the most powerful Earthian computer programme. In short, it is the merest of parochial illusions – though one often entertained by philosophers from Kant to van Fraassen – to think that reality must somehow be adapted to the range of human cognitive faculties or the scope of human knowledge-acquisition.

Such is at any rate the realist case according to the first and second lines of argument. However it is a case which still leaves room for the anti-realist's sceptical rejoinder: namely, that no matter how advanced or refined the Martians' perceptual powers, cognitive capacities, computational resources, and so forth, it might yet turn out that they had got things wrong – perhaps fundamentally wrong – at some crucial stage along the way. This is a version of what is sometimes called the 'sceptical meta-induction', that is to say, the argument that we cannot be rationally justified in supposing the truth of our present-best scientific theories (or assuming the reality of the various [e.g.] microphysical items to which those theories refer) since so much past scientific 'knowledge' has proved either false or applicable only within certain specified limits.[19] So where the realist uses inductive reasoning to back up her case for the existence of verification-transcendent truths the anti-realist turns this argument around and deploys the same kind of reasoning to show that no such appeal is open to the realist except on pain of ignoring or suppressing the evidence of scientific history to date. Moreover this sceptical response is always possible so long as the realist rests her case on epistemological grounds, that is, on the notion of truth as a matter of optimal or idealised epistemic warrant. For the sceptic then has a handle for arguing that no such appeal can escape the closed circle whereby 'truth' is equated with 'truth for us' (or for some suitably placed observer/knower) and 'reality' with whatsoever counts as 'real' at some limit-point stage of enquiry. In which case the realist's argument misfires since it supports not so much the optimistic meta-induction (i.e., from our knowledge of the growth of knowledge to the existence of verification-transcendent truths) but rather its sceptical or negative counterpart, that is, from the record of past errors to the verdict that we cannot possibly be justified in drawing any such upbeat conclusion. At this point the realist will typically rejoin that any talk of 'past errors' presupposes our now being better placed to understand what they were, how they came about, and why (on just what scientific grounds) we are now entitled to treat them as errors. To which the sceptic will routinely respond that this still leaves our present-best knowledge open to future disconfirmation *for reasons that the realist has herself put forward*, ostensibly as lending support to her case for progress toward truth at the ideal limit but rather (unwittingly) showing it to rest on the shakiest of epistemological foundations.

This is where the realist's third line of argument comes in and also where Dummett's anti-realist case is intended to have its maximum force.

For the issue is now conceived (on the realist side) as having nothing to with any states of knowledge – actual or ideal – that supposedly justify our talk of truth with regard to this or that subject-area. Rather it is thought of as concerning truths that obtain irrespective of whether we happen to know them or could ever acquire any means of finding them out. And of course this claim is just what is denied (indeed rejected as sheerly unintelligible) by the Dummett-type anti-realist. Thus, for instance, in mathematics there are certain theorems – such as Goldbach's famous conjecture that every even number is the sum of two primes – which, according to Dummett, are neither true nor false since they cannot be conclusively proved despite their strong intuitive claims and their having been tested right up to the limit of existing computational techniques.[20] For the realist, conversely, such theorems are either true or false as a matter of objective mathematical fact and quite aside from any merely contingent limits on our powers, methods, or techniques of verification. After all, it is surely a *reductio ad absurdum* of the anti-realist case that it seems to entail that any statement concerning the truth or falsehood of Fermat's last theorem was itself neither-true-nor-false before the theorem was eventually proved and only then acquired a definite (bivalent) truth-value. The same would apply to other mathematical conjectures, like that which holds that the decimal expansion of *pi* contains (say) a sequence of one hundred consecutive sevens. Once again the anti-realist would place this statement among those of the Dummettian 'disputed class', thus decreeing it to lack a truth-value unless and until borne out through the discovery of some ingenious proof-procedure or perhaps through the advent of massively increased computing power. And once again the realist would flatly deny that the truth-value of such well-formed mathematical statements is in any way dependent on our knowing how to prove them or (impossibly) to check out Goldbach's conjecture for every even number in the sequence up to infinity. Rather they are *objectively* true or false quite apart from the state of our current-best knowledge or the limits on what we might be able to achieve under ideal epistemic conditions.[21]

Dummett takes a similar line with regard to historical knowledge and the question what should count as a truth-apt statement or candidate for ascription of bivalent truth/falsehood. Thus unless we can know for sure what happened at some time in the past – through first-hand recollection, eye-witness testimony, documentary evidence, reliable source-texts, or whatever – then quite simply there is no truth of the matter, that is to say, no objective truth-value that would obtain despite our lack of the relevant data.[22] Now it might well be thought that in cases of this sort (e.g., that of Mark Antony's having sneezed or not on the eve of the Battle of Actium) at any rate one of the disjuncts must be true and the other false, irrespective of whether we could ever come up with any evidence upon which to decide the issue. Such is indeed the realist's position: that their truth-value is entirely unaffected by our state of knowledge or ignorance concerning them and therefore that the law of bivalence holds for statements of the disputed class. But on Dummett's account there is no such appeal to a realm of historical truth or falsehood beyond what we are able to verify or falsify by the best means at our disposal. Rather, those statements lack a determinate truth-value and are hence simply not candidates for a bivalent (either-or) logic whose remit extends just so far as the scope of our various knowledge-conducive methods and procedures. 'For the anti-realist', he writes, 'an understanding of such a statement consists in knowing what counts as evidence adequate for the assertion of the statement, and the truth of the statement can consist only in the existence of such evidence.'[23] And again: '[t]he notion of truth, when it is introduced, must be explained, in some manner, in terms of our capacity to recognize statements as true, and not in terms of a condition which transcends human capacities'.[24] Thus any 'gaps in our knowledge' must also be construed as 'gaps in reality' or regions of the past for which we possess no reliable sources of evidence and which therefore – by Dummett's anti-realist lights – cannot be thought of as somehow deciding the veracity (or otherwise) of any statement we make with regard to them.

According to Aristotle such gaps arose only in the case of as-yet unknowable future events, such as the event of a sea-battle's having occurred (or not having occurred) by tomorrow evening or the end of next year. Any statement made now concerning its future occurrence or non-occurrence should properly be held neither true nor false until its truth-value was decided by the passage of time and the way that things turned out. So in this case – with respect to future conditionals – one had better suspend the principle of bivalence and admit some further, indeterminate value such as 'neither-true-nor-false'. For Dummett, however, bivalence fails not only where we lack knowledge of future developments but also where we don't know enough about the past to say with full assurance or demonstrative warrant 'this happened' or 'that didn't happen'. Moreover, on his account, we cannot even say: 'Well, at least there must have been some truth of the matter that would verify or falsify our statement if only all the evidence were in, or if only we had access to the relevant information-sources.' For this is just the point of Dummett's anti-realism: that there simply *cannot be* such a 'truth of the matter' if we lack any means of deciding the issue on evidence either currently to hand or potentially within our epistemic grasp.

It is worth citing Dummett at length on this point since many readers will (I guess) find his position counter-intuitive or downright bizarre. Thus:

> [r]ealism about the past entails that there are numerous true propositions forever in principle unknowable. The effects of a past event may simply dissipate. . . . To the realist, this is just part of the human condition; the anti-realist feels unknowability in principle to be intolerable and prefers to view our evidence for and memory of the past to be constitutive of it. For him, there cannot be a past fact no evidence for which exists to be discovered, because it is the existence of such evidence that would make it a fact, if it were one.[25]

Now of course there is a problem for the realist if she places too much emphasis on the idea of unevidenced or unknowable 'facts'. For, as anti-realists are quick to point out, a 'fact' is an item of knowledge that has to be expressed (or expressible) in language and which therefore cannot be conceived as existing in a realm of objective truth quite apart from our various information-sources, proof-procedures, investigative methods, and so forth. Thus Dummett's case can be seen as amounting to a version – a logico-semantic variant – of Kant's transcendental-idealist approach to the problem of knowledge. On this view the only adequate response to Humean scepticism is to take it that 'reality' is in some sense a construct of our human faculties or cognitive powers but a construct which cannot rationally be subject to doubt since it defines the very 'conditions of possibility' for knowledge and experience in general.[26] Where the transcendental realist goes wrong – or lays himself open to the sceptic's rejoinder – is in positing a realm of objective (recognition-transcendent) truths which by very definition we cannot know since they are thought of as standing outside and beyond the furthest capacities of human cognitive grasp.[27] However it is clear from the subsequent history of debate on this topic that Kant's 'solution' to the problem of knowledge has most often given rise to sceptical doubts of just the kind that his philosophy was intended to assuage. For if truth and reality are ultimately framework-relative – relative (that is) to the framing conditions of human perception and knowledge – then of course the sceptic can always argue that those conditions are not (as Kant thought) deducible on sheerly *a priori* grounds but are rather 'internal' to the various schemes by which we make sense of them at various times and in various cultural contexts.

Dummett is very far from embracing any such cultural-relativist conclusion. Indeed it is a main plank in his Fregean philosophy of language and logic that the meaning of statements is a function of their truth-conditions and that we couldn't make a start in acquiring language or learning to recognise those conditions if their truth-value were relativised (as thinkers like Quine would have it) to the whole system of currently-accepted beliefs.[28] Still he goes a long way in this direction – like Kant before him – by internalising truth to the methods, procedures, and standards of verification which effectively decide what shall count *for us* as a truth-apt statement or hypothesis. Hence Dummett's anti-realist claim with respect to statements concerning past events, that is, that they are candidates for bivalent truth or falsehood just insofar as we possess the kind of evidence that enables us to reach some definite verdict. From which it follows that the vast majority of such possible statements – those for which we possess no decisive warrant either way – must be treated as strictly neither-true-nor-false since they bear upon an 'indeterminate' region of history where the evidence is lacking and we are hence not entitled to posit the existence of truths beyond our epistemic ken. So if we just don't know (and could not possibly know in the nature of the case) whether Julius Caesar offered up a *sotto voce* prayer to the gods before crossing the Rubicon then it is wrong – a 'metaphysical' delusion – to assume that there must be some objective truth of the matter that is fixed for all time despite our inability ever to settle the issue.

His realist critics find this argument counter-intuitive to the point of manifest absurdity, while Dummett himself has expressed concern with regard to its seeming logical consequence that the 'reality' of past events can amount to no more than a backward projection of our present-day knowledge-constitutive interests and priorities. In some passages he seems to take a fairly moderate 'interpretivist' view, that is, that what changes with the passage of time is the meaning or significance we attach to those events, or the kinds of salient detail and narrative structure that we impose on the 'raw data' of an otherwise inchoate historical record. This version of the argument would probably be acceptable to most philosophers of history and working historians. However there are passages in Dummett where he appears to take the more extreme anti-realist view that *past events themselves* – and the 'fact' of their either having occurred or not – must be thought of as somehow radically dependent on our present state of knowledge or evidence concerning them. This idea of retroactive causation is of course highly problematic and gives rise to a range of well-known time travel paradoxes that have lately been explored not only by philosophers but also by science-fiction writers and makers of films like *Back to the Future* and *Sliding Doors*. Thus, for instance, they involve the surely unthinkable 'possibility' of travelling back in time and committing some act – such as murdering one's own father before one was conceived – that would reduce the whole notion to a logical absurdity. All the same, as I have said, there are essays by Dummett, for example, 'Can an Effect Precede its Cause?' and 'Bringing About the Past', where he is clearly more than half-way convinced that it does make sense (and indeed follows logically from an anti-realist standpoint) to postulate the existence of retroactive causation.[29]

Dummett's thinking here has various sources, among them the Oxford idealist philosopher John McTaggart – who argued for the 'unreality' of time or the existence of multiple observer-relative time-series – and perhaps certain quantum-related conjectures about faster-than-light 'communication' between particles that have once interacted and thereafter remain in a remotely 'entangled' state at any distance of space-like separation.[30] For, according to the theory of Special Relativity, the speed of light is the absolute constant which determines all relative spatio-temporal locations, so that any process of causal propagation which exceeds that velocity will in effect be travelling 'backwards in time'.[31] Also there is a marked theological strain to some of Dummett's reflections on this topic, as for instance when he writes about the temporal logic of an activity such as praying, or whether it could ever be rational (say) for a father to pray that his son should not *already* have been killed in battle or met with some other misfortune.[32] That he finds nothing illogical about the belief that such prayer may indeed be causally efficacious – since presumably God is not bound by the restrictive conditions of human temporal experience – is perhaps an indication that Dummett's anti-realism is motivated as much by doctrinal commitments of a religious character as by 'purely' philosophical or logico-semantic considerations. Be that as it may, there is a good deal of evidence in his writing that Dummett is willing to endorse the idea that past effects may indeed have present causes, or that it can make sense – paradoxically enough – to think of present actions or prayerful endeavours as 'bringing about the past'.

All the same Dummett does show signs of anxiety elsewhere that such thinking might have other, less benign implications, especially when conjoined with certain politically-inspired agendas for re-writing or 'revising' the record of historical events. This problem is all the more acute for Dummett as a left-liberal thinker who has been much involved in public campaigns for the improvement of race-relations and the effort to counter various forms of racially-motivated violence and prejudice. Thus it cannot have failed to strike him that any argument for the unreality (or malleability) of past events might all too readily be taken up and exploited to tactical advantage by right-wing 'revisionist' ideologues or downright perverters of historical truth. To my knowledge the only passage in his work where Dummett explicitly raises this kind of issue is the Preface to his early book on Frege where he records having discovered – almost by accident – that Frege held some repugnant views of a racist and antisemitic character.[33] Nevertheless, he argues, Frege's work in philosophy of language, logic, and mathematics was so technical and hence so utterly remote from his political beliefs that the work – and Dummett's exposition of it – is in no way compromised or rendered ideologically suspect. Other writers have taken a sharply opposed view, among them the feminist historian of logic Andrea Nye, who enlists Frege as her most extreme representative of a tradition of male-dominated logical thought the very nature of which – as she sees it – is to reinforce the norms of a narrow, patriarchal, ruthlessly abstract, and emotionally crippling mindset.[34] Thus Frege's work in the philosophy of logic cannot (*contra* Dummett) be neatly detached from what we know about his 'private' psychopathology and socio-political beliefs. In short, Nye totally rejects the idea that we can or should draw any kind of distinction between the value of a thinker's work as measured by specialised (discipline-specific) criteria and its value – or cost – to himself and others as a matter of humanly-accountable interests and concerns.

However my main interest here is not so much with this particular dispute over Frege and the autonomy of logic as with the general issue as to whether certain fairly 'technical' philosophic doctrines, such as Dummett's anti-realism, can or should be assessed for their bearing on issues outside that specialised domain. As we have seen, Dummett's case is one that claims warrant on linguistic, logical, epistemic, and metaphysical grounds, but which can also be related to a certain understanding of the limits on timebound human knowledge *vis-à-vis* God's omniscient power to survey and comprehend the totality of truths *sub specie aeternitatis*. This emerges most clearly in his argument for the retroactive efficacy of prayer, a thesis that must appear flatly paradoxical when construed from a realist standpoint regarding the fixity of past events, yet which may be thought to pose no such intractable problems when treated in Dummettian verificationist terms. Yet there is reason to think that this idea of retroactive causal influence is one that carries other, less welcome implications, among them (not least) the scope it offers for various kinds of ideologically-inspired historical revisionism. So one might at least question whether Dummett's anti-realism can stand on its merits as a thesis in philosophy of language and logic quite apart from all merely 'extraneous' considerations such as those briefly outlined here. And one can do so, I would claim, without going anywhere near as far as an out-and-out sceptic like Nye in her absolute refusal to separate the work from the life, or issues of logical validity and truth from issues of personal psychopathology.

III

My point is that any argument against anti-realism on philosophical grounds will have to do more than come up with sundry reasons for thinking it an undesirable belief or a doctrine liable to various kinds of abusive or manipulative treatment. That is to say, it will need to show *also* that anti-realism cannot be consistently maintained as a matter of philosophic principle without running into much deeper problems than any that the realist has to face under pressure from the anti-realist (or 'constructive empiricist') quarter. I have already outlined the terms of this debate and will therefore now offer just a brief recapitulation. What the realist typically affirms is (1) the existence of a mind-independent reality whose nature, structure, constituent properties, causal powers, microphysical attributes, etc., are discovered (not projected or invented) through the best methods and procedures of the natural sciences; (2) the existence of objective (recognition-transcendent) truth-values which attach to any well-formed scientific statement and which hold quite apart from the scope or limits of our present-best (or even best-possible) state of knowledge; (3) the belief that mature scientific theories give a true – not just (as van Fraassen would have it) an 'empirically adequate' – description of the way things stand with respect to physical reality; and (4) the additional requirement that any such theory should *explain* the various observed phenomena by offering a causal (i.e., depth-ontological) account which likewise exceeds the restrictive conditions laid down by empiricists from Hume to the present.[35] Anti-realism comes in different strengths, as we have seen, but mostly involves a rejection of (1) since those properties, powers, attributes, etc., are taken as 'internal' or 'relative' to our various theories or classificatory schemes; a denial of (2) since we cannot make sense of 'truths' that exceed our best evidence or methods of verification; a refusal to countenance (3) on the grounds that truth *just is* 'warranted assertibility' which in turn comes down to a matter of respecting the best empirical evidence; and lastly as against (4) a scepticism with regard to causal powers or depth-explanatory hypotheses which views them as merely an unfortunate regression to bad old 'metaphysical', scholastic, or 'essentialist' habits of thought.[36] To all of which the realist will typically respond that if scientific knowledge were indeed thus restricted – or its claims scaled down in keeping with these stringent sceptical demands – then we should be left totally unable to explain how science has achieved a whole range of signal advances that amount to a point-for-point refutation of the anti-realist case.

No doubt this is one of those classic philosophical disputes – like the freewill *versus* determinism issue or that concerning mind/body dualism – where thinkers are so deeply divided that there seems little hope of resolving the question or converting either party to the other's point of view. Still in this case the two positions are clearly defined and to that extent capable of testing against the evidence as concerns their rival descriptive and explanatory merits. Hilary Putnam put the 'positive argument for realism' in a passage from one of his early essays which he has since found reason to retract (or at any rate to hedge around with various sceptical doubts) but which still makes its point with exemplary force. 'Realism', he wrote,

> is the only philosophy that doesn't make the success of science a miracle. That terms in mature scientific theories typically refer . . ., that the theories accepted in a mature science are typically approximately true, that the same term can refer to the same thing even when it occurs in different theories – these statements are viewed by the scientific realist not as necessary truths but as part of the only scientific explanation of the success of science, and hence as part of any adequate scientific description of science and its relations to its objects.[37]

This passage has become something of a *locus classicus* in the realism/anti-realism debate. Thus it is regularly cited by opponents (like van Fraassen) as a cautionary instance of the kinds of problem that the realist must always run into when he tries to explain the 'success' of science in terms which effectively beg the whole question as to just what constitutes 'success' and just what is required by way of scientific 'explanation' beyond the empiricist's plain demand for predictive-observational warrant. Indeed, as I have said, Putnam has himself undergone various changes of mind during the thirty-odd years since he wrote this passage, retreating first to a standpoint of so-called 'internal' (i.e., framework-relative) realism, and thence to a range of pragmatist or 'commonsense' positions which in his view offer the only way out of such pointless 'metaphysical' disputes.[38]

Still we are not obliged to accept this retreat – very largely under pressure from sceptical arguments like those summarised above – as representing a hard-won gain in wisdom on Putnam's part or a belated recognition that the realist argument just won't work. Rather we can take it as oddly missing the point of his own best previous insight, that is to say, Putnam's powerful statement of the case for scientific realism as 'the only philosophy that doesn't make the success of science a miracle'. Of course this would amount to no more than a piece of gratuitous arm-waving were it not backed up by detailed examples from the history of the natural sciences and also by a worked out realist theory of truth, meaning, and reference of the kind that Putnam glancingly alludes to in the above-cited passage. However both requirements are adequately met in the writings of his early period where Putnam develops just such a theory and applies it convincingly to a wide range of scientific case-studies from fields such as subatomic physics and molecular biology.[39] Indeed –

as I have argued at length elsewhere – there is a constant tension in his later work between Putnam's residual realist convictions and his countervailing sense of the need to make terms with a range of adversary viewpoints.[40] At any rate there is no good reason to suppose that Putnam's change of mind was forced upon him by the superior strength of opposing anti-realist arguments, rather than resulting from a kind of attrition – or a readiness to see all around the issue – brought about by constant exposure to them.

Moreover anti-realists, van Fraassen in particular, have a curious habit of adducing examples which on the face of it would seem to count strongly against their own favoured approach. Thus, for instance, van Fraassen invites us to consider the two sentences 'all solid spheres of enriched uranium (U235) have a diameter of less than one mile' and 'all solid spheres of gold (Au) have a diameter of less than one mile.'[41] The causal realist (or believer in 'laws of nature') will say that these sentences differ crucially with regard to their respective truth-values or validity-conditions. The second is a matter of contingent fact, namely, that there is just not enough gold in all the world to make up a sphere that large. The first, on the other hand, is a truth that follows from certain scientifically-established facts about the subatomic structure of enriched uranium, that is, that it will reach critical mass and create a massive explosion when assembled in very much smaller quantities. Early Putnam would have counted this a case of '*a posteriori* necessary truth', that is, the kind of truth which has to be discovered through a process of empirical enquiry but which nonetheless holds as a matter of necessity in this and all worlds that resemble our own in the relevant (physical) respects. So it is distinguished on the one hand from those kinds of *a priori* necessary truth that hold good across all logically possible worlds, and on the other from contingent matters-of-fact (like the relative scarcity of gold) which just happen to obtain in our own or any world where gold is likewise in short supply. Van Fraassen will have none of this causal-realist and modal-logical talk, convinced as he is that we can give just as good (or empirically adequate) an account of the enriched-uranium case while eschewing all reference to causal powers, microstructural features, or other such 'occult' hypotheses. However there is something distinctly perverse about a theory that raises this self-denying ordinance to a high point of philosophic principle, thus rejecting any inference to the best (most rational) explanation as to why there just cannot, in the nature of things, be a sphere of that size and of that physical composition.

As with many of his arguments this results partly from van Fraassen's adherence to the orthodox quantum-theoretical view according to which any 'hidden-variables' theory (i.e., any appeal to 'common-cause' explanations) will at best merely match the empirical data and at worst (if realistically construed) give rise to additional problems like that of faster-than-light interaction between widely separated particles. Thus 'as a practical maxim, the principle of the common cause may well be operative in science – but not as a demand for explanation which would produce the metaphysical baggage of hidden parameters that carry no new empirical import'.[42] Also he takes it that such explanations are deterministic in character and thus apply only (if at all) to macrophysical objects and events. That is, they can have no valid application in the quantum-physical domain since here – according to the orthodox theory – everything is a matter of intrinsic probability (rather than mere lack of knowledge or uncertainty on our part) which firmly rules out any explanation along 'classical' determinist lines. In Putnam's case likewise the change of mind in his later work goes along with a growing emphasis on the problems that quantum mechanics is assumed to create for a realist and causal-explanatory approach to issues in philosophy of science.[43] And this despite the fact – as both he and van Fraassen would readily acknowledge – that orthodox quantum theory has as yet come up with no remotely adequate proposal for explaining how and where the transition occurs from indeterminate quantum states to the realm of macrophysical reality where we just don't witness such weird phenomena as Schrödinger's 'superposed' (dead-and-alive or neither-dead-nor-alive) cat.[44]

So there is – to repeat – something odd about an argument which takes these unresolved (maybe unresolvable) issues from orthodox quantum theory and erects them into a full-scale case against causal realism and inference to the best explanation. At any rate van Fraassen can scarcely be justified in appealing to the probabilistic character of events at the subatomic (quantum) level in support of his refusal to apply such a causal explanation to the claim that there cannot anywhere exist a sphere of enriched uranium more than one mile in diameter. For whatever the presumptive probability-weighting that any *single* atom in the sphere will (or will not) decay within a given period of time – the half-life of enriched uranium – still it is a fact that beyond a certain volume it will reach critical mass and thus (unlike the sphere of gold) blow itself and a good deal else to smithereens. My point in all this is that one should not be over-impressed by arguments for anti-realism (or constructive empiricism) which extrapolate too quickly from the quantum to the macrophysical domain. For those arguments get things curiously back-to-front by endorsing a deeply problematical theory – orthodox quantum mechanics – and deploying it as knock-down 'evidence' against some of the best-tried methods and procedures of physical science. Besides, there exists an alternative account (Bohm's hidden-variables theory) which perfectly matches the established quantum predictive-observational results – thus meeting van Fraassen's empiricist requirements – yet which also delivers an intelligible realist and causal-explanatory picture with no such burden of unresolved conceptual dilemmas.[45] That van Fraassen and Putnam reject this solution is I think more a matter of orthodox prejudice (or anti-realist inclination) than a verdict forced upon them by the sheer weight of quantum-physical evidence. In Putnam's case this is all the more striking for his having come up at an earlier stage with such powerful arguments for causal realism as the only theory which didn't make the success of science a downright miracle.

Quantum anti-realism has this much in common with its various positivist, empiricist, or instrumentalist precursor movements in the history and philosophy of science. That is to say, it mistakes our *present lack of knowledge* with regard to certain aspects of microphysical reality for the *absolute in-principle impossibility* that we could ever achieve a more complete understanding or one that would justify our taking a realist view of those items (such as subatomic particles) that figure in our current best theories. This was the main point at issue between Einstein and Bohr when the former insisted – and the latter denied – that there must be some deep further fact about quantum mechanics that would finally resolve the measurement-problem and (most importantly for Einstein) allow for the assignment of objective truth-values to statements concerning conjugate variables such as particle position and momentum.[46] It is mostly assumed – on the orthodox account – that Bohr came off best in these debates and hence that any Bohm-type alternative theory which claims to provide a more 'complete' interpretation must be ruled out as conflicting with the range of established predictive-observational data. This assumption was bolstered by von Neumann's famous mathematical 'proof' that no hidden-variables theory could possibly match those data without creating yet further (strictly insoluble) interpretative problems.[47] It was also at one time considered to gain strong support from Bell's demonstration that any such theory would *either* be in conflict with the basic principles of quantum mechanics *or* involve certain classically-unthinkable consequences such as nonlocal causality or superluminal action-at-a-distance.[48] Yet there is now general acceptance that von Neumann's proof was conceptually flawed and that Bell, so far from rejecting the causal-realist alternative, in fact declared strongly in its favour and thought (like Bohm) that nonlocality was a small price to pay in comparison with the various conceptual dilemmas imposed by the orthodox theory.[49]

So it is far from clear why an erstwhile realist like Putnam should take those dilemmas as simply inescapable and, moreover, as requiring that realism be abandoned (or at any rate heavily qualified) not only with respect to quantum phenomena but also with respect to macrophysical objects and events. After all, even Bohr acknowledged that there *must* be some cut-off point on the micro-to-macro scale at which quantum effects such as superposition or wave/particle dualism gave way to determinate (classically decidable) states such as position, momentum, or – *pace* van Fraassen – the physical necessity that a lump of enriched uranium will either explode or not explode depending on whether its compacted volume has reached critical mass. That the orthodox theory has conspicuously failed to explain how or where that line can be drawn is among the most powerful arguments against it and in favour of Bohm's alternative. Also it is reason for looking askance at any sceptically inclined philosophy of science, such as van Fraassen's, which derives far-reaching consequences from the 'evidence' of orthodox quantum theory. The same applies to any approach, like Putnam's, which finds itself driven to kindred conclusions – in his case, one suspects, somewhat against the residual realist grain – through acceptance of that same orthodox account. In both cases there is a curious tendency to ignore the single most vexing dilemma with quantum mechanics – the measurement-problem – and thus to assume that any limits on our knowledge encountered in the microphysical domain must somehow carry across and entail corresponding limits at the macrophysical level.[50] But this is a wholly unwarranted assumption even if – as remains very much open to doubt – the orthodox theory is 'complete' (or incapable of a Bohm-type realist reinterpretation) as applied to quantum-physical phenomena.

One argument that realists are wont to bring up in this context is that scientific knowledge has typically advanced through certain well-defined stages of increasing rational confidence with regard to the existence of such recondite entities as molecules, atoms, electrons, neutrinos, or quarks. Thus, for instance, the atomist hypothesis starts out with the purely speculative claims of the ancient Greek atomists; acquires a somewhat greater (though still highly speculative) measure of explanatory power among early-modern 'corpuscularian' natural philosophers; assumes a decisive theoretical role with the advent of Dalton's revolution in chemistry; is further borne out by its detailed specification in Mendeleev's Periodic Table of the Elements; and eventually – despite the doubts expressed by sceptics from Mach to van Fraassen – arrives at a stage where the reality of atoms is not only a basic presupposition of physics but also a truth confirmed by observation through electron microscopes or manipulation by means of nanotechnology.[51] Corresponding to these stages is the history of changing attitudes (or degrees of belief) which scientists and philosophers have been justified – or rationally warranted –

in adopting toward the atomist hypothesis. Thus the sequence goes, roughly speaking, from noncommittal entertainment of a far-out conjecture to qualified acceptance on reasoned (though still conjectural) grounds, and thence through various subsequent stages of instrumentalist, positivist, empiricist, and lastly full-fledged realist commitment. This story could of course be repeated in much the same form with respect to molecules though the details would change – or the chronology shift toward recent, present-day, or (indeed) future developments – in the case of subatomic particles such as electrons, positrons, neutrinos, and quarks. Still the main point holds: that progress in science has most often gone along with this kind of steadily increasing *and rationally justified* confidence in the reality – as opposed to the heuristic or merely instrumentalist role – of suchlike 'unobservable' items.

Hence the strong reluctance among physicists like Einstein, Schrödinger, Bell, Bohm and others to accept (by orthodox fiat) that quantum mechanics necessarily entailed a drastic, irreversible break with the history of scientific progress to date. Hence also, as I have argued, the dubious logic of a case such as van Fraassen's which extrapolates from certain unresolved problems with orthodox quantum theory in order to make realism look metaphysically extravagant by comparison with constructive empiricism, thereby (in effect) casting doubt on that entire well-documented history. The same can be said of Dummett's anti-realist programme, despite its different logico-linguistic orientation and its adopting what seems a more modest, that is, less doctrinally committed approach. For in his case also there is a standing presumption that truth with respect to any given subject-domain is always a metaphysically-loaded notion, one that exceeds the verificationist appeal to warranted assertibility, and should therefore be confined to that relatively narrow class of statements for which we possess (or could come to possess) some decisive means of ascertainment. Otherwise we have to do with statements of the so-called 'disputed class', statements that lack any truth-value despite their appearance of making a claim which must be objectively true or false quite apart from such issues concerning the extent of our present-best knowledge. Thus – to take an aptly-chosen example from Scott Soames – the realist would assert that there *must* be some truth of the matter (albeit unbeknownst to us) as regards the existence or non-existence of a solar system in some remote part of the expanding universe beyond radio-telescope reach.[52] And of course the anti-realist would deny this claim as one that could not possibly possess any kind of epistemic warrant and must therefore be taken as belonging to the 'disputed' (i.e., non-bivalent) class.

It seems to me that the realist is right about this and likewise about any number of well-formed statements – scientific, mathematical, historical, and so on – whose truth-value we are unable to determine for various reasons but of which we can say (unequivocally affirm) that they are *either* true *or* false as a matter of objective necessity. No doubt a more adequate response to Dummett would need to follow his own prescription by testing the scope and limits of realism in these and other specific areas of enquiry. Thus, for instance, Dummett has a strong case for maintaining his anti-realist approach when it comes to human dispositional attributes or aspects of moral character (like courage) where we don't have evidence to back them up since, so far as we know, the person in question has not been tested in the right sorts of circumstance.[53] So if Jones has had a pretty easy life up to now and never been placed in any kind of threatening or morally challenging situation then the statement 'Jones is courageous!' can fairly be construed as lacking an objective (verification-transcendent) truth-value. That is to say, it is not merely that we (his acquaintances) have no reliable evidence to go on but also that Jones himself is unable to say hand-on-heart 'I'm courageous!', since the virtue in question is of a kind that can only exist – or be properly self-attributed – when realised under suitable conditions. So in this sort of case, where moral qualities or attributes are concerned, the anti-realist has a strong point and the realist will have her work cut out if she takes an adversary line.

However she will be on much firmer ground in denying that the same argument applies to dispositional properties of a physical kind such as the fragility of glass, the solubility of gold in dilute nitric acid, or the tendency of phosphorus to ignite when exposed to friction-generated heat in the presence of oxygen and absence of conditions (like its having been just previously plunged in water) that would affect the outcome.[54] Some philosophers – van Fraassen among them – regard such talk of causal 'dispositions' (realistically construed) as just another showing of the quaint belief in occult 'forces' presumed to explain this or that feature of human experience.[55] Hence Richard Rorty's *ne plus ultra* version of the anti-realist approach, namely his idea that 'the notion of reality as having a "nature" to which it is our duty to correspond is simply one more variant of the notion that the gods can be placated by chanting the right words'.[56] So the realist would be lapsing into primitive habits of thought if she supposed that causal explanations might appeal to certain microphysical attributes – the molecular structure of glass or the subatomic structure of gold, nitric acid, phosphorus, or oxygen – so as to account for the above-mentioned phenomena. This comports with van Fraassen's preference for avoiding any recourse to modal or subjunctive-conditional locutions – 'such-and-such *would* have happened had such-and-such conditions obtained' – insofar as these are taken to entail the existence of properties (causal powers) that exceed the strict empiricist remit. In Dummett's work also there is a strong suggestion that the case with causal explanations of this sort is analogous to the case with avowals of moral character, temperament, or virtue like 'Jones is courageous!' Thus both require that we draw a clear line between statements borne out by the empirical evidence and statements which lack any truth-value for want of empirical confirmation. But then there could be no legitimate appeal to *any* kind of causal-explanatory theory in the physical sciences beyond what is allowed for on the Humean account of 'constant conjunction' or observed regularity. Which of course is no 'explanation' whatsoever, given Hume's idea of inductive reasoning as a flagrant instance of the *post hoc, propter hoc* fallacy. Rather – as the realist will be quick to remark – it amounts to a full-scale sceptical argument against the validity of causal explanation in general and thus looks very like a *reductio ad absurdum* of the whole empiricist position.

IV

There is a passage from one of van Fraassen's more polemical essays which links up in an interesting way with Dummett's example of courage as an attribute that has no reality (or assignable truth-value) beyond its observable manifestation under the right conditions. The passage is worth quoting at length since it shows very clearly how anti-realism trades on a regular confusion between the issue of what is objectively the case quite aside from our knowledge concerning it and what we can justifiably assert on the best evidence to hand. Thus:

> [i]f I believe a theory to be true and not just empirically adequate, my risk of being shown wrong is exactly the risk that the weaker, entailed belief will conflict with actual experience. Meanwhile, by avowing the stronger belief, I place myself in the position of being able to answer more questions, of having a richer, fuller picture of the world . . . But, since the extra opinion is not additionally vulnerable, the risk is – in human terms – illusory, and *therefore so is the wealth*. It is but empty strutting and posturing, this display of courage not under fire and avowal of additional resources that cannot feel the pinch of misfortune any earlier.[57]

What is remarkable here is the impassioned tone of van Fraassen's address – despite that archly ironic final sentence – and his suggestion that the realist is *morally* (as well as metaphysically and logically) at fault in presuming to occupy the high ground in these debates about scientific knowledge. For if the situation is indeed as it appears from a constructive-empiricist standpoint then anyone who espouses realism with respect (say) to subatomic entities, causal dispositions, microphysical structures, and so forth, is gaining no more than he truly deserves for taking such a merely notional 'risk'. In short, he is a character like Dummett's Jones whose courage has never been put to the test, or again, more to the point, like Shakespeare's Ensign Pistol in *Henry the Fifth* whose braggadocio (or 'empty strutting and posturing') is a sure sign that he lacks any such quality. All the same van Fraassen's rhetorical flourish might prompt us to question whether this is not a case of the pot calling the kettle black, or the boot belonging firmly on the other foot. That is to say, there is something excessively strained and paradoxical about his claim that a commitment to the reality of those items that figure in our current-best scientific theories (and to the truth of statements concerning them) is at best a kind of Dutch courage and at worst a kind of skulking behind the lines while others more bravely face up to the absence of grounds for indulging any such delusive belief. After all, on van Fraassen's own account, the realist stance is one that leaves us 'in the position of being able to answer more questions, of having a richer, fuller picture of the world'.[58] In his view that picture involves assumptions which cannot stand up to critical scrutiny since they go beyond anything remotely defensible on constructive-empiricist grounds. Yet it is odd to say that this 'extra opinion' (i.e., the realist commitment) is not 'additionally vulnerable', that the risk involved 'is – in human terms – illusory', and that therefore so is the imagined 'wealth' that supposedly accrues from this 'richer, fuller picture of the world'. For the realist *does* take an additional risk in flouting the constructive empiricist's veto on existence-claims that exceed the range of direct observational evidence or the anti-realist's veto on ascriptions of objective truth-value which exceed those of warranted assertibility. But she does so *not*, as van Fraassen would have it, out of some merely redundant display of 'courage not under fire' or boldness that cannot 'feel the pinch of misfortune' any more than is felt by the cautious adherent to an outlook of constructive empiricism. Rather she accepts that there *is* an extra risk involved – that of being ultimately proved wrong in this stronger ontological commitment – but that such is the inevitable cost to be borne by anyone (scientist or philosopher) who wishes their beliefs to be put to the test rather than hedged around with protective disclaimers.

Thus it is simply not the case, as van Fraassen asserts, that 'if I believe a theory to be true and not just empirically adequate, my risk of being shown wrong is exactly the risk that the weaker, entailed belief will conflict with actual experience'.[59] For this is to pre-judge the issue on terms laid down by the constructive empiricist, that is, on the assumption that it cannot make sense to suppose the existence of objective truth-values or to think that there might be aspects of reality that elude our best-attainable methods of proof or verification. I think that critics of this doctrine are right when they charge it with adopting just the kind of shifty compromise tactic that Osiander first devised in his Preface to Copernicus's *De Revolutionibus*, and that Galileo was reluctantly persuaded to accept by the iron fist of papal authority in the velvet glove of Cardinal Bellarmine's accommodating ruse.[60] That is, it amounts to a secularised (and hence an oddly under-motivated) version of the strategy forced upon early modern science by the need to avoid a head-on collision with the dictates of orthodox religious faith. In its original form this strategy entailed giving up any claim to truth as regards the heliocentric hypothesis and treating it rather as a theory which professed no more than to 'save the appearances', or to match the given observational data while remaining diplomatically unconcerned with the reality 'behind' those appearances. Since then it has re-emerged in various guises, some of them – as in the case of Pierre Duhem – still bearing the mark of a strong theological persuasion, while others (from Mach, *via* the Logical Positivists, to van Fraassen) would clearly repudiate any such idea of extraneous doctrinal commitment.[61] With Dummett, as I have said, there is a similar case to be made when he argues from the limits of human knowledge (construed in verificationist terms) to the logical necessity of accepting an anti-realist position which equates those limits with the range of statements to which truth-values can properly be assigned. However my point is that these various doctrines involve a degree of scepticism which can scarcely be accounted for except in terms of some predisposed aversion to the very idea that science has to do with objective truths which we are sometimes (not always) able to discover through the best methods of disciplined enquiry and inference to the most rational explanation.

Then again, there is the case of Paul Feyerabend who seems (characteristically) to have swung right across from one to the other position on this issue. Thus in Feyerabend's early writing one finds a whole series of polemical attacks on the notion that science should rest content with an appeal to the observational evidence or an empiricist approach that in principle abjures any risky commitment to the objective truth-value of statements concerning, for example, the nature of quantum-physical reality. He is particularly fierce against the orthodox (Copenhagen) quantum theory with its resolute refusal to venture any answer to these questions beyond what is empirically borne out by the range of 'uninterpreted' measurements and predictions. Worst of all – according to

Feyerabend – is the verificationist proposal to abandon a bivalent logic of truth and falsehood in response to any problems or anomalies thrown up by those same quantum data. 'It is evident,' he writes, 'that this sly procedure is only one (the most "modern" one) of the many devices that have been invented for the purpose of saving an incorrect theory in the face of refuting evidence and that, consistently applied, it must lead to the arrest of scientific progress and to stagnation.'[62] In other words it is a handy device – like Osiander's trick with the Copernican theory or Bellarmine's advice to Galileo – for pre-empting any awkward conflicts that might arise if one took those hypotheses at face (realist) value rather than assessing them merely in terms of their empirical adequacy. Yet in his later work, as a self-professed 'epistemological anarchist', Feyerabend famously argues that Galileo fudged the evidence in various ways, that the Church authorities were justified (by their own theologico-political lights) in opposing any realist construal of the evidence, and that it is only in the smugness of orthodox scientific hindsight that we regard Galileo as a hard-pressed champion of truth and reason against the forces of religious bigotry. Indeed he goes so far as to urge, in an open letter, that the Church should even now stick to its doctrinal guns and not cave in under pressure to recant its original edict.[63]

This might seem strangely at odds with Feyerabend's earlier position, that is, his espousal of a realist approach that demands a full commitment to bivalent (objective) truth-values and which – to repeat – finds no room for any 'sly procedure . . . invented for the purpose of saving an incorrect theory in the face of refuting evidence'. However his apparent *volte-face* is readily explained by the fact that Feyerabend's 'realism' was always adopted more on pragmatic or strategic grounds than as a matter of philosophic principle. Thus when he excoriates the notion of 'saving appearances' – for example, by renouncing realism or bivalent logic – as one that inevitably leads to the 'arrest of scientific progress and to stagnation' what Feyerabend chiefly objects to is the missed opportunity for genuine dispute among the maximum range of beliefs-held-true by advocates of different (strictly incommensurable) theories. In other words it is a pretext for maintaining that scientific 'truths' are as many and various as the clashes of belief between believers in astronomy and astrology, or 'orthodox' (Western) medical science and faith-healing, or meteorology and raindance ritual as a means of ensuring the best chances of a profitable harvest. What is nowhere involved is the status of those theories conceived in terms of objective (verification-transcendent) truth or falsehood. This is why Feyerabend can veer right across to treating the issue of Galileo *versus* the Catholic Church as a question that might just as well be decided by the interests of social stability, that is, what involved least challenge or disruption to the currency of accepted belief, as by any appeal to the notional reality 'behind' empirical appearances. It is also why his arguments have exerted such a widespread appeal among social constructivists, cultural relativists, and advocates of the (so-called) 'strong programme' in science studies and the sociology of knowledge.[64]

This all sheds a very different light on van Fraassen's idea that scientific realism amounts to no more than 'empty strutting and posturing, [a] display of courage not under fire and avowal of additional resources that cannot feel the pinch of misfortune any earlier'.[65] For one thing it makes the point that anti-realism goes along very nicely with a readiness to endorse doctrinal positions – like that of the Catholic Church – which rely more on suasive techniques (or the presence of an ideological thought-police) than on standards of truth or rational inference to the best explanation. For another, it shows how easily the tables can be turned so as to cast the realist in the role of dogmatic upholder of orthodox 'truth' and the sceptic – or constructive empiricist – as one who sensibly avoids such dogmatic commitments and acknowledges the non-finality of scientific knowledge as we currently regard it. Yet of course it is just the realist's point that our beliefs in this domain always stand open to correction since their truth or falsity is an objective matter and hence in no way decided by the limits of our present-best understanding or verification-procedures. Still less is it dependent on those various ideological motivating interests which strong sociologists typically treat as the deciding factor in cases of dispute between rival scientific theories or paradigms.[66] For this is to embrace a thoroughgoing version of the sceptical-relativist doctrine that truth *just is* whatever counts as such by the interpretative lights of some dominant consensus, community, or interest-group.

At any rate the example of Galileo *versus* the Catholic Church should give pause to those – among them neo-pragmatists like Rorty – who claim that such thinking promotes a more open, dialogical exchange of views among parties to the ongoing 'cultural conversation'. In fact it is more likely, on this evidence, to work out as an argument in favour of just those communities which have the power to impose their convictions, whether through a range of well-tried suasive techniques or by sheer *force majeure* with punitive sanctions attached. Thus Rorty's seemingly benign appeal to the manifest virtues of 'North-Atlantic postmodern bourgeois liberal pragmatist' culture – virtues which he takes to be best embodied in present-day US society – is one that may well have a different (more threatening) ring to those outside the charmed circle of accepted values and beliefs.[67] Of course these issues are fairly remote from the arguments brought by van Fraassen in support of his constructive-empiricist approach, or by Dummett in making the case for anti-realism on 'technical' (i.e., logico-semantic) grounds. All the same, there is room for doubt when they both assert – van Fraassen more explicitly – that realism involves a false display of 'courage not under fire' or a risk of merely notional 'extra resources' (epistemic and moral) whose credit is overdrawn from the outset. For this is to get the matter back-to-front insofar as the realist *does* take additional risks by staking her claim on the existence of entities, microphysical properties, causal powers, and the objective truth-value of statements concerning them. No doubt those risks will appear just so much 'empty strutting and posturing' from the viewpoint of a constructive-empiricist approach which rejects any thought of a reality 'beyond' observational appearances, or a Dummett-type anti-realist approach that finds no use for any notion of truth beyond the range of verifiable statements or candidates for 'warranted assertibility'. However these doctrines are closely related to that other, more overtly accommodationist strategy whose advocates – from Osiander down – have most often wished to 'save appearances' in the twofold sense of conserving the empirical data while avoiding any conflict with the prevalent (scientific or theologico-political) belief-systems of their day. That this was also a chief motivating factor in acceptance of the orthodox (Copenhagen) quantum theory is a case that has been argued with eloquent zeal by Karl Popper and also, though to very different ends of his own, by Feyerabend in the above-cited essay.[68]

So there is reason to reject van Fraassen's idea of the moral as well as intellectual and methodological bankruptcy of realist arguments in philosophy of science. However, as I have said, what is chiefly required by way of defending those arguments is not so much a plucky avowal of courage under fire (to adopt his favoured polemical terms) but a case-by-case assessment of the rival positions across various disciplines and areas of enquiry. Take for instance Dummett's anti-realist contention with respect to mathematical truth, that is, that it cannot make sense to think of certain well-formed but as-yet unproven theorems (like Goldbach's Conjecture) as somehow 'objectively' true or false despite our possessing no adequate proof-procedure or powers of computational grasp. There is an interesting passage where Dummett compares the argument for realism with respect to mathematical 'entities' (numbers, sets, classes, functions, etc.) with the argument for realism concerning astrophysical objects and events. 'The Platonist metaphor,' he writes, 'assimilates mathematical enquiry to the investigations of the astronomer; mathematical structures, like galaxies, exist, independently of us, in a realm of reality which we do not inhabit but which those of us who have the skill are capable of observing and reporting on.'[69] There are two main points that the realist might wish to make about this passage. One is that the issue is somewhat skewed by Dummett's assumption that realism and platonism are pretty much synonymous terms in the philosophy of mathematics. Yet – as some have argued, Kurt Gödel among them – this requires that the realist must take on board all the problems of a full-fledged platonist metaphysics, not least the strictly unintelligible notion of our somehow having contact with abstract entities like numbers through a mode of quasi-perceptual grasp such as Plato envisaged with his doctrine of 'forms' or 'essences'. In Gödel's words:

> mathematical intuition need not be conceived of as a faculty giving an *immediate* knowledge of the objects concerned. . . . Rather, they, too, may represent an aspect of objective reality, but, as opposed to sensations, their presence in us may be due to another kind of relationship between ourselves and reality.[70]

This non-platonist (or modified platonist) version of mathematical realism has been strongly defended by a number of recent advocates including Roger Penrose and Jerrold Katz.[71] At any rate it offers a well-developed alternative to Dummett's idea that the realist must be in the grip of some naive illusion which leads her to think of us as somehow surveying the domain of numbers or set-theoretical relations just as we might survey the heavens in search of a known or unfamiliar galaxy.

However there is a second point about the passage from Dummett which takes us to the heart of these issues. What he chiefly rejects in the realist ('Platonist') conception of mathematical enquiry is the idea that numbers, sets, or other such abstract 'entities' are *there to be discovered* – like galaxies – insofar as they 'exist, independently of us, in a realm of reality which we do not inhabit but which those of us who have the skill are capable of observing and reporting'.[72] On the one hand this captures Dummett's objection to realism as involving the belief in recognition-transcendent truths, or truths that obtain quite apart from our best-available methods of proof and verification. On the other it expresses his equally firm conviction that the kinds of observational warrant we may have for affirming the existence of galaxies visible from our terrestrial location – or perhaps from a voyaging space-probe in radio contact – are *not* the kinds of warrant we could ever have for asserting mathematical truths. This latter point the realist can readily grant once relieved of the Platonist burden, that is to say, the impossible task of explaining how our minds achieve quasi-perceptual contact with a range of purely abstract entities. However she will look more askance at Dummett's claim that realism 'assimilates mathematical enquiry' to the sorts of discovery that astronomers make when they survey some *humanly observable* portion of the universe, that is to say, some region that falls within reach of our technologically assisted powers of observation. For it is just this kind of epistemic restriction that the realist most strongly disavows, committed as she is to the existence of truths – whether with respect to galaxies or mathematical theorems – which depend not at all on our capacities for finding them out. This point is best made by Soames's example (cited above) concerning the objective truth or falsity of a statement to the effect that there exists a solar system in some portion of the expanding universe which lies beyond reach of our present or future-best means of radio-telescope surveillance. Thus Dummett is misconstruing the realist position when he takes it to apply to a 'realm of reality' which we 'do not inhabit' but are none the less capable of 'observing and reporting on'. What this analogy does, in effect, is talk the realist down from a belief in objective (recognition-transcendent) truths to a belief in that far more limited class of truths which conform to the conditions that he (Dummett) requires for warranted assertibility. And from here it is no great distance to the view that mathematical as well as astronomical truths are restricted to the range of truth-evaluable statements for which we possess some established proof-procedure or means of verification.

V

The best short answer to Dummett's position is to be found in a passage by Soames which makes the point by way of a formal argument concerning the different orders of transfinite numbers and the impossibility that any collection of statements could express the entire range of mathematical truths or valid propositions. Thus:

> a proposition can be true even if it has never been expressed by an actual utterance. It is also not absurd to suppose that it can be true even if there is no sentence that expresses it. For example, for each of the nondenumerably many real numbers, there is a proposition that it is greater than or equal to zero. If each sentence is a finite string of words drawn from a finite vocabulary, then the number of propositions outstrips the denumerable infinity of sentences available to express them – that is, there are truths with no linguistic expression. Moreover, if languages are man-made constructions, then propositions that are expressed by sentences could have been true even if no sentences had expressed them. For example, the proposition that the sun is a star could have been true even if no one and hence no sentence had existed to express it.[73]

The last example here takes us back from mathematics to astronomy and brings out very sharply the contrast with Dummett's way of thinking. Thus its truth-value is fixed by an objective (observer-independent) fact, that is, that the sun is a star, just as – in Soames's other example – it is either true or false (objectively so) that there exists a duplicate solar system in some remote or epistemically inaccessible region of the universe. At this point the anti-realist will most likely remark that 'facts' are after all linguistic or discursive entities and hence that we cannot think of statements as somehow (tautologically) 'corresponding to the facts'. However this ignores – or conveniently sidesteps – the realist's central claim, that is to say, her contention that truth in such matters is fixed independently of any conditions (epistemic, linguistic, or whatever) which happen to apply in our present or even best-possible future state of knowledge.

Of course there are thinkers, Dummett among them, to whom this will seem so far from self-evident as to constitute a kind of logical absurdity, a claim to 'know' (or to have good grounds for asserting) that which by very definition exceeds the furthest bounds of humanly attainable knowledge. Nor could the realist entertain much hope of converting Dummett from his hard-won philosophical position by remarking on the implausibility – as well as the anthropocentric bias – of a theory that confounds ontological with epistemological issues, or which fails to conceive that there might (indeed must) be a multitude of truths unknown or unknowable to human enquirers. It is just as unlikely that anyone could convert van Fraassen by pointing to various well-documented cases – such as the atomist hypothesis – where scientific progress can best be measured by the passage from a purely instrumentalist outlook, *via* an intermediate stage of qualified realist commitment, to the point where by far the most rational option is full-fledged realism with respect to the entities in question. What is so odd about van Fraassen's programme is that it fastens on the earliest (least advanced) phase in this typical pattern of development and treats it as the basis for a full-scale exercise in restricting or demoting the claims of scientific truth. In response the realist will most likely fall back upon some version of the 'no miracles' argument proposed by thinkers like Richard Boyd and early Putnam.[74] That is, she will advert to the sheer self-evidence of scientific progress – or (not to beg the ethical issue) of advancement in certain well-defined areas of knowledge – for which there is no accounting, miracles apart, if one eschews a convergent-realist approach based on the principles of causal reasoning and inference to the best explanation. Nor is this merely a fallback option in the sense of evading the central philosophic issue as concerns our knowledge of the growth of knowledge and what has proved its worth as a valid scientific theory. For indeed, as Putnam says, we cannot make sense of the history of science to date except on the assumption that 'terms in mature scientific theories typically refer . . ., that the theories accepted in a mature science are typically approximately true, [and] that the same term can refer to the same thing even when it occurs in different theories'.[75]

However the realist's crucial point is that we might just be wrong about the theories that undergird our present-best science and yet, for precisely that reason, be right to claim that truth in such matters is in no way recognition-dependent or tied to criteria of epistemic warrant. Rather it is decided by the way things stand in physical reality or in a realm of nonphysical objective truths, for example, those of mathematics that are wholly unaffected by whatever we might think or be able to establish concerning them. Of course the anti-realist may choose to discount this argument, just as the sceptic may dig in and profess to doubt the reality of an 'external world', other minds, or any event that is supposed to have occurred more than one second ago. But there can then be no reason to regard anti-realism as anything more than a technical update – or a sophisticated logico-semantic variant – on themes that have always been the sceptic's stock-in-trade and which even the sceptic is compelled to renounce (as Hume famously admitted) as soon as he leaves the study.

References

1. See especially Michael Dummett, *Frege: philosophy of language*, 2nd edn (London: Duckworth, 1981).
2. Gottlob Frege, 'On Sense and Reference', in P. T. Geach and M. Black (eds), *Translations from the Philosophical writings of Gottlob Frege* (Oxford: Blackwell, 1952), pp. 56–78.
3. Ludwig Wittgenstein, *Philosophical Investigations*, trans. G. E. M. Anscombe (Oxford: Blackwell, 1958).
4. Dummett, *Truth and Other Enigmas* (London: Duckworth, 1978).
5. Dummett, *The Logical Basis of Metaphysics* (London: Duckworth, 1991).
6. Bas van Fraassen, *The Scientific Image* (Oxford: Clarendon Press, 1980); also *Laws and Symmetry* (Clarendon Press, 1989).
7. See for instance the essays collected in A. J. Ayer (ed.), *Logical Positivism* (New York: Free Press, 1959).
8. van Fraassen, *The Scientific Image*, p. 8 (Note 6, above).
9. Ibid., p. 12.
10. Ibid., p. 72.
11. See especially van Fraassen, *Laws and Symmetry* (Note 6, above).
12. Van Fraassen, *The Scientific Image*, p. 203 (Note 6, above).
13. See Ernst Mach, *The Science of Mechanics* (London: Watts, 1893); also, for a lively and informative critical account, C. J. Misak, *Verificationism: its history and prospects* (London: Routledge, 1995).
14. See for instance D. M. Armstrong, *Universals and Scientific Realism*, 2 vols (Cambridge: Cambridge University Press, 1978); J. Aronson, R. Harré and E. Way, *Realism Rescued: how scientific progress is possible* (London: Duckworth, 1994); Michael Devitt, *Realism and Truth*, 2nd edn (Princeton, NJ: Princeton University Press, 1991); Jarrett Leplin (ed.), *Scientific Realism*

(Berkeley & Los Angeles: University of California Press, 1984); Karl Popper, *Realism and the Aim of Science* (London: Hutchinson, 1983); Peter J. Smith, *Realism and the Progress of Science* (Cambridge: Cambridge University Press, 1981).

15. Paul Churchland, 'The Ontological Status of Observables: in praise of the superempirical virtues', in P. M. Churchland and C. M. Hooker (eds), *Images of Science: essays on realism and empiricism, with a reply from Bas C. van Fraassen* (Chicago: University of Chicago Press, 1985). See also Christopher Norris, 'Anti-Realism and Constructive Empiricism: is there a (real) difference?' and 'Ontology according to van Fraassen: some problems with constructive empiricism', in *Against Relativism: philosophy of science, deconstruction and critical theory* (Oxford: Blackwell, 1997), pp. 167–95 and 196–217.
16. See Notes 1, 4 and 5 above.
17. Crispin Wright, *Realism, Meaning and Truth*, 2nd edn (Oxford: Blackwell, 1993).
18. See entries under Note 14, above; also William P. Alston, *A Realist Theory of Truth* (Ithaca, NY: Cornell University Press, 1996).
19. See especially Larry Laudan, 'A Confutation of Convergent Realism', *Philosophy of Science*, Vol. 48 (1981), pp. 19–49.
20. Dummett, *Elements of Intuitionism* (Oxford: Oxford University Press, 1977).
21. See for instance Jerrold J. Katz, *Realistic Rationalism* (Cambridge, MA: MIT Press, 1998).
22. Dummett, *Truth and Other Enigmas* (Note 4, above).
23. Ibid., p. 155.
24. Dummett, *The Seas of Language* (Oxford: Clarendon Press, 1993), p. 75.
25. Dummett, *The Logical Basis of Metaphysics*, p. 7 (Note 5, above).
26. Immanuel Kant, *Critique of Pure Reason*, trans. N. Kemp Smith (London: Macmillan, 1964).
27. See for instance Hilary Putnam, *Reason, Truth and History* (Cambridge: Cambridge University Press, 1981).
28. Dummett, *Frege: philosophy of language* (Note 1, above).
29. Dummett, 'Can an Effect Precede its Cause?', 'Bringing About the Past', and 'The Reality of the Past', in *Truth and Other Enigmas*, pp. 319–32, 333–50 and 358–74.
30. For further discussion see Christopher Norris, 'Can Logic be Quantum-Relativized? Putnam, Dummett and the "Great Quantum Muddle" ', in *Quantum Theory and the Flight from Realism: philosophical responses to quantum mechanics* (London: Routledge, 2000), pp. 194–230.
31. See for instance Tim Maudlin, *Quantum Non-Locality and Relativity: metaphysical intimations of modern science* (Oxford: Blackwell, 1993) and Michael Redhead, *Incompleteness, Nonlocality and Realism: a prolegomenon to the philosophy of quantum mechanics* (Oxford: Clarendon Press, 1987).
32. See Note 29, above.
33. Dummett, *Frege: philosophy of language* (Note 1, above).
34. Andrea Nye, *Words of Power: a feminist reading of the history of logic* (London: Routledge, 1990).

35. See entries under Note 14, above; also J. L. Aronson, 'Testing for Convergent Realism', *British Journal for the Philosophy of Science*, Vol. 40 (1989), pp. 255–60; Gilbert Harman, 'Inference to the Best Explanation', *Philosophical Review*, Vol. 74 (1965), pp. 88–95; Peter Lipton, *Inference to the Best Explanation* (London: Routledge, 1993); Wesley C. Salmon, *The Foundations of Scientific Inference* (Pittsburgh, PA: University of Pittsburgh Press, 1967).
36. See Dummett, *Truth and Other Enigmas* (Note 4 above); Michael Luntley, *Language, Logic and Experience: the case for anti-realism* (London: Duckworth, 1988); Neil Tennant, *Anti-Realism and Logic* (Oxford: Clarendon Press, 1987); Wright, *Realism, Meaning and Truth* (Note 17, above).
37. Putnam, *Mathematics, Matter and Method* (Cambridge: Cambridge University Press, 1975), p. 73.
38. See Norris, *Hilary Putnam: realism, reason and the uses of uncertainty* (Manchester: Manchester University Press, 2002).
39. Putnam, *Mind, Language and Reality* (Cambridge: Cambridge University Press, 1975).
40. See Norris, *Hilary Putnam* (Note 38, above).
41. van Fraassen, *Laws and Symmetry*, p. 27 (Note 6, above).
42. van Fraassen, *The Scientific Image*, p. 31 (Note 6, above).
43. See especially Putnam, *Realism and Reason* (Cambridge: Cambridge University Press, 1983).
44. See John A. Wheeler and W. H. Zurek (eds), *Quantum Theory and Measurement* (Princeton, NJ: Princeton University Press, 1983); also van Fraassen, *Quantum Mechanics: an empiricist view* (Oxford: Clarendon Press, 1992).
45. See David Bohm, *Causality and Chance in Modern Physics* (London: Routledge & Kegan Paul, 1957); David Bohm and B. J. Hiley, *The Undivided Universe: an ontological interpretation of quantum theory* (London: Routledge, 1993); James T. Cushing, *Quantum Mechanics: historical contingency and the Copenhagen hegemony* (Chicago: University of Chicago Press, 1994); and Peter Holland, *The Quantum Theory of Motion* (Cambridge: Cambridge University Press, 1993).
46. Albert Einstein, B. Podolsky and N. Rosen, 'Can Quantum-Mechanical Description of Reality be Considered Complete?', *Physical Review*, series 2, Vol. 47 (1935), pp. 777–80; Niels Bohr, article in response under the same title, *Physical Review*, Vol. 48 (1935), pp. 696–702; Bohr, 'Conversation with Einstein on Epistemological Problems in Atomic Physics', in P. A. Schilpp (ed.), *Albert Einstein: philosopher-scientist* (La Salle: Open Court, 1969), pp. 199–241; also Arthur Fine, *The Shaky Game: Einstein, realism, and quantum theory* (Chicago: University of Chicago Press, 1936); Don Howard, 'Einstein on Locality and Separability', *Studies in the History and Philosophy of Science*, Vol. 16 (1985), pp. 171–220.
47. See G. Birkhoff and J. von Neumann, 'The Logic of Quantum Mechanics', *Annals of Mathematics*, Vol. 37 (1936), pp. 823–43.
48. J. S. Bell, *Speakable and Unspeakable in Quantum Mechanics: collected papers on quantum philosophy* (Cambridge: Cambridge University Press, 1987).
49. See Note 45, above.

50. See Wheeler and Zurek (eds), *Quantum Theory and Measurement* (Note 44, above).
51. See for instance M. Gardner, 'Realism and Instrumentalism in Nineteenth-Century Atomism', *Philosophy of Science*, Vol. 46 (1979), pp. 1–34; also Mary Jo Nye, *Molecular Reality* (London: MacDonald, 1972) and J. Perrin, *Atoms*, trans. D. L. Hammick (New York: van Nostrand, 1923).
52. Scott Soames, *Understanding Truth* (Oxford: Oxford University Press, 1999).
53. Dummett, *Truth and Other Enigmas*, pp. 14–17 (Note 4, above).
54. See for instance Rom Harré and E. H. Madden, *Causal Powers* (Oxford: Blackwell, 1975); Wesley C. Salmon, *Scientific Explanation and the Causal Structure of the World* (Princeton, NJ: Princeton University Press, 1984); Brian Skyrms, *Causal Necessity* (New Haven: Yale University Press, 1980); and M. Tooley, *Causation: a realist approach* (Oxford: Blackwell, 1988).
55. van Fraassen, *Laws and Symmetry* (Note 6, above).
56. Richard Rorty, *Objectivity, Relativism, and Truth* (Cambridge: Cambridge University Press, 1991), p. 80.
57. van Fraassen, 'Empiricism in the Philosophy of Language', in Paul Churchland and Clifford Hooker (eds), *Images of Science: essays on realism and empiricism, with a reply from Bas C. van Fraassen* (Chicago: University of Chicago Press, 1985), p. 255.
58. Ibid., p. 255.
59. Ibid., p. 255.
60. See for instance Alexandre Koyré, *Galilean Studies* (Brighton: Harvester, 1978) and various contributions to P. Machamer (ed.), *The Cambridge Companion to Galileo* (Cambridge: Cambridge University Press, 1998).
61. See Pierre Duhem, *To Save the Appearances: an essay on the idea of physical theory from Plato to Galileo*, trans. E. Dolan and C. Maschler (Chicago: University of Chicago Press, 1969); also entries under Note 13, above.
62. Paul K. Feyerabend, 'Reichenbach's Interpretation of Quantum Mechanics', *Philosophical Studies*, Vol. XX (1958), pp. 45–62; p. 50.
63. See Feyerabend, *Science in a Free Society* (London: New Left Books, 1978); also *Against Method* (New Left Books, 1975).
64. See for instance Barry Barnes, *About Science* (Oxford: Blackwell, 1985); David Bloor, *Knowledge and Social Imagery* (London: Routledge & Kegan Paul, 1976); Steve Fuller, *Philosophy of Science and its Discontents* (Boulder, CO: Westview Press, 1989); and Steve Woolgar, *Science: the very idea* (London: Tavistock, 1988).
65. See Note 57, above.
66. See Note 64, above; also Steven Shapin and Simon Schaffer, *Leviathan and the Air-Pump: Hobbes, Boyle, and the experimental life* (Princeton, NJ: Princeton University Press, 1985) and Steve Woolgar (ed.), *Knowledge and Reflexivity: new frontiers in the sociology of knowledge* (London: Sage, 1988).
67. See especially Rorty, *Contingency, Irony, and Solidarity* (Cambridge: Cambridge University Press, 1989) and *Objectivity, Relativism, and Truth* (Note 56, above).
68. Karl Popper, *Quantum Theory and the Schism in Physics* (London: Hutchinson, 1982); also Note 62, above.

69. Dummett, *Truth and Other Enigmas*, p. 229 (Note 4, above).
70. Kurt Gödel, 'What is Cantor's Continuum Problem?', in Paul Benacerraf and Hilary Putnam (eds.), *The Philosophy of Mathematics: selected essays*, 2nd edn (Cambridge: Cambridge University Press, 1983), pp. 470–85; p. 484.
71. Roger Penrose, *Shadows of the Mind: a search for the missing science of consciousness* (London: Vintage, 1995); Katz, *Realistic Rationalism* (Note 21, above).
72. Dummett, *Truth and Other Enigmas*, p. 205 (Note 4, above).
73. Soames, *Understanding Truth*, p. 19 (Note 52, above).
74. See Richard Boyd, 'The Current Status of Scientific Realism', in Jarrett Leplin (ed.), *Scientific Realism* (Berkeley & Los Angeles: University of California Press, 1984), pp. 41–82.
75. Putnam, *Mathematics, Matter and Method*, p. 73 (Note 37, above).

Chapter Two

Response-Dependence: the current debate in review

I

Just recently a number of philosophers have offered what they take to be a new solution – or at any rate a promising line of approach – to the issue between realist and anti-realist conceptions of knowledge and truth. This involves the idea of 'response-dependence' as a means of explaining how certain statements can be thought of as candidates for ascriptions of truth or falsity while also necessarily involving some appeal to the scope and conditions of human perceptual or cognitive grasp.[1] Such an approach has most often been adopted – at least since Locke – in debates about the status of 'secondary qualities' like colour, taste, odour, texture, or heat and cold, the latter construed in phenomenological (i.e., experiential) terms rather than defined scientifically, for instance as a function of the mean kinetic energy of molecules. Thus secondary qualities are those that result from an interaction between perceiver and object perceived, rather than existing *either* as objective (mind-independent) physical properties *or* as purely subjective qualia that have no 'reality' except as registered by this or that human sensorium. According to Locke:

> [t]he ideas of primary qualities of bodies are resemblances of them, and their patterns do really exist in the bodies themselves, but the ideas produced in us by these secondary qualities have no resemblance of them at all. There is nothing like our ideas existing in the bodies themselves. They are, in the bodies we denominate from them, only a power to produce those sensations in us; and what is sweet, blue, or warm in idea is but the certain bulk, figure, and motion of the insensible parts, in the bodies themselves, which we call so.[2]

On this basis we can usefully distinguish between areas of discourse (such as those concerning primary qualities like shape and size) where we can properly claim to *detect* what is the case with respect to an observer-independent physical domain and areas of discourse (such as those concerning colour) where our judgements involve a perceptual registration of imputed properties or qualities which cannot be assigned any such objective status. These latter sorts of judgement must always have reference, whether overt or implicit, to what would be the case for a suitably placed and fully sentient observer under optimum sensory conditions or excluding any circumstance (hallucination, abnormal background lighting, heat-haze phenomena, etc.) that would lead them to mistake or misdescribe the quality in question.[3]

So one major purpose of this theory is to show how properties can be ranged on a scale that permits us to distinguish 'detectivist' from 'projectivist' orders of truth-claim, or those whose veridical warrant derives from the way things stand with respect to a world of objective (response-independent) properties and those whose assertibility-conditions cannot be specified without some appeal to the register of duly normalised human responses. Moreover, so its proponents would claim, the theory has a wide range of applications beyond the traditionally recognised range of secondary qualities, that is, those having to do with colour, taste, odour, and other such modes of sensory perception. Thus it might point the way toward an account of moral judgements that incorporates a strong normative appeal to widely shared values and beliefs yet which doesn't let go of the equally powerful conviction that such judgements are nonetheless subject to appraisal on rational-evaluative grounds.[4] Or again, it might provide a response-dependent but not merely subjectivist account of what constitutes a good joke or a genuinely comic situation. That is to say, the criteria for finding something funny or not in the least amusing – like those for judging some particular action worthy of moral praise or blame – are not such as could yield any sure technique for *detecting* such properties in the instance to hand. Rather they belong to that class of judgements which involve an appeal to certain shared norms of communal response that define *what counts* among those qualified to judge as a comic (or morally evaluable) case in point. And if the instance of comedy seems scarcely plausible – since 'normal' responses vary so widely across differences of culture, age-group, gender, individual temperament, and so forth – then perhaps it is best treated as a limit-case example which can usefully serve to fix the conditions for other, more relevant cases.[5]

Mark Johnston has done much to promote this idea of response-dependence as an answer to various worrisome issues in ontology, epistemology, and philosophy of mind. As he puts it:

> [i]f the concept associated with the predicate 'is C' is a concept interdependent with or dependent upon concepts of certain subjects' responses under certain

conditions, then something of the following form will hold *a priori*: x is C if in conditions K, Ss are disposed to produce x-directed response R (or: x is such as to produce R in Ss under conditions K).[6]

Or again, in Philip Pettit's slightly less cumbrous phrasing: the description 'response-dependent' is one which can usefully be deployed 'to pick out those terms and concepts that are biconditionally connected, as an *a priori* matter, with certain more or less primitive responses: in particular, with responses of a perceptual or affective character'.[7] Still there are certain further requirements that have to be met if a concept is to qualify as response-dependent in a properly substantive and non-trivial sense of that term. One is that it cannot simply be a matter of some vague or open-ended specification such as 'whatever it takes' in order for red objects to be recognised as red or – if this approach is extended to issues in moral philosophy – for praiseworthy acts to be duly acknowledged as meriting moral approbation. Thus, for instance, it is no use saying that a subject *S* is properly equipped to judge and that conditions K are the right sorts of condition under which to exercise that judgement just so long as the result of *S* + *K* is a correct (= communally sanctioned) usage of the colour-term or moral-evaluative predicate in question. Rather the specification must be one that explains *just what it is* about *S* that makes her a competent or reliable judge in such matters, and also *just what it is* about the normal set of conditions *K* that serves to distinguish them from other, that is, non-standard or distorting conditions.

In Crispin Wright's words, this entails that the criteria for *S* and *K* should 'not be filled out trivially', or in such a way that they 'overtly or covertly specify as the conditions and subjects whatever conditions and whatever subjects are required to get it right'.[8] And again:

> they must be specified in sufficient detail to incorporate a constructive account of the epistemology of the judgements in question, so that not merely does a subject's satisfaction of them ensure that the conditions under which she is operating have 'whatever-it-takes' to bring it about that the judgement is true, but a concrete conception is conveyed of what it actually does take.[9]

So in the case of correct colour-term usage what we need is a detailed description of the factors that make for veridical judgements of colour, such as: perceived by a normally sighted or non-visually-impaired observer under optimal conditions (say at noon on a lightly clouded summer's day) and in the absence of any disturbing factor – like a shadow-casting object or proximal light-source – that could interfere with the subject's capacity to recognise green objects as green, red objects as red, etc. And in the case of moral-evaluative judgements one would likewise have to offer a substantive (non-trivial) account of *what it is* about *S* and *K* – the subject concerned and the given situation – which gives them a certain normative or benchmark status as compared with other possible modes or conditions of response. Only thus can one save the *a priori* biconditional – 'x is C if and only if in conditions *K*, *S*s are disposed to produce x-directed response R' – from collapsing into manifest circularity or amounting to the merely tautologous (definitional) truth that subjects and conditions must be counted normal just in case the conjunction of *S* + *K* produces a correct, that is, normal attribution of predicate C to object or situation *x*. So the main requirement for ascriptions of response-dependence is that the property in question can be shown to depend not only on certain features intrinsic to the object or situation concerned but also on certain *substantive and constitutive* features of a normal (non-deviant or favourably placed) mode of human response. Alex Miller makes a similar point when he talks about 'conceptually structured' properties which cannot be thought of as existing 'out there' in a realm of objective (response-independent) reality but which are always already subject to judgement under the forms and conditions of human perceptual or epistemic grasp. Thus a property is conceptually structured 'when there is an *a priori* and *non-trivial* connection between the facts about its instantiation and at least some of our judgements to the effect that the property is instantiated'.[10] This he takes to rule out any treatment of such properties that would regard them as fit candidates for 'tracking' or 'detecting', that is to say, as possessing an objective character to which our judgements must duly correspond, rather than as constituted, at least in part, by the nature and structure of those same judgements.

Miller, like Johnston, expresses the hope that an approach to these issues *via* the theory of response-dependence can help to resolve many of the problems that have dogged epistemology ever since Locke and which have lately been posed with particular force by Michael Dummett's global challenge to realism on logico-semantic grounds. Thus, to Dummett's way of thinking, it simply cannot make sense to assert the existence of verification-transcendent truths or, more precisely, to take the view that well-formed statements belonging to the 'disputed class' (i.e., whose truth-value we are unable to establish) can nonetheless be true or false – objectively so despite our lack of knowledge concerning them.[11] This restriction applies pretty much across the board, from unproven mathematical theorems (such as Goldbach's Conjecture that every even number is the sum of two primes), to statements concerning remote astrophysical objects and events, or historical assertions – like 'Julius Caesar coughed six times as he crossed the Rubicon' – for which we possess no evidence. The realist thinks it sheerly self-evident that such statements *must* be either true or false (i.e., conform to the classical law of bivalence) just so long as they are well-formed and make some intelligible claim with regard to some specified fact of the matter.[12] From her standpoint it is nothing short of absurd that statements like these should be thought of as dependent for their truth-value on our happening to possess a proof-procedure for some mathematical theorem, or radio-telescopic evidence for statements concerning distant astronomical objects, or eye-witness testimony for Caesar's state of health on the day in question. What decides the issue of their truth or falsehood is whether (unbeknownst to us) every even number *is* the sum of two primes, or whether, for instance, there *does* in fact exist a duplicate solar system in some remote region of the universe, or whether Julius Caesar *did* in fact cough six times on his way across the river. However the anti-realist finds it just as absurd – indeed philosophically unthinkable – that we should raise that issue in relation to statements that exceed, transcend, or elude our utmost powers of ascertainment. Rather we should treat them as strictly non-bivalent (that is to say, undecidable) on the best evidence to hand, and therefore as neither true nor false so far as we can possibly tell. Otherwise we shall end up in the surely impossible predicament of claiming to know – to have good grounds for stating – what lies beyond our furthest epistemic grasp or scope of warranted assertibility.

It is at this point that the advocates of a response-dependent account enter their claim to have discovered an alternative approach that avoids the twin extremes of hardline 'metaphysical' realism on the one hand and outright projectivism on the other. In their view the realist goes wrong – yields too many hostages to sceptical fortune – through adopting an objectivist notion of truth whereby the truth-value of our various judgements or statements is placed altogether beyond epistemic reach or beyond what should ultimately count as 'best opinion' among those qualified to judge. Hence, Miller thinks, the ease with which anti-realists can regularly win at this game simply by remarking that such truths are unknowable by very definition and can thus do nothing to bolster the realist's case. However there is no need for the realist to find herself driven into this corner if she will only concede the point about response-dependence, that is, the surely non-threatening point that a great many of our truth-apt statements have their truth-values jointly fixed or decided through certain facts concerning the properties of things (or situations) along with certain facts concerning our perceptual or conceptual grasp of those properties. Where the realist makes her big mistake is in thinking that any such recourse to the notion of response-dependence is a move that plays straight into the sceptic's hands by giving up the idea of objective truth-values that could always, in principle, transcend what counts as 'best opinion' or even, at the limit, idealised epistemic warrant. Yet, in Miller's view, this anxiety stems from a false (and, moreover, an unhealthily 'sublimated') conception of knowledge and truth which leaves the realist cruelly exposed to all manner of well-practised anti-realist rejoinders. Where it chiefly gets a hold is through the basic thought that if our judgements are to track real-world properties or claim cognitive access to them then those properties must be thought of as 'conceptually unstructured', that is, as existing just as they are quite apart from (or independently of) any contribution that we might ourselves make through the process of perceptual cognition or conceptual uptake. But in that case the realist is once again stuck with the strictly insoluble problem of explaining how we could ever gain knowledge or form reliable judgements concerning a reality that lies *ex hypothesi* outside and beyond our furthest epistemic reach. So she would do much better, Miller advises, to drop this unworkable objectivist requirement and adopt a response-dispositional account that rejects any hardline anti-realist position while acknowledging the extent to which certain properties are conceptually structured. For it then becomes possible to work out the details of a more moderate (non-self-defeating) version of realism which can put up a strong defence against the standard range of sceptical counter-arguments.

Miller has a nice passage making this point which I shall cite at length because it captures the gist of a good many arguments, by Wright and others, which are rarely put with such clarity and force. 'The idea is as follows', he writes:

> [i]n our pre-theoretic, pre-philosophical thinking, we have a perfectly healthy desire for a degree of independence between our judgements and the facts which those judgements are capable of tracking. When we do philosophy, this healthy desire becomes sublimated into an *unhealthy philosophical conception* of what this independence has to consist in. So just as Gustav Mahler's perfectly healthy respect for women becomes sublimated into an unhealthy syndrome known as the Virgin Mary complex, our own perfectly healthy desire for a measure of independence between the knower and what is known becomes sublimated into the idea that the properties which the judgements of the knower cognitively access have to be conceptually unstructured.[13]

Miller follows John McDowell (who in turn follows Wittgenstein) in tracing this pathological condition to the idea of a 'super-rigid rail' or a piece of 'super-rigid machinery' that somehow has to guide our various processes of deductive inference, mathematical reasoning, scientific theory-construction, etc., if we are to get things truly and objectively right rather than 'right' by our own communal or practice-based criteria.[14] Such is the 'superlative conception' of rules which, according to Wittgenstein, makes it an absolute mystery how we could ever know what rule-following involved or when we were following the correct rule as distinct from some nonstandard or deviant and yet (on its own terms) perfectly consistent alternative.[15] Anti-realist arguments have been motivated chiefly by this and kindred problems concerning our epistemic access to truths or rational decision-procedures which the realist holds to be objectively valid and hence independent of our various knowledge-constitutive uses and practices.

For some – McDowell among them – the Wittgensteinian 'paradox' about rule-following is a false dilemma that can best be resolved by seeing how the very conception of a rule (e.g., a simple arithmetical rule like addition or subtraction) is such as to extend as a matter of objective necessity into regions beyond any finite or presently graspable range of application. Thus, according to McDowell, 'the idea of ratification independence is itself just part of the idea of meaning's normative reach', whether in the case of mathematics or with any such recursive procedure (such as speaking in accordance with the rules of grammar) that requires something more than an ad hoc grasp of what works on this or that particular occasion.[16] For others – more impressed by Wittgenstein's sceptical argument – it is a genuine problem as to what could ever *count* as correctly 'following a rule' since our standards of correctness cannot derive (on pain of infinite regress) from any appeal to some higher-level rule that would decide the issue as between variant construals.[17] On this view there is simply no conceiving how a normative practice might be somehow capable of laying down rules (or 'super-rigid' tracks) that effectively determined the outcome in advance for all future applications. Nor could an adequate answer be obtained by enquiring what an expert mathematician or a competent speaker of English *had in mind* when they produced a valid mathematical result or a grammatically well-formed sentence. For of course this answer runs straight into trouble with Wittgenstein's 'private language' argument, that is say, his insistence that any such appeal to a realm of inner goings-on or events in the mind of individual agents is incapable of resolving the issue since (1) it gives rise to the same kind of infinite regress, and (2) it provides no 'public' (shared or communicable) set of criteria whereby to adjudicate from one case to the next.[18] Hence Kripke's 'sceptical solution' to Wittgenstein's sceptical dilemma, namely the idea that it is communal warrant – the existence of some shared or agreed-upon way of proceeding – that alone makes sense of our various linguistic, mathematical, and other practices.

The idea of response-dependent properties or predicates is often put forward as a means of avoiding what many philosophers (McDowell and Wright among them) regard as the unsatisfactory nature of this last-ditch appeal to communal sanction as the arbiter of meaning, validity, and truth. McDowell suggests that a return to Kant – or to a suitably 'detranscendentalised' version of Kant's arguments in the First *Critique* – is the best way to go when confronted with issues like the rule-following paradox or the idea that 'nothing works' in philosophy of mathematics since objectivity can be bought only at the cost of placing truth beyond human knowledge and knowledge can be bought only at the cost of renouncing any claim to objective truth.[19] Thus Kant was on the right track, so McDowell thinks, when he explained how knowledge comes about through a synthesising power of judgement that involves the jointly operative powers of 'receptivity' and 'spontaneity' and which thereby enables us to bring intuitions under concepts in an act of achieved cognitive grasp.[20] However there are problems with McDowell's reading of Kant, not least its appeal to those notoriously murky passages where Kant falls back on the Imagination – that 'mysterious power buried in the depths of the soul' – by way of accomplishing the required link between two such disparate 'faculties' as those of sensuous (phenomenal) intuition and conceptual understanding.[21] Moreover there is the awkward fact that Kant's entire argument in the First *Critique* rests crucially on his claim for the *a priori* self-evident character of certain primordial intuitions – like the truths of Euclidean geometry or Newtonian space-time physics – which were later shown to lack any such ultimate or strictly indubitable warrant.

II

All the same McDowell's line of argument has seemed distinctly promising to those, like Miller, who think that it provides a useful starting-point for a theory of response-dependence which cuts out the Kantian transcendental talk while still providing all the 'objectivity' we need in order to resist the more extreme varieties of sceptical or anti-realist doctrine. Thus Miller cites McDowell:

> [u]nderstanding is a grasp of patterns that extend to new cases independently of our ratification, as required for meaning to be other than an illusion (and – not incidentally – for the intuitive sense of objectivity to have a use); but the constraints imposed by our concepts do not have the platonistic autonomy with which they are credited in the picture of the super-rigid machinery.[22]

And again: '[i]t is wrong to suppose that platonism is implicit in the very idea that meaning and intention contain within themselves a determination of what counts as accord with them'.[23] That is, we can take Kant's lead – on a suitably 'naturalised' construal – and thus come to see that the standard of correctness in speaking grammatically, performing an arithmetical calculation, or drawing a deductive inference is dependent in part (and in varying degree) on the normative character of best judgement with respect to the rule-governed practice or procedure in question. Just as the ascription of colour-predicates retains this crucial normative aspect *despite* involving some reference to the observer and the circumstances under which the colour is perceived so likewise the ascription of truth-predicates in other areas of discourse can be thought to involve an element of response-dependence *without* thereby giving up all claim to correctness or objectivity.

No doubt the weighting will vary from one instance to another, so that secondary qualities like colour will be taken to depend much more on the phenomenology of observer-response while primary qualities like shape and size will be taken to possess a more objective – independently ratifiable – character. Furthest out toward this latter (minimally response-dependent) end of the scale will be standards of correctness or valid reasoning as applied to logic, mathematics, or the formal branches of the exact sciences. Indeed they would have to be counted strictly off-the-scale if conceived in realist (i.e., recognition-transcendent) terms.[24] Even so, Miller argues, we should do much better to reject this realist view since it gives rise to all those well-known problems concerning the impossibility of our having epistemic access to truths that by very definition must elude our utmost powers of rational or evidential grasp. Thus he finds it 'puzzling' that McDowell should still want to talk about the *objectivity* of mathematics, logic, and certain other (for instance grammatical) rules or recursive procedures despite his awareness of the difficulties to which this objectivist conception gives rise. After all, '[w]hat can the "platonistic autonomy" alluded to in Wittgenstein's picture of the "super-rigid rail" consist in, if not the objectivity of meaning as characterised by Wright?'[25] For Wright, as for Miller, the chief purpose of adopting a response-dispositional account is to avoid precisely this stark choice (as McDowell appears to conceive it) between objective truth-values that stand altogether beyond epistemic reach and a communitarian or practice-based approach that opens the way to all manner of far gone cultural-relativist conclusions.

Thus (Miller again): '[h]ow . . . can McDowell reject platonism without thereby also rejecting the objectivity of meaning?'[26] Yet it soon becomes clear that this is a rhetorical question designed to elicit an affirmative answer, that is, a solution to the rule-following paradox and other sceptical worries that would adopt something like McDowell's line of argument while successfully managing to avoid both horns of the objectivist/communitarian dilemma. 'By sketching an alternative to Wright's anti-realist construal of response-dependence, I will suggest that there is a notion of platonism which is, plausibly, the proper target of the rule-following considerations, but whose rejection nevertheless leaves scope for the retention of the objectivity of meaning.'[27] This alternative is the kind of 'humanised platonism' – Miller's term – which holds that certain properties and predicates are 'conceptually structured' (or response-dependent) but all the same sees no reason to deny that they possess properly objective criteria of valid application. Such a humanised platonist approach would also have the therapeutic virtue of weaning us off that 'sublimated conception of cognitive access' which Miller regards as philosophically unhealthy, like Mahler's sublimation of his respect for women into a perverse and psychologically damaging form of the Virgin Mary complex. It would thereby release us from the chronic misconception that objectivity is an all-or-nothing affair, and that the cost of resiling from a full-scale commitment to the existence of conceptually unstructured (recognition-transcendent) properties or predicates is a collapse into some wholesale version of epistemological relativism.

'This explains', Miller writes, 'how the objectivity of meaning can be retained, even while the spurious autonomy of the super-rigid-rule-as-rail is consciously rejected.'[28] In other words one can have a perfectly workable conception of objectivity – of what it takes for our various statements and beliefs to be reliably truth-tracking – without going in for the sublimated version which supposes truth to be 'objective' in a sense that places it forever beyond reach of our epistemic powers. Thus the problem about rule-following would simply disappear in so far as it could then be shown to result from the false dichotomy presumed to exist between standards prescribed by some 'super-rigid' concept of absolute procedural correctness and conventions laid down by the standards that apply in this or that community of usage. All that is needed in order to resolve Wittgenstein's paradox is the straightforward acceptance that certain predicates are conceptually structured and that this does nothing to impugn or undermine their objective truth-value. Indeed it is in the very nature of these predicates – prototypically colour-term ascriptions – that they *must* involve some such appeal to what counts as an instance of the property in question as perceived by a normally equipped observer under normal (adequately specified) ambient conditions. What marks them out as conceptually structured is the close connection that can be shown to exist between 'the system of relationships among the things that may possess that property and our *concept* of that property'.[29] And what makes the connection something more than a matter of habitual associative linkage or Humean 'constant conjunction' is the fact that it enters necessarily (that is, as a matter of *a priori* warrant) into any judgement we can form concerning such matters. A property is conceptually structured, in Miller's account, 'when there is an *a priori* and *non-trivial* connection between the facts about its instantiation and at least some of our judgements to the effect that the property is instantiated'.[30]

Thus the task for philosophy – though also, one might think, for the physical sciences where the property in question falls within their remit – is to spell out the various physical factors and perceptual conditions that decide what shall count as a normal judgement in any given case. Only then can the theory amount to something more than a trivial claim to the effect that 'red objects are those that elicit the predicate "red" from normally sighted observers under whatever lighting conditions it takes', or 'rough textures are those that prompt the "roughness"-response in feelers with normal tactile sensations under standard (however specified) physical circumstances.' Otherwise there could be no substantive point in adducing the universally quantified *a priori* biconditional, that is, the response-dependence thesis that for any predicate P as applied to x P should be taken as conceptually structured if and only if the criteria for its correct application include some strictly indispensable appeal to the response of a normal and suitably placed observer as well as to the properties of x that reliably trigger or elicit that response. What gives this theory its philosophic bite – or saves it from empty circularity – is the fact that it can claim such *a priori* warrant even while still leaving room (in principle at least) for any number of detailed specifications with regard to what counts in perceptual terms as 'normal' or 'suitably placed'. Thus it promises to resolve the dilemma posed by Dummett-style anti-realism, namely that objectivity is bought only at the cost of renouncing (humanly attainable) knowledge and knowledge secured only on condition that we give up conceiving truth as a matter of objective (recognition-transcendent) correspondence with the way things stand in reality. Rather we should see that this is just another manifestation of the sublimated 'super-rigid rail' idea which assumes that correctness must be a matter of accurately 'tracking' those facts that confer an objective truth-value on our judgements, and moreover that 'the thing tracked or accessed has to be independent of the tracker or accesser'.[31] If we can just let go of that false supposition – the source of all our epistemological woes – then (Miller claims) there is nothing to prevent us from adopting a response-dependence theory which takes full account of the contribution made by our various cognitive inputs while blocking the sceptic's standard move, that is, his appeal to the rule-following paradox and other such pseudo-dilemmas. For these latter sorts of argument derive their force from the notion that rules (like meanings or concepts) can be valid only insofar as they possess a rigidly determinative character which stands somehow *outside and above* any particular act of judgement and which is thereby able to provide in advance for all future cases and occasions.

So it is that Kripke can press home his Wittgenstein-derived sceptical point about the infinite regress that threatens when we think to specify rules for the proper application of rules, or when we try to solve the problem by asking what rule-followers must have in mind when they manage to apply the correct rule. But this will seem a problem only if one is still in the grip of that 'sublimated' Platonist conception of rules which equates their objectivity with their holding-good quite apart from any input (or conceptual structure) that we or other subjects may bring to them. On this account, 'we can think of our judgements about the instantiation of a property as capable in principle of tracking or cognitively accessing the facts about its instantiation only if the property in question is conceptually unstructured'. On the humanised Platonist account, conversely, we can 'think of ourselves as tracking or cognitively accessing the facts about the instantiation of conceptually *structured* properties'.[32] What this amounts to, in effect, is yet another version of Kant's central argument in the First *Critique*, namely that our only hope of defeating the sceptic is to give up any thought of our somehow having access to an order of objective (mind-independent) reality. Rather we should accept the idea that all our judgements are 'conceptually structured' in various ways, whether through conforming to our basic *a priori* intuitions of space and time or through falling under certain likewise *a priori* concepts such as that of causality.[33]

The Kantian connection is more explicit in McDowell but also plays a strong background role in the thinking of Johnston, Miller, Wright and other advocates of response-dependence as an answer to epistemological scepticism in its current anti-realist (i.e., logico-semantic) guise. Thus the present-day equivalent of Kant's answer to the Humean sceptic is the claim put forward by these thinkers that we just needn't worry about the lack of objective (recognition-transcendent) truths with regard to certain areas of discourse since the areas concerned are precisely those where our judgements are subject to normative criteria deriving from the very nature and structure of what counts as an adequate cognitive response. Moreover, this still leaves room for the possibility of getting things wrong, for example, through perceiving objects or colours under less-than-ideal optical conditions or – in the case that most interests Miller – through our failing to follow the correct rule as distinct from all the other, more-or-less plausible rules that might be adduced so as to justify an aberrant result. In short, there is no reason to suppose that by giving up the 'Sublimated Platonist' conception in favour of a 'Humanised Platonist' approach we are driven to relinquish the very idea of objective validity and truth. What it means, less drastically, is coming to acknowledge that the sublimated conception was always a non-starter (since it played straight into the sceptic's hands) and that we lose nothing, and indeed gain a great deal, by accepting this sensibly scaled-down alternative conception.

So the chief claim for response-dispositional theories is that they offer an argument that is able to confront and, in some cases, to accommodate the anti-realist challenge with regard to objective (recognition-transcendent) truths while at the same rejecting those more extreme varieties of anti-realist thought which conclude that truth can never be more than a matter of communal warrant or accredited 'best opinion'. Thus, in Miller's words:

> Rejection of this idea [i.e., the sublimated 'super-rigid rail'] does not involve rejection of the idea that we track or cognitively access the requirements of rules, where those requirements are independent of human judgement in the sense of independence central to Humanised Platonism: our judgements about the applicability of the semantic predicate which encapsulates the imposed requirement can still come apart from the fact of that semantic predicate's applicability when the non-trivially specified ideal conditions do not obtain. We can thus still see ourselves as sometimes tracking or cognitively accessing the requirements of rules that reach ahead to separate as yet unactualised behavioural episodes into those that do, and those that do not, normatively accord with the relevant rule. This explains how the objectivity of meaning can be retained, even while the spurious autonomy of the super-rigid-rule-as-rail is consciously rejected.[34]

In which case there is simply no need to accept Kripke's 'sceptical solution' to Wittgenstein's sceptical paradox about rule-following, that is, the idea that since justifications must always run out at some point in the otherwise infinite regress of rules for the application of rules for the application of rules (and so forth), therefore we have no choice but to repose on the communitarian appeal to 'practices' or acculturated 'forms of life'. What the Humanised Platonist approach allows us to see is that such practices can indeed go wrong by certain standards of cognitive accountability that are *not* super-rigid in the sublimated (scepticism-inducing) way but which can nonetheless be specified with adequate precision and taken to provide adequate criteria for deciding what counts (or fails to count) as correctly following a rule. All that drops out on this de-sublimated view of the relevant truth-conditions is the idea that objectivity *must* be a matter of tracking or cognitively accessing facts which *cannot* be conceptually structured since their being so would compromise, negate, or undermine the very claim to objectivity of judgement. Yet of course – as the sceptic will be swift to remark – that claim is self-undermining in so far as objectivity by very definition (or by this definition at least) rules out any proper or permissible appeal to the structures and modalities of human judgement. Hence the importance, as Miller sees it, of asserting the alternative 'Humanised Platonist' view according to which we can still have objectivity in a perfectly acceptable sense of that term while avoiding the sceptical nemesis embraced by upholders of the hardline (sublimated) platonist conception.

Hence also his disagreement with those, like Wright, who espouse a version of response-dependence theory but who view it very often as yielding more hostages to sceptical fortune than Miller thinks either desirable or necessary.[35] Thus, '[a]ccording to Wright's anti-realist, the conclusion that if there were semantic facts they would be in principle undetectable is nothing to worry about, not because semantic discourse can be given a satisfying non-factualist construal, but rather because such semantic facts as there are are susceptible to a fundamentally *non-detectivist* epistemology'.[36] However, as Miller sees it, this argument throws away the chief benefit of a response-dispositional account, that is to say, the possibility it holds out of explaining how our judgements can be *both* responsive to 'best opinion' under certain specified optimal conditions *and* capable of tracking (or detecting) such concepts or rules as can properly be thought to possess an objectively valid character beyond any practice-based conception of veridical warrant. Thus:

> on the Humanised Platonist conception of tracking we deliberately separate the idea that best opinions play an extension-determining role from the idea that they constrain rather than track the facts about the extension of the relevant predicate; in Humanised Platonism we view best beliefs as playing a constraining role with respect to the applicability of a predicate *only in virtue of the fact that they infallibly track its extension*'.[37]

This might look suspiciously like having one's cake and eating it – invoking 'best opinion' so as to provide for a response-dependent account while also insisting (through those metaphors of 'tracking' and 'detection') that best opinion somehow *cannot be wrong* when applied to a suitable range of predicates or properties. However Miller can always reply that his is the best (indeed the only adequate) truth-preserving approach since the alternatives fall out between a 'sublimated' realist conception that places truth beyond our utmost epistemic reach and a full-fledged anti-realist theory that restricts truth to whatever we can know – or reliably assert – within the limits imposed by our present-best means of recognition or verification. Thus the virtue of adopting a 'Humanized Platonist' outlook is that it manages to head off the

Wittgenstein–Kripke sceptical challenge by saving the required objectivity of certain rules, concepts, and meanings while nonetheless stopping well short of the claim that such objectivity precludes their being in any way conceptually structured. All that is needed in order to achieve this desirable result is a distinction between two ideas of 'independence' or 'autonomy', those which can be taken 'to characterise the Humanised and Sublimated conceptions respectively'. On the latter account objectivity drops out as soon as one concedes – with regard to some particular area of discourse – that correctness in matters of factual statement or rule-following practice involves some appeal to response-dependent or conceptually structured predicates. On the former account, conversely, objectivity remains very much in the picture even though the relevant standards or conditions of correctness are such as cannot be specified without making that appeal.

III

This is why, according to Miller, 'the proper target of the rule-following considerations is the Sublimated Conception of cognitive access'.[38] What it enables us to see is that the 'rigid-rail' idea of objectivity has driven philosophers into the cleft stick of supposing that correctness in judgement must *either* be a matter of our somehow having epistemic access (*per impossibile*) to recognition-transcendent truths *or* be equated with the deliverances of 'best opinion', taken to determine, rather than to track, the extension of our object-terms and predicates. In which case, quite simply, we could not be wrong in applying any rule or concept that conformed to the standards or practices laid down by existing communal warrant. However this amounts to just another version of Kripke's 'sceptical solution' whereby there is *nothing more* to the business of correctly following a rule – of continuing a sequence of numbers in the 'right' way or coming up with the 'right' answer to some question in elementary arithmetic – than producing a response that counts as correct by those same communal lights.[39] Thus Kripke's sceptical solution entails that the assertibility-conditions for a sentence such as '68 + 57 = 125' cannot be specified in any other way than by saying (like Wittgenstein) 'this game is played!' or 'correct according to the rules that apply in the language-game of elementary arithmetic'.[40] However such an argument goes clean against the strong (and surely justified) intuition that arithmetical truth *cannot* be merely a matter of our sentences coming out right with respect to some practice that prevails within this or that community of judgement. Rather, as Miller contends, there has to be provision for the standing possibility of our actually getting things wrong, or even – at the limit – for 'best opinion' somehow to come apart from the truth-conditions for valid arithmetical reasoning. After all, it is a consequence of Kripke's sceptical 'solution' to the rule-following paradox that arithmetical statements can only have conditions of warranted assertibility (not truth), and moreover that any issue concerning their correctness can only be referred to best opinion as defined in communal or practice-relative terms.

This follows, to repeat, firstly from the infinite-regress argument about rules for the proper application of rules, and secondly from the Wittgensteinian premise that there is no introspectible or deep further 'fact' about a competent arithmetician and language-user that would make it infallibly the case that she understood the '+'-sign to signify *addition* in the standard (arithmetically correct) sense. Thus, according to Kripke, it is impossible that any such appeal to some vague inner realm of meanings, intentions, mental contents, propositional attitudes, or whatever, should somehow provide the kind of normative force required to make sense of the claim for arithmetical objectivity or truth. At this point we may be tempted to suggest that meaning addition by '+' is a *sui generis* 'primitive state', one that is 'not to be assimilated to sensations or headaches or any "qualitative" states, nor to be assimilated to dispositions, but a state of a unique kind of its own'.[41] However (Kripke counters) this response, though strictly irrefutable, is also manifestly a counsel of despair insofar as 'it leaves the nature of [that] postulated primitive state – the primitive state of meaning addition by "+" – completely mysterious. It is not supposed to be an introspectible state yet supposedly we are aware of it with some fair degree of certainty whenever it occurs.'[42] From which he concludes that there is simply no alternative to the communitarian conception of correctness in rule-following since such correctness cannot be *either* a matter of our cognitively accessing truths (or objective validity-conditions) that lie beyond our utmost epistemic reach *or* a matter of our having privileged epistemic access to a realm of meanings, concepts, and intentions that determines what shall count as a correct application of the rule.

So far at least Miller agrees with Kripke: that neither of these conceptions can possibly work, the first because it means we could *never be right* (epistemically justified) in asserting some objective truth of arithmetic, and the second because it means we could *never be wrong* insofar as correctness would amount to no more than accordance with private (incommunicable) mind-states which licensed any number of alternative 'rules' for applying the '+'-sign or other such operators. However, Miller argues, 'the two proposals considered here by Kripke . . . are exhaustive only if the following assumption is obligatory: *that the range of inner states that are introspectible is limited to those possessed of a distinctive qualitative phenomenology*.'[43] That is to say, Kripke takes it that the sole alternative to a hardline (super-rigid-rail or 'sublimated' platonist) conception of objectivity is one that must involve a surely 'desperate' appeal to some wholly indefinable state of inner experience which cuts the speaker or reasoner off from any standards of correctness other than those supplied by her private beliefs or intuitions. Yet 'why should we make this assumption?' Miller asks. And again, more specifically: '[w]hy cannot we conceive of understanding as irreducible, introspectible, and yet as possessing no distinctive qualitative phenomenology?'[44] After all there is no reason – Kripkean (or 'Kripkensteinian') prejudice aside – to conclude that those alternatives exhaust the field and that the only way to go once disabused of the super-rigid-rail and private-introspectionist fallacies is to fall back on the idea of communal warrant as our last best hope of salvaging some workable (albeit practice-relative) conception of what it means to follow a rule.

Hence Miller's 'Humanised Platonist' theory of cognitive access, one that seeks to avoid this false dilemma by invoking a dimension of response-dependence which allows such access through the role of best opinion in deciding the applicability of certain predicates yet which also conserves the possibility of correctness (and error) by explaining how best opinion may either track or 'come apart' from objective truth-conditions. Thus:

> [t]he proposed account . . . which I shall suggest as an alternative to the Sublimated Conception is designed, in its application to the inner, to make sense of this possibility, in a manner that avoids the charges of irrefutability and mystery-mongering, as well as the other problems that beset the two non-reductionist solutions rejected by Kripke.[45]

What this involves is the claim – the distinctively Kantian claim – that our judgements can be shown to possess all the 'objectivity' required to combat scepticism just so long as our account of them incorporates some reference to the intersubjectively valid conditions of knowledge and experience in general. That is, we lose nothing through the turn to response-dependence – just as Kant thought we lost nothing through the turn to transcendental idealism – since what is given up in both cases is the self-contradictory notion that we might somehow have knowledge of a sheerly objective (noumenal) reality which *by very definition* eludes our utmost powers of perceptual and conceptual grasp. Quite the opposite, in fact: we regain the world (or save knowledge from the threat of Humean scepticism) by producing *a priori* arguments to the effect that the realm of phenomenal appearances could not be other than it is for knowers such as ourselves equipped with certain likewise *a priori* (knowledge-constitutive) modes of apprehension. Thus for Kant, famously, the only answer to the epistemological sceptic is one that abjures any question concerning our 'knowledge of the external world' except insofar as that knowledge is construed as having to do with the conditions of possibility – the operative scope and limits – of conceptual understanding as applied to the manifold of sensuous or phenomenal intuitions. To suppose that knowledge must surely consist in *something more* – in our somehow having access to 'objective' truths outside or beyond those conditions – is to fall straight into the sceptic's trap since he can always show this supposition to rest on a downright self-contradictory claim. So the realist (Kant's 'empirical realist' who takes this position to be perfectly consistent with the tenets of transcendental idealism) can best avoid making that fatal mistake by conceding that reality is always apprehended under the forms and modalities of human knowledge but nonetheless maintaining – as against the sceptic – that our judgements may be correct or otherwise insofar as they accord (or fail to accord) with the conditions for optimal response as defined by just those forms and modalities.

In short, Kant's argument bears a marked resemblance to Miller's claim for the problem-solving virtues of a 'Humanised Platonist' approach, that is, for a duly qualified version of the response-dependence theory which allows us to retain what is right about the 'tracking' or 'detectivist' conception of truth while permitting us to jettison the super-rigid-rail along with its various unwanted (scepticism-inducing) implications. Indeed, given time, one could pursue the analogy further and remark how Kant's position was arrived at, like Miller's, through perceiving both the problems that arose with any purely rationalist (or objectivist) theory of knowledge and those which resulted from adopting an empiricist approach that reduced knowledge to the Humean 'theatre' of fleeting sensory impressions.[46] However this comparison also suggests that any difficulties with Kant's purported solution are very likely to emerge once again, albeit in somewhat different (i.e., 'detranscendentalised') form, when a similar solution is nowadays attempted by theorists of response-dependence. Thus the greatest problem that Kant bequeathed to subsequent defenders of realism in various fields – especially mathematics and philosophy of science – was just the problem that he claimed to have resolved in the First *Critique*, namely that of showing how our judgement could be held accountable to standards of objectivity and truth even while maintaining that those standards must themselves conform to the scope and limits of cognitive judgement.[47] The history of subsequent attempts to resolve it starts out with Fichte, Schelling and the debate between 'subjective' and 'objective' idealists and continues nowadays not only among devoted

Kantian exegetes but also among those, like McDowell, who take a lead from Kant in their epistemological endeavours.[48] Hilary Putnam has undoubtedly tried longest and hardest to square some version of 'internal' (i.e. framework-relative) realism with a due regard for our powerful intuition that there must be objective truth-values that transcend best opinion even in the limit of idealised epistemic or rational acceptability.[49] So when Miller suggests (*contra* Kripke) that 'we can have a healthy measure of independence between our judgements and the properties which they cognitively access, without requiring that the properties in question be conceptually unstructured' he is resuming an issue that has preoccupied thinkers of otherwise very diverse philosophical persuasion.[50]

McDowell is most explicit in proposing that we look back to those passages of Kant where knowledge is taken to result from the exercise of judgement, itself involving the jointly operative powers of 'receptivity' and 'spontaneity', or the bringing of sensuous intuitions under adequate concepts through an act of synthesis that inherently eludes our conscious awareness yet which somehow underlies and makes possible our entire range of cognitive dealings with the world. 'If we restrict ourselves to the standpoint of experience itself', McDowell writes,

> what we find in Kant is precisely the picture I have been recommending: a picture in which reality is not located outside a boundary that encloses the conceptual sphere . . . The fact that experience involves receptivity ensures the required constraint from outside thinking and judging. But since the deliverances of receptivity already draw on capacities that belong to spontaneity, we can coherently suppose that the constraint is rational; that is how the picture avoids the pitfall of the Given.[51]

Thus we can keep what is most useful in Kant's picture – the idea of 'receptivity' and 'spontaneity' as jointly involved in the act of cognitive judgement – while rejecting the whole 'transcendental' apparatus through which Kant claims to deduce the *a priori* 'conditions of possibility' for knowledge and experience in general. For unfortunately, as McDowell sees it,

> Kant also has a transcendental story, and in the transcendental perspective there does seem to be an isolable contribution from receptivity. In the transcendental perspective, receptivity figures as a susceptibility to the impact of a supersensible reality, a reality that is supposed to be independent of our conceptual activity in a stronger sense than any that fits the ordinary empirical world.[52]

However, he thinks, there is nothing to be lost – and much to be gained – by tactfully ignoring this whole 'metaphysical' dimension of Kant's thought and making the most of those other passages in the First *Critique* that stress the reciprocal interinvolvement of 'receptivity' and 'spontaneity'. What this Kantian approach enables us to see is that philosophers from the Logical Positivists down have gone badly wrong and run into all manner of insoluble antinomies by supposing that the 'problem of knowledge' can be adequately addressed without taking account of judgement as an intermediary power that provides the missing link between empirical intuitions and concepts of understanding. Thus:

> [t]he original Kantian thought was that empirical knowledge results from a co-operation between receptivity and spontaneity. (Here "spontaneity" can be simply a label for the involvement of conceptual capacities.) We can dismount from the seesaw if we can achieve a firm grip on this thought: receptivity does not make an even notionally separable contribution to the co-operation.[53]

In which case we can have all the philosophic benefits of Kant's 'Copernican revolution' without ever getting our fingers caught in all that clanking and functionally otiose machinery of 'transcendental' justification.

However there are problems with McDowell's argument which go right back to those obscure passages in the First *Critique* where Kant talks of judgement – the joint product of receptivity and spontaneity – as involving the exercise of 'imagination', which faculty he describes in turn as a mysterious 'art buried in the depths of the soul', prerequisite to our every act of cognitive judgement yet forever beyond reach of conceptual understanding.[54] Also there is the difficulty of conceiving how judgement can be subject to empirical constraints if – as McDowell puts it in the above-quoted passage – 'reality is not located outside a boundary that encloses the conceptual sphere.' To be sure the passage then goes on to assert, as if in response to this anticipated objection, that '[t]he fact that experience involves receptivity ensures the required constraint from outside thinking and judging.' Yet any force that this rejoinder might be taken to possess is once again thrown into doubt, or so it might seem, by McDowell's immediate qualifying statement that 'since the deliverances of receptivity already draw on capacities that belong to spontaneity, we can coherently suppose that the constraint is rational; that is how the picture avoids the pitfall of the Given.'[55] What he has in mind here is Wilfrid Sellars's oft-cited attack on the 'myth of the Given,' that is, the naive empiricist appeal to an ultimate or bedrock level of experience or sense-certainty which exists quite apart from the various theories or conceptual constructions that we place upon it.[56] Thus McDowell's argument – like that of the response-dependence theorists – can be seen as an attempt to avoid this pitfall by invoking 'spontaneity' as the mind's contribution to a process which cannot be treated in any such reductively empiricist terms since it requires that 'receptivity' (or sensory uptake) be thought of as *always already* informed by the concepts, categories, and organising structures that constitute our knowledge and experience.

Still it is hard to see how McDowell's account can effectively deliver on its promise to do full justice not only to the role of judgement in achieving all this but also to the realist's standing demand that any such account make room for objectivity in a stronger sense, that is, as in principle allowing the existence of truths that transcend our present-best or even best-possible powers of recognition. Not that McDowell is unaware of this likely challenge from the realist quarter. Indeed, as he says,

> [i]t can be difficult to accept that the Myth of the Given is a myth . . . It can seem that we are retaining a role for spontaneity but refusing to acknowledge any role for receptivity, and that is intolerable. If our activity in empirical thought and judgement is to be recognizable as bearing on reality at all, there must be external constraint. There must be a role for receptivity as well as spontaneity, for sensibility as well as understanding. Realizing this, we come under pressure to recoil back into appealing to the Given, only to see over again that it cannot help. There is a danger of falling into an interminable oscillation.[57]

What is required, therefore, is an account of judgement that would prevent this oscillation from ever taking hold – or philosophers from getting stuck on the seesaw – by insisting once again that the 'two' powers are inextricably bound up together and that 'receptivity does not make an even notionally separable contribution to the co-operation'.[58] That they have to be described in such misleadingly dichotomous terms is merely a result (so McDowell implies) of the need to think our way through and beyond a burdensome inheritance – most recently that of logical empiricism – which makes it well-nigh impossible to find a more adequate vocabulary in which to discuss such issues.

IV

All the same one may doubt whether McDowell himself and the response-dependence theorists have yet managed to dismount from the seesaw or to damp down its movement to the point where they (or a select representative) could sit at one end and a realist at the other without giving rise to yet further violent oscillations. Where the problem lies, yet again, is in the idea that judgement can somehow *contain* or *encompass* whatever it is that confers truth upon our statements, or, as McDowell rather tortuously puts it, that 'reality is not located outside a boundary that encloses the conceptual sphere'. For in that case spontaneity must have the upper hand over receptivity, and judgement be taken as determining, not tracking, what shall ultimately count as a matter of 'objective' truth. That is to say, if 'the given' is indeed just a mythical construct, and moreover if the empirical 'constraints' on our acts of judgement are themselves always already conceptually structured, then there would seem nothing to prevent spontaneity from reaching all the way out to those various 'objects' – whether numbers, sets, astronomical bodies, or factual states of affairs – which the realist takes to be wholly independent of our judgements or best beliefs concerning them. Indeed one purpose of McDowell's argument 'is to bring out how difficult it is to see that we can have both desiderata: both rational constraint from the world and spontaneity all the way out'.[59]. But this difficulty is sure to result from any response-dependence theory that promotes 'spontaneity' to the point of arguing that constraints on our judgement can only be conceived as a matter of 'rational constraint from the world'. For the way is then open for the anti-realist to counter that whatever provides a 'rational' check on our spontaneous judgements or modes of response must always already be subject to conceptual structures which effectively determine (rather than track) the constitution of 'objective' reality. And from here it is but a short distance to the claim – which McDowell and the response-dependence theorists are mostly eager to disown – that truth in such matters *just is* a question of best opinion or warranted assertibility.

Their keenness to disown it stems chiefly from a growing dissatisfaction with Dummett-style anti-realism on the part of thinkers like Crispin Wright who were once (not so long ago) strongly drawn in that direction.[60] Thus one argument that figures prominently in the response-dependence literature is that a theory of knowledge cannot be adequate to our standing intuitions in this regard if it fails to make some room for the realist case that there must surely be a great many truths – mathematical, scientific, historical and so forth – which in no way depend on our present or future ability to find them out. However, this allowance makes for a degree of tension (the precise degree varying from case to case) with their general commitment to response-dependence as a theory that promises to resolve the issue – or to split the difference – between realists and anti-realists. That is to say, there is a constant tendency, as I have noted in McDowell, to press this resolution toward the response-dependence end of the scale and thus to define 'objective' truth in terms of what properly counts as such for a suitably placed observer or knower under optimal epistemic conditions. Nor is this bias at all surprising given that the theory has developed in the main as a corrective to certain perceived excesses of the anti-realist position yet one that continues to accept its chief tenet, that is, the inherently problematic character of any attempt to specify truth-conditions beyond those provided by best opinion or warranted assertibility. Hence McDowell's problem in explaining how objective truth can somehow remain in the picture even though 'spontaneity' – or the mind's contribution through the act or process of conceptual judgement – must be taken to reach 'all the way out' and thus to determine or constitute reality insofar as we can possibly conceive it. Wright states the issue in the form of a rhetorical question that captures precisely this dilemma imposed by the logic of anti-realism. 'How can a sentence be undetectably true,' he asks, 'unless the rule embodied in its content – the condition which the world has to satisfy to confer truth upon it – can permissibly be thought of as extending, so to speak, of itself into areas where we cannot follow it and thus determining, without any contribution from ourselves or our reactive natures, that a certain state of affairs complies with it?'[61] To which the implied correct answer must be 'It cannot,' since any positive response would entail the existence of some 'super-rigid machinery' or 'superlative conception' of rules which transcended the limits of human judgement or epistemic grasp and thus failed to comply with the requirements of a response-dependent account.

No doubt (Wright concedes) there are areas of discourse where those requirements don't apply and where the truth of certain statements must be thought of as holding irrespective of any 'contribution from ourselves or our reactive natures'. One of them would seem to be mathematics – or at least the basic axioms of Peano arithmetic – since, according to Wright, 'in shifting to a broadly intuitionistic conception of, say, number theory, we do not immediately foreclose on the idea that the series of natural numbers constitutes a real object of mathematical investigation, which it is harmless and correct to think of the number theoretician as explaining'.[62] Even so Wright's endorsement of the realist construal as 'correct' is offset by his describing it as 'harmless', that is to say (one might reasonably infer) as an attitude adopted more for the sake of facilitating commerce with those notionally 'real' entities than out of any principled commitment to the view that mathematical truths are objective in the verification-transcendent sense of that term. There is a similar ambivalence about Wright's idea that the realist's demands might be satisfied – or her anxieties laid to rest – by introducing the idea of 'superassertibility' for the class of statements that intuitively strike us as possessing objective truth- or falsehood-values even though (at the limit) they involve some normative appeal to best opinion or to judgements arrived at under optimal epistemic conditions. For here again, Wright concedes, there is room for disagreement as to just how this claim is to be interpreted, with the realist likely to say: 'it is because certain statements (in the discourse in question) are true that they are superassertible,' while the advocate of a response-dependence approach is most likely to counter: 'it is because they are superassertible that such statements are true.'[63]

Clearly Wright's aim is to find some workable *modus vivendi* that would allow the realist her 'correct' (or at any rate 'harmless') belief in the objectivity of arithmetic without thereby precluding the appeal to response-dependence where it most matters, that is, as regards those other plausibly truth-apt areas of discourse which can nonetheless be held to require some reference to optimised judgement or best opinion. However it is not so clear that this aim can be achieved on the terms laid down by Wright's idea of 'superassertibility' as a kind of quasi-objective or limit-case condition that would split the difference between both parties. Thus, according to Wright, a statement may properly count as superassertible 'if and only if it is, or can be, warranted and some warrant for it would survive arbitrarily close scrutiny of its pedigree and arbitrarily extensive increments to or other forms of improvement of our information'.[64] In other words it is the same criterion that 'internal realists' such as middle-period Putnam apply when they speak of truth, in Peircean terms, as that which is ultimately 'fated' to be known when all the evidence is in and when that evidence is subject to rational assessment under ideal epistemic conditions.[65]

This consequence emerges most explicitly when Wright remarks that superassertibility 'is also, in a natural sense, an *internal* property of the statements of a discourse – a projection, merely, of the standards, whatever they are, which actually inform assertions within the discourse', and moreover that '[i]t supplies no external norm – in a way that truth is classically supposed to do – against which the internal standards might *sub specie Dei* themselves be measured, and might rate as adequate or inadequate.'[66] So the realist can take little comfort from Wright's apparent concession to the case for objectivity in certain areas of discourse – like elementary number-theory – where she will surely want to claim that response-dependence is out of the picture since truth in such matters has nothing to do with our present-best state of knowledge or range of currently available proof-procedures. For it is just her point that these truths are evidentially (or epistemically) unconstrained, that is to say, that a well-formed arithmetical statement is one whose truth-conditions are decided by the way things stand with respect to numbers and the various operations (adding, subtracting, multiplying and so forth) which produce – or sometimes fail to produce – correct arithmetical results. Furthermore those results are correct, or otherwise, not merely as a matter of assertoric warrant according to best opinion or the deliverance of optimised epistemic judgement but as a matter of objective (i.e., recognition-transcendent) truth.[67] Nor can such statements be treated as 'super-assertible' in Wright's carefully specified sense of that term, that is, as possessing a determinate truth-value just in case our warrant for asserting or denying them would hold good to the utmost of our capacity for devising new and more refined or powerful proof-procedures. For once again the realist will be quick to respond that this provision falls crucially short of what it means to assert an arithmetical fact such as '68 + 57 = 125'. Rather, she will insist, the truth-value of that statement has *nothing whatsoever* to do with our epistemic warrant for asserting it even when the notion of warrant is hypothetically extended – as in Wright's alternative account – so as to allow for its having been tested right up to the limit of best opinion among those best qualified to judge. For this would still leave open the (albeit maximally remote) possibility that their judgements might be systematically distorted or subject to some humanly undetectable deficit in our powers of numerical calculation.

Thus, according to the realist, any fact about what counts – or might ultimately count – as truth among qualified experts cannot properly be taken as deciding the issue with regard to the truth or falsity of statements in arithmetic or in other such areas of discourse where objective (i.e., non-response-dependent) standards apply. After all, the whole debate about anti-realism started out with Dummett's development of the case as a generalisation from the intuitionist approach to philosophy of mathematics, that is to say, his argument that here (as elsewhere) the principle of bivalence necessarily fails when applied to statements for which we lack any adequate proof-procedure or evidential grounds.[68] What Wright appears to have chiefly in view with his proposal of 'superassertibility'-conditions is an approach that would somewhat mollify the realist by removing the sting from Dummett's more extreme formulations – as Dummett likewise seems willing to do in his recent discussions of this topic – while not yielding ground on the crucial issue as to whether 'objectivity' is *always* to some extent a matter of best opinion or idealised epistemic warrant.[69] Hence Wright's suggestion that 'in shifting to a broadly intuitionist conception of, say, number theory, we do not immediately foreclose on the idea that the series of natural numbers constitutes a real object of mathematical investigation'.[70] Yet of course the most controversial feature of Dummett's anti-realist approach that it *does* quite explicitly foreclose on any conception of mathematics that would entail the existence of objective truths exceeding our powers of computational grasp or our best available proof-procedures. From which it follows that the question as to just what *counts* as a 'real object of mathematical investigation' can be settled only with reference to the scope and limits of our knowledge concerning it. However in that case the 'broadly intuitionist conception' that Wright still espouses is one that cannot be brought into line with a realist conception of mathematical truth, except insofar as it treats the latter as a 'harmless' (and to that extent 'correct') way of thinking adopted in order to explain what it is that number theoreticians talk about when they purport to talk about numbers.

Wright is perfectly clear about this when he specifies – following Dummett – that realism with respect to any given area of discourse presupposes a relationship between a statement and its truth-maker such that the truth-maker 'is quite independent of our standards of appraisal' since it belongs to an order of objective reality 'on which we impinge only in an (at most) detective role'.[71] Thus, according to the realist, truth in such areas must be thought of as evidentially and epistemically unconstrained, and correct judgement conceived as tracking it rather than assigning truth-values in conformity with best opinion. However this cannot be the case with statements whose warrant or truth-aptness consists in their being 'superassertible' in Wright's sense of that term. For such statements are by very definition candidates for assessment as true or false only insofar as they elicit a definite response to one or the other effect from those who are properly qualified to judge in virtue of possessing the right kinds of perceptual or cognitive equipment and deploying it under optimal conditions relative to the 'area of discourse' in question. So it makes no difference, from a realist viewpoint, if those conditions are specified with reference to an ideal limit of epistemic warrant rather than a merely *de facto* or presently existing state of knowledge. All that is accomplished by Wright's shift to the notion of 'superassertibility' is a means of effectively deferring the issue while continuing to insist – with the Dummett-type anti-realist – that truth in such matters must *at the limit* be somehow evidentially or epistemically constrained. And it is just this claim that the realist finds utterly implausible, whether applied to statements in arithmetic like those of elementary number-theory or to a great many well-formed (truth-apt) statements in the physical sciences and other disciplines, among them that of historical enquiry.

No doubt it may be said that Wright's concessions to a realist (or quasi-realist) approach in the case of mathematics are expressly intended to defuse this issue through the idea that discourses are ranged on a scale of greater or lesser 'objectivity' depending on whether best opinion plays a minimal or a maximal role in deciding what counts as an instance of correct judgement. At one end of the scale best opinion could be seen as *tracking* or *detecting* truth while at the other it would wholly *determine* the truth of some proffered statement or assertion. Mathematical discourse might thus be taken as belonging to the former class while his favoured examples of the latter type are the discourses of comedy and morals, each of which, in Wright's view, involves an irreducible appeal to what is considered funny or judged right or wrong by widespread assent among those who possess a fair claim to pronounce on the matter. With respect to such cases, 'on a wide range of construals . . . evidence transcendence is simply not in view'. And again: 'at first approximation . . . comic discourse is disciplined by the objective of irreproachability in the light of a community of comic sensibility'.[72] Not that Wright is renouncing any notion of rightness or good judgement in such matters, as can be seen from his claim that individual reactions to comedy are 'disciplined' by wider (communal) patterns of response and have for their 'objective' – itself a pointedly ambiguous choice of term – the ideal of 'irreproachability' relative to best opinion in the matter. All the same, he suggests, there is something decidedly implausible about claiming that everyone who had heard a certain joke or watched a certain TV comedy series could be wrong in thinking it funny (or otherwise) by some objective standard against which their responses could be measured and found wanting. So in this sort of case, according to Wright, best opinion must be taken as the ultimate court of appeal since there is just no way that its verdict could be countermanded or its judgement overturned by reference to some higher (i.e., non-response-dependent) tribunal.

The same goes for ethics, he thinks, at least on that 'wide class of construals' which take ethical judgements to issue from a general commitment to certain beliefs, values, and priorities whose claim on our moral and social consciences is a matter of intersubjective consensus rather than objective truth. Here again it would be odd – indeed a kind of moral arrogance – for any member of some such community to say that all the others were wrong or marching out-of-step with his or her own irreproachable standards of judgement. So in these two cases – comedy and morals – we should take it that truth is determined, not tracked, by the deliverances of best opinion and that qualified judges are those who exhibit just the kinds of response that count as valid among fellow-members of the relevant community or cultural collective. Which is also to say that any *properties* possessed by comic or moral discourse are not the sorts of property that could ever be 'detected' or somehow (impossibly) discovered to exist quite apart from our more-or-less adequate, sensitive, or culturally informed responses to them. Rather they are properties that depend entirely on their being recognised by human agents with a certain range of normative values and beliefs which equip them to respond in appropriate ways to a given situation with comic potential or to a given predicament – real or imagined – with the potential to evoke various (maybe conflicting) moral sentiments. I use the term 'sentiment' here because Wright's characterisation of moral discourse is one that inclines more toward an affective (Humean) account of the moral 'passions' than toward any objectivist (e.g., Kantian) ethical theory. It also stands in marked tension with the kind of ethical realism that would account for moral judgements – to the extent that they are warranted or justified – in terms of our more-or-less developed capacity for responding to certain real-world situations (such as that in Nazi Germany or apartheid South Africa) in a way that takes due stock of their impact on the realities of human life as lived under given material or socio-political conditions.[73]

However there are passages in Wright where he *does* cite this as a reason for doubting that the case for response-dependence in moral-evaluative contexts can be treated as directly or straightforwardly analogous to the case with our perceptions of colour, taste, or other such Lockean secondary qualities. On the contrary, he suggests, moral judgements are more like judgements of primary qualities (such as shape) insofar as they require that *something* hold firm – that there exists some stability of reference – despite and across any shifts of perspective such as that involved in viewing an object from different angles or a given situation from different moral standpoints. Thus: 'the evident *prima facie* analogy is not with *Red* but with *Approximately Square*, when amended to include a condition of stability in shape'.[74] And again:

> moral qualities are not like secondary qualities in the crucial respect: the extension of the truth-predicate among ascriptions of moral quality may not be thought of as determined by our best beliefs – or, at least, the case for thinking otherwise would have to be a different one. The reason, as with judgements of approximative shape, is because whether such a belief is *best* depends on antecedent truths concerning shape/moral status. Second, and for that reason, judgements of moral quality cannot *inherit* objectivity in the way in which . . . judgements of secondary quality can. They cannot do so because the inheritance can only be from the psychological and from the other types of C-condition in a relevant biconditional. And, in the moral case, some of the other C-conditions will themselves be moral. So the mix of subjectivity and objectivity is simply not as in the case of secondary qualities. The comparison is misconceived, and can only encourage a misplaced confidence in the objectivity of morals.[75]

What is most striking about this passage is the way that it turns around in mid-course from an argument *for* the (relative) objectivity of moral judgements and *against* their response-dependent character by analogy with perceptions of colour to an argument *against* the 'objectivity of morals' and *for* the idea of C-conditions (i.e., optimal conditions for a competent subject to arrive at the right sorts of judgement) as decisive in the moral case. Thus it starts out from the basic conviction that there has to be room for moral judgements to diverge from the deliverance of 'best belief' since otherwise they would be wholly fixed or determined – like correct attributions of 'red' – by the way things stand with respect to some (duly normalised) range of moral responses on the part of certain subjects under certain conditions. Yet clearly this is *not* the way we think about moral judgements insofar as (1) they can always go against some dominant consensus of opinion, and (2) they must always be responsive to something – that is, some morally evaluable state of affairs – the character of which is not *determined by* but itself sets the relevant *standards for* any judgement we may make concerning them. So Wright would appear in agreement with those – ethical realists among them – who reject any version of response-dependence theory as applied to moral judgements since it tends on the one hand to over-emphasise the role of 'best opinion' in fixing the reference of moral terms and on the other to restrict sharply any scope for the exercise of responsible judgement in matters that exert a claim on our moral conscience above and beyond whatever normally counts as an optimal mode of response. Thus, in the moral case, 'appropriate receptivity may differ from what suffices in the case of colour precisely by involving some explicit distance from what is typical of moral responses in our culture, or in another'.[76] Which would seem to require that any adequate theory should acknowledge both the degree of objectivity required for any adequate account of moral judgement and also the extent to which moral judgements (unlike perceptions of colour) can possess justificatory warrant even if they diverge from the standard range of recognised 'correct' attributions.

Hence Wright's idea that a certain class of (duly qualified) primary qualities such as 'approximately square' might be better suited to serve as analogies for the moral case than those secondary qualities – like 'red' – whose reference is fixed according to the standard quantified biconditional, that is, as a matter of correctness according to normal perceptions under normal perceptual conditions. For by shifting the emphasis in this direction (toward the 'objective' end of the scale) we can see how moral judgements differ decisively from perceptions whose correctness must be taken to depend on their conforming to certain observer-relative even if intersubjectively valid modes of response. Thus 'the satisfaction of the C-conditions in *Approximately Square* [is] not independent of the extension of shape concepts', just as 'the satisfaction of the C-conditions in *Moral* is not independent of the extension of moral concepts – *S*'s moral suitability, in particular, is itself, presumably, a matter for moral judgement'.[77] In other words – or so it seems – Wright's point in all this is to meet the ethical realist more than half-way by conceding – as against any strong version of the response-dependence thesis – that standards of correctness in moral judgement have more to do with their truth-tracking virtue or responsiveness to morally salient aspects of some given situation rather than with their effectively determining (as in the case of colour-perception) what shall qualify as a correct judgement. However this is not the way that Wright's argument goes. For it is just his point – *contra* the moral objectivist – that moral judgements are unlike perceptions of colour to the extent that they cannot 'inherit objectivity' in the same way that statements such as '*x* is red' derive their correctness-conditions from the fact (as expressed by the duly provisoed and quantified biconditional) that '*x* appears red to visually normal or unimpaired observers under normal lighting conditions' (etc. etc.). And if *this* is the relevant standard of 'objectivity' – one that makes it dependent on normalised modes of perceptual-cognitive grasp – then clearly moral judgements cannot be candidates for objective status. They cannot be so, to repeat, 'because the inheritance can only be from the psychological and from the other kinds of *C*-condition in a relevant biconditional'.[78] And since, in the case of moral judgements, 'some of the other *C*-conditions will themselves be moral', therefore 'the mix of subjectivity and objectivity is simply not as in the case of secondary qualities'. That is to say, what chiefly distinguishes moral judgements from instances of colour-perception is their lack of just that 'objectivity' that comes of a firm grounding in the repertoire of duly normalised human responses under duly normalised perceptual-cognitive conditions. In which case any over-strong analogy between these cases – or any argument that doesn't make full allowance for the different 'mix' of subjective and objective components – must indeed run the risk, as Wright says, of 'encourag[ing] a misconceived confidence in the objectivity of morals'.[79]

However, once again, this shows very clearly how a response-dependence-oriented approach will always tend to redefine 'objectivity' on its own preferential terms, here by equating it with just that kind of intersubjectively specified stability of reference that secures the normative character of judgements like 'x is red', or 'x tastes sweet', or 'x feels rough to the touch'. And, of course, if statements like these are taken as the reference-class, then there will seem little hope of securing such 'objective' status for judgements of the kind: 'Apartheid was wicked', 'George W. Bush's economic policies are socially divisive and morally wrong', or 'it is right to maximise equality of opportunity across the widest possible range of class and income-groups'. Wright's chief argument against the 'objectivity of morals' is that moral statements resist treatment in terms of the standard biconditional formula unless the relevant C-conditions, that is, the conditions for a normal (or optimal) response are taken to include some moral-evaluative predicates. Thus, on his account, they differ decisively from statements concerning secondary qualities like colour whose specification includes *both* a reference to their response-dependent character *and* to a certain dispositional feature of certain objects (e.g., red balloons or London buses) which prevents any such threatening circularity. But this is just to set things up in such a way that the colour instance is taken as paradigmatic and any version of moral realism or objectivism treated as a failed candidate for treatment on the same terms.

What is more, it produces some curious claims as to which other areas of discourse should likewise be thought of as failing the objectivity-test under these terms and conditions. Thus:

> the *self-containment* of moral epistemology – the circumstance that judging that a moral judgement has a proper pedigree will involve moral judgement – has at least a *prima facie* analogue in mathematical judgement – something whose fundamentally anthropocentric character, if that is the right sort of view of it to take, ought to be consistent with its enjoyment of a fairly robust species of objectivity. So that may yet be the more illuminating tradition of comparison to explore – if a comparison is wanted at all.[80]

It is hard to know just what to make of all these tentative suggestions, semi-disclaimers, qualifying clauses, and so forth. However one notion that does come across is that of moral epistemology as sharing a certain salient feature with the discourse of mathematics, namely its character of 'self-containment' or the fact that its truth-conditions cannot be specified without some presumptively circular appeal to standards of validity that have no reference outside or beyond the discourse itself. According to Wright this means that mathematical judgements are 'anthropocentric' insofar as their correctness can only be a matter of conformity with certain humanly instituted rules, procedures, or criteria for valid application. All the same, he concedes, this idea must make room for a 'fairly robust species of objectivity' if it is going to capture our basic intuitions with regard to the nature of mathematical truth. Yet it is hard to see how this can be the case – how the truth of such statements as '68 + 57 = 125' can be objective in anything like the required sense – given the idea of such truth as dependent on our 'anthropocentric' (human, all-too-human) powers of mathematical grasp. Maybe this is not the right 'view of it to take', as Wright cagily admits. But it *is* very much the viewpoint implied by his comparison between mathematical and moral judgements as both 'self-contained' in the sense of allowing no legitimate appeal – like that which applies in the case of colour-term usage – to conditions of correctness that involve some reference to standards of 'objective' (non-self-referring) validity or truth. And this despite his clear acknowledgement elsewhere that there is something decidedly counter-intuitive about any conception of mathematical correctness that doesn't make room for the standing possibility of widespread error or of human judgements as 'coming apart' from what is truly (objectively) the case. All the same – as emerges startlingly to view in that remark about the 'anthropocentric' character of mathematical discourse – Wright's approach is one that inclines very much toward the right-hand (i.e., perceiver-relative) side of the biconditional formula and which hence manifests a marked bias against the idea of truth-values as holding independently of 'best opinion' or optimal epistemic warrant.

V

In his later work Wright seems keen to deflect this objection from the realist quarter by acknowledging the range of different criteria or validity-conditions that should properly be taken to apply in various disciplines or areas of discourse.[81] Thus, for instance, he concedes that moral judgements require something more than the appeal to standards of communal acceptability if they are to offer any grounds for principled resistance to a dominant (maybe systematically distorted) consensus of opinion. On the face of it this sliding-scale theory is well-equipped to sustain a sensibly pluralist approach, that is, one that takes response-dependence as intrinsic to all our moral judgements but which nonetheless allows for some measure of ethical realism short of that required by the hardline objectivist in matters of ethical evaluation. However this is not how his argument works out, as can be seen from what he says elsewhere concerning the resemblance between moral and comic 'communities' of judgement and the impossibility, in either case, of conceiving that there might be some grounds of appeal beyond such a communitarian conception of right or appropriate response. As with mathematical judgements, so here: what looks like a move toward meeting the realist on terms that she could reasonably accept turns out to be a move that effectively reasserts the anti-realist case by treating her claims as always subject to the deliverance of best opinion or communal warrant. Or again: just as the move to intuitionism in number-theory still allows us (harmlessly) to think of the series of natural numbers as a 'real object of mathematical investigation' while remaining uncommitted as regards the existence of objective truth-values, so likewise in the case of moral judgement we can have all the quasi-'realism' we want just so long as it entails no commitment to anything stronger in the way of legitimising warrant. This implication is reinforced by the idea of moral judgement as bearing close comparison with our response to comic situations, since there is surely something absurd (even comical) in the notion that our sense of humour might be subject to standards of correctness transcending those that actually decide whether we happen to find something funny or not.

In short, there is a constant bias in Wright's treatment of these issues that shifts the emphasis from a realist to an anti-realist construal, whatever the particular 'area of discourse' under review. And this despite his no doubt genuine desire to accommodate those strong realist intuitions which often run counter to the kind of argument that he finds altogether more convincing from a philosophic standpoint. This tendency is already obvious in Mark Johnston's writings on response-dependence, a main point of reference for much that has later been written on the topic by Wright, Miller and others. Thus, according to Johnston, 'response-dispositional' properties can best be defined as 'properties identified, a priori, as dispositions to elicit certain specified cognitive or affective responses under suitable (substantially specified) circumstances in suitable (substantially specified) subjects'.[82] What is chiefly of note in this passage is first the running together of 'cognitive' and 'affective' responses as if they could be treated pretty much on a par with respect to their truth-conditions, and second his assumption that the 'properties' which elicit them can somehow be identified *a priori* – that is, as a matter of necessary (presuppositional) truth – despite the requirement that responses and properties should both receive an adequate or 'substantial' specification. It seems to me that these two features of Johnston's argument are indicative of much that is problematic about the current literature on response-dependence in various contexts of debate. That is to say, this approach has an inbuilt bias toward just those 'properties' that can most readily be thought of as response-dependent on any plausible construal, that is, features of the world as perceived by sentient creatures such as ourselves with a certain range of presumptively normal responses under given conditions.

The example of colour-terms tends to take pride of place since our perception of colours has standardly figured – at least since Locke – as the prototype instance of a secondary quality that cannot be adequately specified in physicalist terms but which always involves some ultimate reference to the subjective or phenomenological dimension of human experience. (Consider if you will the famous hypothetical test-case of Mary the colour-scientist who 'knows' everything there is to be known about optics, waveband theory, reflectance, refraction, the neurophysiology of colour-perception, and so forth, but who happens to be colour-blind and therefore cannot *know* – in a qualitative sense – what is meant when other non-expert types knowingly refer to the colour 'blue'.[83]) However this fondness for colour as a privileged example goes along with a general shift toward the subjective end of the scale or toward those cases which give the best hold for a generalised theory that demotes objectivity in favour of a strong response-dispositional approach. Thus the idea of moral values as construable in realist terms is effectively ruled out by classing them together with so-called comic 'properties' and hence excluding them from consideration as suitable candidates for ascription of objective truth or falsehood. Moreover this approach gains added support from the notion that response dependent properties are connected as a matter of strictly *a priori* warrant with those statements or judgements that count as correct among members of the relevant norm-providing community. For insofar as their correctness by communal standards is such as to exclude the very possibility that they might be wrong – that the norms in question might themselves be deviant or erroneous – then of course it is a sheerly self-evident truth that things *just are* as they are perceived or considered to be according to best opinion. Indeed the standard forms of quantified biconditional could better be described as analytic rather than *a priori* since they hold as a matter of logical necessity once it is allowed that correct judgements (thus defined) simply *cannot do other* than pick out the appropriate (response-dependent) properties or qualities.

However, as I have said, it then becomes a puzzle as to how the right-hand side of the biconditional can be given an adequate (substantive or non-trivial) specification and thus avoid the charge that this whole line of argument amounts to no more than an exercise in circular reasoning. That is, if the argument goes through as a matter of *a priori* self-evidence then there is no need to specify just what it is about the relevant (biconditionally linked) properties and responses that warrants or explains their jointly counting as an instance of correct judgement. In which case the theorist might just as well proclaim that this thesis is valid merely in virtue of its logical form for every judgement that involves the ascription of certain predicates to certain objects or events, and which moreover enjoys the kind of normative status that places its truth beyond doubt for all qualified perceivers or judges. A consequence of this is to blur the distinction – which Wright elsewhere seems eager to uphold – between (1) properties like physical shape or mathematical correctness which plausibly involve an appeal to objective truth-conditions, (2) qualities like colour that plausibly involve some reference to given perceptual norms, and (3) qualities such as comic potential – or the disposition to make us laugh – which fail to meet conditions (1) or (2) on account of their largely culture-specific or temperamental character. For Wright's whole approach is such as to privilege an epistemic conception of truth (i.e., one tailored to the scope and limits of humanly attainable knowledge) over any alethic or objectivist conception that involves the existence of truth-values beyond those warranted by best opinion with respect to some given area of discourse.[84] This is why, as we have seen, he introduces the idea of 'superassertibility' as a means of countering realist objections by allowing that truth may elude or transcend any merely *de facto* consensus of 'best opinion' while nonetheless keeping it within the range of idealised epistemic warrant. Thus there is always the explicit or implicit appeal to a community of duly qualified subjects whose qualification as regards the particular case in hand *just is* their readiness to issue statements that satisfy the relevant biconditional.

This explains what I have described as the marked tendency, in Wright and others, to make out the argument for response-dependence in a way that constantly extends its reach into areas of discourse that would otherwise appear prime candidates for treatment in terms of objective (recognition-transcendent) truth-values. It also explains the dissatisfaction that ethical realists have felt when confronted with an argument that leaves little room for distinguishing between the kinds of criteria that properly apply in the case of moral evaluation and the kinds of shared reactive disposition that may account for our laughing at the same sorts of thing just so long as we and others have enough in common (age, class, cultural background, temperament) to be on roughly the same comic wavelength. Here again there is a notable failure to allow that best opinion cannot do all the work and that there might exist certain limit-case instances – such as that of a community wholly given over to barbarous or inhumane practices – which would warrant our asserting the existence of truths unacknowledged or unrecognised by any member of that community. Thus the argument is at risk of endorsing those cultural-relativist appropriations of Wittgenstein which deny that we can ever be justified in criticising practices, beliefs, or value-systems other than our own since by so doing we manifest a failure to grasp those criteria for moral judgement that come from our sharing some particular 'language-game' or communal 'form of life'.[85] Epistemologically speaking it is a close relative of Dummett's anti-realist position, that is to say, his logico-semantic variant on the verificationist doctrine which entails the inadmissibility of truth-claims transcending the limits of attainable knowledge or epistemic warrant. Moreover it falls in readily enough with that 'Kripkensteinian' approach to issues in the philosophy of mathematics and logic which conceives of correctness in rule-following as at bottom just a matter of behaving in accord with the practices that standardly count as correct by our best communal lights.

To be sure, Wright does make allowance for the fact that different 'areas of discourse' involve different kinds of truth-claim or orders of validity. These latter extend all the way from instances of straightforward response-dependence to instances of 'superassertibility' where truth is a matter of idealised epistemic warrant and – beyond that – to areas of discourse which satisfy the conditions for 'cognitive command', that is to say, for the greatest degree of objectivity consistent with a theory which still makes room for some contribution (however minimal) on the right-hand side of the quantified biconditional. 'When a discourse exhibits Cognitive Command,' Wright specifies, 'any difference of opinion will be such that there are considerations quite independent of the conflict which, if known about, would mandate withdrawal of one (or both) of the contending views.'[86] However there is still that saving clause – 'if known about' – which draws the line so as to admit truths that fall within the compass of optimised epistemic warrant and so as to exclude any notion of truths that might in principle transcend or elude the best efforts of human enquiry. And this concession is all that anti-realists require in order to press home their case, whether on Kripkensteinian rule-following grounds or with reference to Dummett's more generalised (logico-semantic) version of the argument. At any rate there is ample reason to think that response-dependence theory is not so much an answer – or a viable alternative – to these various sceptical doctrines as another 'sceptical solution' (like Kripke's) that leaves all the problems very firmly in place.

References

1. See for instance Jim Edwards, 'Best Opinion and Intentional States', *Philosophical Quarterly*, Vol. 42 (1992), pp. 21–42; Richard Holton, 'Reponse-Dependence and Infallibility', *Analysis*, Vol. 52 (1992), pp. 180–84; Mark Johnston, 'Dispositional Theories of Value', *Proceedings of the Aristotelian Society*, Vol. 63 (1989), pp. 139–74, 'How to Speak of the Colours', *Philosophical Studies*, Vol. 68 (1992), pp. 221–63, and 'Objectivity Refigured: pragmatism without verificationism', in J. Haldane and C. Wright (eds), *Realism, Representation and Projection* (Oxford: Oxford University Press, 1993), pp. 85–130; Alex Miller, 'Rule-Following, Response-Dependence, and McDowell's Debate with Anti-Realism', *European Review of Philosophy*, Vol. 3 (1998), pp. 175–97; Philip Pettit, 'Realism and Response-Dependence', *Mind*, Vol. 100 (1991), pp. 597–626, *The Common Mind: an essay on psychology, society, and politics* (Oxford: Oxford University Press, 1992), 'Are Manifest Qualities Response-Dependent?', *The Monist*, Vol. 81 (1998), pp. 3–43, and 'Noumenalism

and Response-Dependence', *The Monist*, Vol. 81 (1998), pp. 112–32; Mark Powell, 'Realism or Response-Dependence?', *European Review of Philosophy*, Vol. 3 (1998), pp. 1–13; Peter Railton, 'Red, Bitter, Good', *European Review of Philosophy*, Vol. 3 (1998), pp. 67–84; Ralph Wedgwood, 'The Essence of Response-Dependence', *European Review of Philosophy*, Vol. 3 (1998), pp. 31–54; Crispin Wright, 'Moral Values, Projection, and Secondary Qualities', *Proceedings of the Aristotelian Society*, Supplementary Vol. 62 (1988), pp. 1–26, 'Realism, Antirealism, Irrealism, Quasi-Realism', *Midwest Studies in Philosophy*, Vol. 12 (1988), pp. 25–49, 'Euthyphronism and the Physicality of Colour', *European Review of Philosophy*, Vol. 3 (1998), pp. 15–30, and *Truth and Objectivity* (Cambridge, MA: Harvard University Press, 1992).

2. John Locke, *An Essay Concerning Human Understanding*, ed. A. S. Pringle-Pattison (Oxford: Oxford University Press, 1969), Book II, Chap. 8, Sect. 15, p. 69.
3. See Johnston, 'How to Speak of the Colours' and other entries under Note 1, above.
4. See for instance Railton, 'Red, Bitter, Good' and Wright, 'Moral Values, Projection, and Secondary Qualities' (Note 1, above); also Michael Smith, *The Moral Problem* (Oxford: Blackwell, 1994).
5. For further discussion see Wright, *Truth and Objectivity* (Note 1, above).
6. Johnston, 'Dispositional Theories of Value', p. 141 (Note 1, above).
7. Pettit, 'Terms, Things, and Response-Dependence', *European Review of Philosophy*, Vol. 3 (1998), pp. 55–66; p. 55.
8. Wright, *Truth and Objectivity*, p. 112 (Note 1, above).
9. Ibid., p. 112
10. Alex Miller, 'Rule-Following, Response-Dependence, and McDowell's Debate with Anti-Realism', p. 177 (note 1, above).
11. See especially Michael Dummett, *Truth and Other Enigmas* (London: Duckworth, 1978) and *The Logical Basis of Metaphysics* (Duckworth, 1991); also Michael Luntley, *Language, Logic and Experience: the case for anti-realism* (London: Duckworth, 1988); Neil Tennant, *Anti-Realism and Logic* (Oxford: Clarendon Press, 1987); Timothy Williamson, 'Knowability and Constructivism: the logic of anti-realism', *Philosophical Quarterly*, Vol. 38 (1988), pp. 422–32; and Crispin Wright, *Realism, Meaning and Truth*, 2nd edn (Oxford: Blackwell, 1993).
12. See for instance William P. Alston, *A Realist Theory of Truth* (Ithaca, NY: Cornell University Press, 1996) and Scott Soames, *Understanding Truth* (Oxford: Oxford University Press, 1999).
13. Miller, 'Rule-Following, Response-Dependence, and McDowell's Debate with Anti-Realism', p. 178 (Note 1, above).
14. John McDowell, 'Intentionality and Interiority in Wittgenstein', in K. Puhl (ed.), *Meaning Scepticism* (Berlin: de Gruyter, 1991), pp. 148–69 and 'Meaning and Intentionality in Wittgenstein's Later Philosophy', *Midwest Studies in Philosophy*, Vol. 17 (1992), pp. 40–52.
15. Ludwig Wittgenstein, *Philosophical Investigations*, trans. G. E. M. Anscombe (Oxford: Blackwell, 1953), Sects 201–92 *passim*; also Kripke, *Wittgenstein on Rules and Private Language* (Blackwell, 1982); Bob Hale, 'Rule-Following, Objectivity, and Meaning', in Hale and Crispin Wright

(eds), *A Companion to the Philosophy of Language* (Blackwell, 1997), pp. 369–96; John McDowell, 'Wittgenstein on Following a Rule', *Synthèse*, Vol. 58 (1984), pp. 325–63; Alexander Miller and Crispin Wright (eds), *Rule-Following and Meaning* (Teddington: Acumen, 2001).

16. McDowell, 'Meaning and Intentionality in Wittgenstein's Later Philosophy', p. 149 (Note 14, above).
17. See especially Kripke, *Wittgenstein on Rules and Private Language* (Note 15, above).
18. Wittgenstein, *Philosophical Investigations*, Sects 269–94 *passim*.
19. McDowell, *Mind and World* (Cambridge, MA: Harvard University Press, 1994). For the argument that 'nothing works' in philosophy of mathematics, see Paul Benacerraf, 'What Numbers Could Not Be', in Paul Benacerraf and Hilary Putnam (eds), *The Philosophy of Mathematics: selected essays*, 2nd edn. (Cambridge: Cambridge University Press, 1983), pp. 272–94; also various essays collected in Putnam, *Mathematics, Matter and Method* (Cambridge University Press, 1975).
20. Immanuel Kant, *Critique of Pure Reason*, trans. Norman Kemp Smith (London: Macmillan, 1964).
21. Kant, 'Transcendental Aesthetic', in *Critique of Pure Reason*, pp. 65–82. See also Christopher Norris, 'McDowell on Kant: redrawing the bounds of sense' and 'The Limits of Naturalism: further thoughts on McDowell's *Mind and World*', in *Minding the Gap: epistemology and philosophy of science in the two traditions* (Amherst, MA: University of Massachusetts Press, 2000), pp. 172–96 and 197–230.
22. McDowell, 'Wittgenstein on Following a Rule', p. 353 (Note 15, above).
23. McDowell, 'Intentionality and Interiority in Wittgenstein', p. 168 (Note 14, above).
24. See entries under Note 12, above; also Jerrold J. Katz, *Realistic Rationalism* (Cambridge, MA: MIT Press, 1998).
25. Miller, 'Rule-Following, Response-Dependence, and McDowell's Debate with Anti-Realism', p. 176 (Note 1, above).
26. Ibid., p. 176.
27. Ibid., p. 176.
28. Ibid., p. 196.
29. Ibid., p. 177.
30. Ibid., p. 177.
31. Ibid., p. 177.
32. Ibid., p. 178.
33. Kant, *Critique of Pure Reason* (Note 20, above).
34. Miller, 'Rule-Following', pp. 195–6 (Note 10, above).
35. Wright, *Truth and Objectivity* (Note 1, above).
36. Miller, 'Rule-Following', p. 186 (Note 10, above).
37. Ibid., p. 193.
38. Ibid., p. 176.
39. Kripke, *Wittgenstein on Rules and Private Language* (Note 15, above).
40. Wittgenstein, *Philosophical Investigations*; also *On Certainty*, ed. G. E. M. Anscombe and G. H. von Wright (Oxford: Blackwell, 1969) and *Lectures on the Foundations of Mathematics*, ed. Cora Diamond (Chicago: University of Chicago Press, 1976).

41. Kripke, *Wittgenstein on Rules and Private Language*, p. 51 (Note 15, above).
42. Ibid., p. 51.
43. Miller, 'Rule-Following', p. 185 (Note 10, above).
44. Ibid., p. 185.
45. Ibid., p. 185.
46. David Hume, *A Treatise of Human Nature* (Oxford: Clarendon Press, 1978).
47. See for instance Frederick C. Beiser, *The Fate of Reason: German philosophy from Kant to Fichte* (Cambridge, MA: Harvard University Press, 1987).
48. Johann Gottlieb Fichte, *The Science of Knowledge with the First and Second Introductions*, trans. and ed. Peter Heath and John Lachs (Cambridge: Cambridge University Press, 1980); F. W. J. Schelling, *System of Transcendental Idealism*, trans. Peter Heath (Charlottesville, VA: University of Virginia Press, 1978); McDowell, *Mind and World* (Note 19, above).
49. See especially Hilary Putnam, *Reason, Truth and History* (Cambridge: Cambridge University Press, 1981); also *Realism and Reason* (Cambridge University Press, 1983); *The Many Faces of Realism* (La Salle, IL: Open Court, 1987); *Representation and Reality* (Cambridge University Press, 1988); *Realism With a Human Face* (Cambridge, MA: Harvard University Press, 1990).
50. Miller, 'Rule-Following', p. 179 (Note 10, above).
51. McDowell, *Mind and World*, p. 41 (Note 19, above).
52. Ibid., p. 41.
53. Ibid., p. 9.
54. See Note 21, above.
55. McDowell, *Mind and World*, p. 41 (Note 19, above).
56. Wilfrid Sellars, *Empiricism and the Philosophy of Mind* (Cambridge, MA: Harvard University Press, 1997).
57. McDowell, *Mind and World*, pp. 8–9 (Note 19, above).
58. Ibid., p. 9.
58. Ibid., p. 8, n. 7.
60. Wright, *Realism, Meaning and Truth* (Note 11, above).
61. Wright, *Truth and Objectivity*, p. 228 (Note 1, above).
62. Ibid., p. 5; see also Wright, *Wittgenstein on the Foundations of Mathematics* (Cambridge, MA: Harvard University Press, 1980).
63. Wright, *Truth and Objectivity*, p. 80 (Note 1, above).
64. Ibid., p. 48.
65. See Note 49, above.
66. Wright, *Truth and Objectivity*, p. 61 (Note 1, above).
67. See Notes 12 and 24, above; also Michael Detlefson (ed.), *Proof and Knowledge in Mathematics* (London: Routledge, 1992) and Philip Kitcher, *The Nature of Mathematical Knowledge* (Oxford: Oxford University Press, 1983).
68. See Note 11, above.
69. See Dummett, *The Logical Basis of Metaphysics* (Note 11, above).
70. Wright, *Truth and Objectivity*, p. 5 (Note 1, above).
71. Ibid., p. 80.
72. Ibid., p. 106.

73. For further discussion of this ethical issue from a range of philosophic viewpoints, see relevant entries under Note 1 (above); also Robert L. Arrington, *Rationalism, Realism and Relativism: perspectives in contemporary moral epistemology* (Ithaca, NY: Cornell University Press, 1989); David O. Brink, *Moral Realism and the Foundations of Ethics* (Cambridge: Cambridge University Press, 1989); Sabina Lovibond, *Realism and Imagination in Ethics* (Oxford: Blackwell, 1983); Smith, *The Moral Problem* (Note 4, above).
74. Wright, 'Moral Values, Projection and Secondary Qualities', p. 23 (Note 1, above).
75. Ibid., p. 24.
76. Ibid., p. 10.
77. Ibid., p. 23.
78. Ibid., p. 24.
79. Ibid., p. 24.
80. Ibid., p. 25.
81. Wright, *Truth and Objectivity* (Note 1, above).
82. Cited by Wright, ibid., p. 136.
83. Frank Jackson, 'Epiphenomenal Qualia', *Philosophical Quarterly*, Vol. 32 (1982), pp. 127–36 and 'What Mary Didn't Know', *The Journal of Philosophy*, Vol. 83, no. 5 (1986), pp. 291–5.
84. See especially Alston, *A Realist Theory of Truth* (Note 12, above).
85. See for instance Peter Winch, *The Idea of a Social Science and its Relation to Philosophy* (London: Routledge & Kegan Paul, 1958).
86. Wright, *Truth and Objectivity*, p. 103 (Note 1, above).

Chapter Three

Green Thoughts in a Moral Shade: anti-realism, ethics and response-dependence

> Meanwhile the Mind, from pleasure less,
> Withdraws into its happiness;
> The mind, that ocean where each kind
> Does straight its own resemblance find,
> Yet it creates, transcending these,
> Far other Worlds, and other seas;
> Annihilating all that's made
> To a green thought in a green shade.
>
> Andrew Marvell, 'The Garden'

I

Wittgenstein's influence remains very strong in recent discussions of response-dependence (henceforth where convenient abbreviated to 'RD') even though some who have written on the topic – Crispin Wright among them – are keen to keep their distance from certain of his claims.[1] Thus Wright quite explicitly rejects Wittgenstein's 'therapeutic' idea that the philosopher's proper concern (insofar as she has one) is to 'give philosophy peace' by helping us to see that all its hyperinduced puzzles and perplexities are merely the result of our chronic 'bewitchment by language' and our consequent proneness to all manner of metaphysical delusions.[2] More than that, he goes some way toward countering those Wittgenstein-derived anti-realist arguments, such as Michael Dummett's, that would deny the existence of recognition-transcendent (i.e., to us unknown or unknowable) truth-values, and would thus make every area of discourse subject to the governing criterion of assertoric warrant or optimised epistemic grasp.[3] This emerges most clearly from Wright's various remarks with regard to mathematics, in particular his statement that in switching to an intuitionist conception of number-theory we need not 'foreclose' on the attractive idea 'that the series of natural numbers constitutes a real object of mathematical investigation', one which moreover 'it is harmless and correct to think of the number theoretician as exploring'.[4] However there is a certain ambivalence (not to say evasiveness) about Wright's phrasing here which can scarcely escape notice. If we take the word 'correct' in that last clause as representing his considered position on the matter then there would seem to be no escaping the conclusion that Wright is a realist (indeed a Platonist) with respect to numbers, sets, and other such mathematical entities. Conversely, if we emphasise the word 'harmless', then the sentence comes out as a qualified endorsement of mathematical realism but one which should in truth give the realist little comfort since it treats her belief in the 'reality' of numbers as a kind of enabling assumption adopted for the sake of procedural convenience. And from here it is no great distance to a fictionalist theory of mathematical 'truth' that would scarcely provide any adequate defence against a Kripke-style sceptical or communitarian 'solution' to the Wittgensteinian rule-following paradox.[5]

Nevertheless Wright is unwilling to go all the way with a fictionalist (or hardline instrumentalist) like Hartry Field who argues that we ought to jettison the belief in objectively-existent numbers, sets, etc., since this realist conception makes it strictly impossible to explain how we could ever acquire knowledge of such abstract (epistemically inaccessible) 'objects'.[6] Thus Field, in Wright's words, 'takes it for granted that the correct account of the truth-conditions of pure mathematical statements has the effect – because of its implication of an objectionably abstract ontology – of putting them beyond establishment by ordinary proof methods'.[7] On this view the only non-objectionable approach is one that dispenses altogether with that abstract ontology and adopts a fictionalist conception where numbers figure only as convenient notations or instrumental posits that happen to serve our purposes in the physical sciences.[8] As I say, Wright is far from convinced by this argument and indeed seems to take it as a handy *reductio* of anti-realism when applied at full strength to number-theory or the truth-claims of mathematics. Yet his reader may likewise be far from convinced that Wright has any adequate counterargument that would hold the line against Field's radically nominalist conclusions or against that strain of sceptical-communitarian thinking that Kripke finds implicit in Wittgenstein's rule-following considerations.[9] Nor is the prospect much improved by his switch to the notion of 'superassertibility' as a means of heading off such sceptical doubts while retaining the response-dependent conception of epistemic warrant as our last best hope of countering the anti-realist challenge. For this answer still fails to meet the realist objection that the truth-value of statements such as '68 + 57 = 125' or 'Every even number is the sum of two primes' depends not at all on our state of knowledge or best opinion concerning them. In the second case – that of Goldbach's Conjecture – the statement possesses an objective truth-value (so the realist will claim) even though that value is as yet (and may forever remain) unknown since no computer-programme however powerful can test it against the infinite sequence of even numbers, and nobody has so far come up with a formalised proof-procedure that would establish its truth or falsehood by some more economical means. Thus to say that its truth is 'super-assertible' – maximally borne out through the corroborative evidence so far acquired through testing the conjecture up to vast numerical limits – is a concession that ultimately counts for nothing on the realist view. For this still makes the truth-value of Goldbach's Conjecture dependent on our computational powers or on the scope and limits of our arithmetical grasp rather than acknowledging, as the realist would have it, that the objective truth (or falsehood) of such well-formed hypotheses might always lie beyond our present-best or even our utmost attainable knowledge.

At this point it may be useful to cite the passage from *Truth and Objectivity* where Wright offers his most detailed specification of the quantified biconditional formula as applied to various response-dependent areas of discourse. The argument goes as follows:

> For all S, P: P if and only if (if CS then RS), where 'S' is any agent, 'P' ranges over all of some wide class of judgements (judgements of colour or shape, or moral judgements, or mathematical judgements, for instance), 'RS' expresses S's having of some germane experience (judging that P, for instance, or having a visual impression of colour, or of shape, or being smitten with moral sentiments of a certain kind, or amused) and 'CS' expresses the satisfaction of certain conditions of optimality on that particular response. If the response is a judgement, then S's satisfaction of conditions C will ensure that no other circumstances could have given the judgement formed a greater credibility.[10]

What is so striking about this passage – as with much of the current literature on response-dependence – is the combination of a highly formalised (logically regimented) mode of expression with a curious tendency to blur distinctions that would otherwise seem absolutely prerequisite to any purposeful thinking about the range of topics in question. Moreover, it is precisely *because* the framing argument operates at such a high level of abstract generality that its application to particular cases – perceptions of colour and shape, moral sentiments, mathematical judgements, amusement at comic situations – seems to treat them all as so many variants on the same basic theme, that is, the response-dependence thesis as a putative solution to various issues that might (on any other construal) be taken to require separate treatment on their own distinctive terms. Thus there is something very odd about a theory that 'ranges over all of some wide range of judgements' and which claims to specify just what it is *in each case* that constitutes the 'having of some germane response' yet which offers no more in the way of such specification than a vague appeal to 'conditions of optimality' that can themselves be specified only through a circular reference to their role in producing just those kinds of germane response.

Nor does it help very much to be told that where the response is a judgement (i.e., a response with certain truth-conditions attached) then 'S's [the agent's] satisfaction of [optimal] conditions C will ensure that no other circumstances could have given the judgement formed a greater credibility'. For this is merely to reiterate the same tautological point, that is, the analytic (self-evident and wholly uninformative) truth that anyone who competently judges this or that to be case under optimally truth-conducive circumstances must for that very reason count as best qualified to judge and hence as immune to challenge, correction, or more expert guidance by anyone else whose opinion has been formed under different and thus (by definition) less advantageous circumstances. When phrased like this – without the apparatus of logical notation – the argument appears just an exercise in tail-chasing circularity or a truism that gains some semblance of content through the appeal to 'substantially specified' provisos respecting both the agent's competence to judge and the relevant circumstantial factors.[11] Yet one looks in vain for anything like such an adequate specification, that is to say, anything more than a series of likewise tautological claims to the effect that – in the case of response-dependent predicates – correctness is necessarily a matter of best opinion and best opinion that which necessarily obtains among knowers or perceivers whose judgements or responses are arrived at under optimal epistemic conditions.

My point in all this is that the lack of 'substantially specified' criteria for response-dependent predicates, properties, or attributes goes along with the tendency (as noted above) to widen the range of candidate instances until it encompasses just about everything from what we find funny to what we find morally good (or repugnant), and thence to what counts as a correct (normal) colour perception or even, at the limit, what counts as a valid mathematical judgement. Philip Pettit raises this concern most explicitly when he asks 'how far realism about any area of discourse is undermined by an admission of response-dependence in this sense', that is, the sense in which, concerning that area, it is impossible for our judgements or predicate-assignments to be mistaken since correct judgement or valid predication is inextricably tied to the normative conditions of human response.[12] As usual in this context Pettit takes the instance of colours and other 'secondary qualities' as a paradigm case where such responses, 'at least under suitable conditions, represent a privileged mode of access: a mode of access that rules out error and ignorance'.[13] Of course, in the case of colour-perception, one can go a long way – as the response-dependence theorists often do – toward filling out the physical specification for what shall count as 'suitable conditions', for example, 'perceived as "red" by a normally sighted observer at noon on a moderately cloudy day with no proximate causes of perceptual error such as heat-haze or the presence of a nearby light-source which creates distorting interference-effects'. Indeed other theorists, Mark Johnston among them, have come up with all manner of ingenious scenarios involving non-standard (perceptually misleading) conditions which can then be added to the list that constitutes an 'appropriately provisoed' biconditional for the predicate or property concerned.[14] That is, these are circumstances in the absence of which the biconditional can be taken to hold *a priori*, or as a matter of sheer self-evidence concerning the correctness of our perceptual judgements and the impossibility of our being in error with respect to such response-dependent predicates and properties. Yet here again there is a certain vagueness or regular slippage in the argument from '*a priori* = analytic and hence definitionally true' to '*a priori* = self-evident to us as normally-equipped cognisers and perceivers whose experience of the world is structured or textured according to certain specifiable conditions of cognitive or affective response'. This latter reading would account for Pettit's reference to a 'privileged mode of access', one that automatically 'rules out error and ignorance' since we *just can't be wrong* – perceptually deluded – concerning those judgements that we arrive at 'under suitable conditions' and are suitably (indeed ideally) placed to report on since after all they belong to our own first-person privileged realm of acquaintance. But if the other (analytic) interpretation amounts, as I have said, to a trivial claim devoid of substantive philosophical content then this alternative reading is problematic on several grounds, not least its appeal to the supposed guarantee of veridical first-person epistemic warrant. For one need not be a card-carrying Wittgensteinian to object that such appeals give rise to a vicious regress and, besides, must be counted strictly unintelligible insofar as they lack any reference to a wider (intersubjectively validated) commonality of judgement.[15]

It seems to me that some of the chief problems with response-dependence theory result from this ambivalent usage of the term *a priori* and its consequent tendency to oscillate between a trivial (merely tautological) sense which deprives the theory of substantive content and a sense in which judgement is taken to play a more active role but only at the cost of extending its powers beyond anything accountable to real-world empirical or objective constraints. Such, as I have argued at length elsewhere, is the problem with John McDowell's attempt to enlist Kant's notions of 'receptivity' and 'spontaneity' as the jointly-operative powers of mind which between them account for our knowledge of the world or our capacity to bring intuitions under concepts through the exercise of cognitive judgement.[16] However, this attempt turns out to produce a similar oscillating pattern of argument, with McDowell – like Kant in certain enigmatic passages of the First *Critique* – unable to provide a convincing account of how the 'two' powers could more properly be thought of as inseparable aspects of the self-same cognitive process and hence failing to hold a balance between its receptive (i.e., empirically constrained) and spontaneous (world-constitutive) modes. Moreover it is 'spontaneity' that tends to assume the dominant role, just as it did in the history of post-Kantian idealist thought which began with Fichte and whose influence can still be felt in the various forms of 'internal'-realist approach that philosophers such as Hilary Putnam have lately espoused as a kind of compromise settlement.[17]

Nor can it be said that the problem is successfully resolved by the theorists of response-dependence when they give up McDowell's Kantian appeal to such dubious 'powers of mind' and elect rather to articulate their case in a logically-regimented language – like Wright's in the passage quoted above – which makes as few concessions as possible to that old (presumptively outmoded) way of thinking. For in their case also there is a constant bias toward conceiving judgement in terms of the mind's reality-constitutive power or its 'spontaneous' capacity to lay down conditions for our 'receptive' openness to the incoming data of sensory perception. Hence, among other things, the emphasis on colour as a prototype instance not only of secondary qualities (traditionally defined) but also of *any* property that can plausibly be treated as involving some appeal to the normative conditions of response among suitably qualified subjects. Thus, on the one hand, judgements of colour are construed as having more in common with affective dispositions – such as finding something comic or melancholy to behold – than would seem at all plausible if one took full account of the latest developments in optics or the relevant branches of neurophysiology. Meanwhile, on the other hand, colour-perception is often invoked as a paradigm case or at any rate a standard point of reference for the discussion of primary qualities (again as traditionally defined) or indeed for the treatment of properties – like that of mathematical truth – which are thereby (supposedly) brought within the ambit of a response-dependent account.[18]

II

So it is that Wright can put his case for extending the quantified biconditional to 'a wide class of judgements' which he takes to include 'judgements of colour or shape, or moral judgements, or mathematical judgements, for instance'.[19] All that is required in order for the biconditional to apply and for the property in question to count as intrinsically response-dependent is that its being correctly picked out should involve the 'having of some germane experience' on the part of a suitably placed subject, such as 'having a visual impression of colour, or of shape, or being smitten with moral sentiments, or amused'.[20] The quoted passages here are all taken from that single compendious sentence – cited five paragraphs above – where Wright lays out his formal statement of the response-dependence (RD) case along with its attendant apparatus of logical symbolism. What is particularly striking about that sentence is the fact that mathematical judgements drop out the second time around and that their place is taken by the psychological state of 'being amused', or of attributing the property 'comic' to some given situation or state of affairs. One could interpret this curious mid-sentence shift of focus either as a shying-away from the idea that mathematical judgements can be treated on a par with the other examples that Wright mentions or, conversely, as a way of making the point that the RD thesis extends right across the range from mathematics to the psychodynamics of comic or other such affective modes of response. On the first interpretation it looks like a sign that the theory has problems (albeit none too clearly acknowledged) with accommodating instances, like that of mathematics, where it is up against powerful countervailing intuitions which require that truth be conceived as something more than the deliverance of best opinion under optimal circumstances. On the second it suggests that an RD approach is intrinsically opposed to the idea that correctness even in mathematical judgements might involve an order of objective (recognition-transcendent) truth that cannot be specified in response-dependent terms. For in that case the point is most effectively made by including in the 'wide range' of RD-specifiable judgements a motley assortment that extends all the way from colour-perceptions to perceptions of shape and thence to mathematics and/or the state of being 'smitten' by moral sentiments or the tendency to laugh when presented with amusing situations. At very least such a claim would raise the question as to whether response-dependence theory can offer a remotely plausible account of what distinguishes the truth-value of mathematical statements from the kind of vaguely normative warrant possessed by a disposition to be amused by certain things that most other people (or anyway those on roughly the same comic wavelength) also find amusing.

Yet it might well be thought that any theory which fails this test – that treats the two cases as in any way comparable – is a theory that has gone seriously wrong by over-extending the scope and pertinence of the RD thesis. Moreover, even if one sets mathematics aside, there is still a large problem with Wright's claim that moral judgements should be treated on a par with our tendency to be amused by certain things since 'on a wide class of construals . . . evidence transcendence is simply not in view' for either area of discourse.[21] For on a different (more discriminate) class of construals it is an error to suppose that moral discourse is response-dependent in anything like the sense of that term which properly applies to jokes or comic situations. No doubt, in some cases, there is a moral dimension to our sense of what counts – what *ought* to count – as a joking matter or as fit material for comic treatment. Thus we may well judge that certain jokes are morally offensive since they exploit various kinds of racial prejudice, or appeal to a depraved conception of human sexuality, or involve making light of events whose enormity is felt to repudiate such comic treatment. Or again, they may strike us as pushing too far with that element of victimage – of collusive third-party scapegoating – which Freud considered a chief source of the somewhat guilty pleasure that we find ourselves taking in some kinds of joke.[22] Of course the pleasure is guilty precisely because our sense of the joke's being off-colour, distasteful or too near-the-knuckle is not enough to prevent us from finding it funny and recounting it again when given half a chance. So clearly the cases of moral judgement and comic response cannot be held altogether distinct or treated as belonging to such different 'areas of discourse' that Wright's equating them amounts to just a kind of crass category-mistake.

Nevertheless there *is* a crucial difference between them, namely that which Peter Railton points out when he remarks that '[w]hat matters [in the moral case] is not who is making the judgement, but *of whom* the judgement is being made, which can be constant across differences in observers'.[23] To this extent it is less like colour-perceptions and more like relational properties such as sweetness or sourness, properties that certainly involve some element of response-dependence – that is, some reference to the state of our taste-buds or associated neurophysiology – but which also involve a seeking-out of those kinds of experience that conduce to our pleasure, satisfaction, or well-being. That is to say, moral judgements have to do with certain properties (of persons, actions, life-chances, or conditions of human flourishing) which cannot be entirely response-dependent even though, to be sure, they cannot be thought of as inhabiting a realm of purely objective values that exist quite apart from humanly-indexed best opinion in the matter.[24] To make them entirely response-dependent would be to say (in effect) that what is good *just is* what is 'good in the way of belief', whatever the belief-community in question or its ideas concerning the nature, value, and proper distribution of human goods. To make them entirely response-*in*dependent would be to place them beyond the sphere of human interests and values, and hence to licence the enforced imposition of value-systems – say religious or political – that claimed to invalidate any such limiting (human, all-too-human) perspective. Rather there is a sense in which moral judgements have to do with our working out the *right* relation to the properties of a life well-lived where 'right' is defined in relational terms as involving both the intrinsic good of certain specified conditions and the fact that those conditions are intrinsic *just by virtue* of their answering to standards of right moral judgement.

Thus, as Railton argues, '[o]ur vocabulary of intrinsic value is primarily geared to the task of asking what to seek and what to avoid, depending on whether it would be (in some sense) a positive or negative thing intrinsically to lead a given life.'[25] And again: it is 'unsurprising' in this case that 'the domain of what is intrinsically good for humans is not rigidly fixed by actual human responses, but reflects instead potentially evolving or changing human responses.'[26] His point is that such evolution could not come about – or be assigned any positive value – except on the assumption that our moral responses are *responses to* some independently-existing (non-belief-relative) standard of human flourishing rather than responses that *themselves determine* what shall properly count as such a standard. If they were 'rigidly fixed' by the evaluative norms of any given moral community then of course its members would be incapable of responding to anything that challenged or contravened the *de facto* consensus of best opinion within that particular community. On the other hand those norms must be thought of as sufficiently robust or well-defined – sufficiently in touch with the interests and values that make for human flourishing – to give them a genuine purchase on our sense of moral right and wrong. What is required is therefore a *relational* conception of the truth-conditions for moral discourse which avoids both the 'strong' (observer-relative) construal of response-dependence and the equally unpalatable idea that moral properties are somehow fixed independently of whatever we think, feel, or believe concerning them.

Thus the realist will argue that pain is intrinsically a bad thing for human beings or other sentient creatures that suffer it and hence that the wanton infliction of pain – its infliction without any justified case for its serving some morally defensible purpose – is likewise an intrinsic evil quite apart from what various individuals (or communities) may happen to think or feel. This situation would not be changed in the least should it happen that our moral sensibilities underwent some drastic change of character so that we came to consider it perfectly acceptable – even virtuous – to inflict suffering on human beings or animals without any attempt at such justification. That human beings experience pain or humiliation under certain conditions or that animals likewise suffer when physically maltreated is a fact wholly independent of our own or other people's judgements in the matter. Yet if the RD thesis in its strong form were applied to the instance of moral discourse then it would follow that any change in our responses – say through some politically motivated drive toward persecuting deviant minorities or some freak of genetic evolution that caused us to become sadistic monsters – must be thought of as entailing a wholesale shift in the standards concerning what properly counts as a good or bad action. Of course there are some – subjectivists, relativists, Nietzschean 'transvaluers of values' – who can see no reason not to grasp this nettle and accept the conclusion (whether anxiously or willingly) that moral judgements *just are* whatever judgements we make according to our 'best', that is, culture-relative or strong-individualist lights.[27] Even so, the ethical realist will claim, their argument can be shown to go wrong – and itself to be a form of delinquent moral reasoning – insofar as it ignores the intrinsic evil of pain, humiliation, and other such degrading experiences which *cannot but* be bad for those who suffer and (by extension) those who wantonly inflict them.

Thus, as Railton says, '[h]uman approbation of its torment would not in the least improve the experience of a dog being kicked or a horse being whipped . . . Rather, it is the intrinsically unliked character of the torment such conduct would cause its recipients – a torment which is unaffected by our attitude – that makes the behaviour wrong.'[28] So there is more than a certain anecdotal piquancy about the story of Nietzsche's rushing out to embrace a donkey that was being beaten in the street before he entered the long period of confinement and (supposed) madness which signalled the end of his writing career as the great antinomian transvaluer of human values. Railton's phrasing is pointedly ambiguous when he talks of 'the experience of a dog being kicked or a horse being whipped' since it seems to have both the primary sense 'that which the animal experiences', and the secondary (yet none the less important) sense: 'that which human beings do or should properly experience when confronted with such instances of wantonly inflicted suffering'. It is in just this way that moral properties and judgements are best thought of as relational, that is, as involving both a reference to real (non-observer-relative) facts about the experience of sentient creatures such as ourselves or non-human animals and a reference to aspects of distinctively human moral awareness that determine what shall count as an adequate response in any given case. The trouble with the strong RD thesis is that it tends to downplay the former requirement by treating moral properties as 'rigidly' specified through the kinds of response they typically evoke, in which case, as I have said, there is simply no room for the claim that some experiences *just are* bad quite apart from whatever we or others may think concerning them. Conversely, the trouble with a strong-objectivist approach to ethical issues is that it finds no place for that essential normative dimension wherein moral judgements necessarily connect with our more-or-less developed powers of responsiveness or our capacity to react in suitable ways to the various cases, actions, or predicaments that confront us. So it is important to get clear about the kind and degree of response-dependence involved and also about the sorts of analogy from other areas of discourse that work – or that signally fail to work – in the case of moral reasoning.

Railton's point is that the RD literature has manifested a strong bias toward colour-perception as a paradigm secondary quality, perhaps (he suggests) because it reflects 'the predominance of vision in human sensory life'.[29] Still we might do better – and avoid some of the above-mentioned philosophic pitfalls – if we took the sensation of taste and its correlative range of qualities (sweetness, bitterness, etc.) as an analogue when thinking about such matters. Thus '"[i]ntrinsic" value is indeed rather like "sweet" and "bitter" – and unlike "red" and "green" – in its relational, functional character and its relation to guiding choice toward the desirable and away from the undesirable'.[30] Here he takes a lead from Sidney Shoemaker who in turn cites Jonathan Bennett on the issue of secondary qualities and how these differ with respect to both the kinds of quality involved and the extent to which they either guide best opinion or have their extension fixed by it.[31] Bennett had offered the example of phenol-thio-uria, a substance that apparently has a bitter taste when sampled by three in every four respondents but which is completely tasteless to the other party. Shoemaker interprets this case as a knock-down argument against the view that taste, like colour, is response-dependent in the strong sense of being rigidly specified by what counts as a normal perception in some suitably equipped subject under optimal epistemic conditions. For what could possibly provide such a 'rigid' set of baseline standards, he asks, when the property in question is so manifestly subject to *differences* in the kinds of response it might evoke, or counterfactual variations which serve to make this point by envisaging a differently weighted distribution of responses among those asked for their opinion.

Thus, putting the case at its most extreme: '[i]f, as the result of selective breeding, or surgical tampering, it becomes tasteless to everyone, I say it has become tasteless. And if more drastic surgical tampering makes it taste sweet to everyone, I say it has become sweet.'[32] Shoemaker's main purpose with this argument is to help us see that certain properties (or qualities) like taste – unlike certain others such as colour – are instrumental in guiding our choices or enabling us the better to pick and choose among various kinds of experience, rather than serving in a purely (or chiefly) informative capacity through their rigid specification in terms of normalised human epistemic response. In short, '[o]ur dominant interest in classifying things by flavour is our interest in having certain taste experiences and avoiding others, and not our interest in what our experiences tell us about other things. With colour it is the other way around . . .'[33] Railton finds this a persuasive analogy in the case of moral judgement since here also it is a question – he thinks – of our coming to recognise the goodness or badness of persons, acts, or dispositions whose nature is such as to elicit praise or blame precisely insofar as we are responsive to (or properly guided by) certain morally salient qualities that are manifest in them.

Still it is difficult to hold this balance without leaning either too far in the direction of a rigidified RD approach that gives the last word to our judgements, or else too far in the opposite direction, that is, toward a strongly objectivist view of moral properties that would minimise their response-dependent character and hence their answerability to human needs, values, and concerns. Thus Railton, having set forth his thesis that moral judgements should be thought of as more like gustatory than visual modes of perception, goes on in the very next sentence to remark that 'moral value has a more complex character, which in certain cases leads it to mimic the rigidification of colour'. After all, 'we use colour terms to assemble information about the world around us for input into deliberation, not to steer choice more directly'.[34] And if they are to function with any degree of reliability in this basic cognitive or property-tracking role then surely we are constrained to think of colours as 'rigidified' at least to the extent that grass remains green or sapphires stay blue despite any more-or-less drastic changes in our perceptual apparatus like those envisaged by Shoemaker. So moral properties have this much in common with colours: that we would not (or should not) regard certain acts as having taken on a different moral character – wanton cruelty to animals, say, as having undergone a change from 'bad' to 'good' or 'morally indifferent' – merely on account of some shift in our views or widespread coarsening of human moral sensibility. In the one case 'changing human colour reception would not change colours', since '[w]e would not want people to *misread* the change in the appearance of grass as a change in its physical constitution and environment'.[35] In the case of moral judgement, likewise, 'changing human sensibilities toward animals would not change the moral badness of wanton cruelty toward them', since '[w]e would not want people to misread the change in their own attitudes as a change in what happens to the beasts themselves'.[36] So there is a sense in which moral values and colours do have something important in common, namely their existing as properties that cannot be treated as entirely response-dependent without thereby inviting the charge of downright epistemic or moral relativism.

III

What is odd about Railton's discussion at this point is that he seems to misinterpret or completely reconstrue the RD theorists' customary usage of the term 'rigid' and its cognates. That is, he construes it as applying to *those properties themselves* (e.g., the intrinsic or objective greenness of grass), rather than applying to the regular correspondence between such *imputed* properties and their disposition to evoke certain kinds of specifiable response in perceivers suitably placed and equipped to register their presence. Yet of course it is just the point of the quantified biconditional approach as theorised by Wright, Johnston and others that it asserts the existence of this *a priori* link between a subject's having of some 'germane experience' (such as the normally-circumstanced perception of green) and the correctness of ascribing some correlative property (greenness) to the object as normally or standardly perceived. Hence the canonical definition of response-dependent properties as those that 'elicit certain specified cognitive or affective responses under suitable (substantially specified) circumstances in certain (substantially specified) subjects'.[37] So it is odd, as I say, that Railton here locates the 'rigidity' of colour-terms – along with moral values – in a realm of objective (response-independent) *facts* about 'green' or 'cruelty toward animals' which inherently transcends and may sometimes refute or discredit any state of best opinion (however widespread) that happens to exist among human perceivers or moral agents. This is not to say that he is wrong in so doing – quite the contrary – but rather that his raising these issues about moral realism in the context of current RD debate has the effect of somewhat skewing his argument and creating a degree of confusion as to just what constitutes a 'realist' approach in various differently specified areas of discourse.

Where this confusion comes in, I suggest, is through the tendency to suppose that *any* standard of correctness in judgement with respect to properties such as shape, colour, moral rightness or wrongness, comic potential, or even mathematical truth must inherently be apt for treatment in response-dispositional terms simply by reason of its making that appeal to some area-specific standard of correctness in judgement. This is why Railton swings right across from claiming that moral properties are *not* like colours (and are more like properties of taste) because they involve a greater scope for learning from experience and guiding our choices in the right direction, to claiming that they *are* like colours in the basic sense of remaining 'rigid' despite any change in our perceptions or judgements concerning them. What prompts this shift of argumentative tack is the way that 'rigidification' is on the one hand treated as a bad thing (a closing-off of the potential for moral growth) when applied to human responses and on the other treated as a good thing (a hedge against moral relativism) when applied to those properties – like kindness or cruelty – that are taken to characterise certain acts quite apart from our perhaps morally delinquent judgements or responses. In the first sense 'rigidification seems . . . inappropriate as a way of capturing the objectivity of moral assessments'.[38] Thus it makes 'objectivity' in the moral sphere too much a matter of getting things right (or wrong) by reference to rigidified modes of response that more properly apply to standards of correctness in picking out secondary qualities – like greenness – which are subject to normative specification in a way that leaves little room for guiding, enhancing, or refining our relevant capacities. In the second (non-RD) sense of the term as Railton deploys it 'rigidification' is taken to denote that range of moral values and properties which *like* greenness or other such attributes is able to stand firm against untoward (humanly degrading) changes in our moral sensibility. To this extent it answers the moral realist's call for a robust conception of such values and properties that rebuts the various present-day forms of emotivist, projectivist, or cultural-relativist thinking. Thus Railton agrees with David Wiggins that if moral values are 'rigidified' in Sense One (i.e., held constant to a fixed range of quasi-perceptual responses) then moral judgement loses all claim to provide a source of guidance or orientation in achieving a better – more developed or humane – repertoire of moral responses.[39] However he also takes Wiggins's point that moral judgements must have validity-conditions that transcend any given such repertoire since otherwise they could amount to no more than expressions of subjective or communally-sanctioned belief. What is not so clear is how these two lines of argument can be fitted together and, if so, how a response-dispositional approach can help to resolve the various problems that arise in making this attempt.

Thus Wiggins cites Bertrand Russell's puzzled yet forceful remark that 'I cannot see how to refute the arguments for the subjectivity of ethical values, but I find myself incapable of believing that all that is wrong with wanton cruelty is that I don't like it.'[40] What Railton (like Wiggins) takes this to mean is that ethical values *can and must* be assigned some distinctive status that removes them from the sphere of subjective preference or individual 'taste' while still making room for that powerful intuition which views them as intrinsically subject to change and development and hence as not 'rigid' in the same way as natural-kind designations or even colour predicates. Here again there is nothing to quarrel with – from an ethical-realist viewpoint – in Railton's understanding of the requirements that bear on an adequate (i.e., sufficiently objective yet also humanly accountable) philosophy of moral values. However, his way of making the point *via* a discussion of response-dependence is one that leads to some curious turns of argument. Take for instance a passage where he follows Wiggins in rejecting the 'rigidified' conception while strongly denying that this necessarily entails any form of ethical relativism. 'Rigidified subjectivism,' Railton writes, 'does indeed yield the result that even if human beings were to undergo some change that would make them approve wanton cruelty, this would not make it morally good. It is the moral approvals and disapprovals of actual humans – including their disapproval of wanton cruelty – that would fix the extension of "morally good".'[41] Yet surely (on a response-dependent account) 'rigidified subjectivism' is just the kind of outlook that *must* inevitably make it the case that any such wholesale change in human moral sensibilities would bring about an equally wholesale change in the moral values or properties involved. That is to say, those 'properties' would themselves be dependent on the values normally assigned to them, and those values would in turn be dependent on – or relativised to – the modes of response that happened to prevail within some given community of moral beliefs. Railton's first sentence in the above-cited passage seems to state the case for moral realism (that goodness or badness are *not* just projections of approving or disapproving attitudes) while asserting – oddly – that this somehow follows from a rigidified subjectivist conception of moral values which would in fact yield just the opposite result. His second sentence seems to cover thought-experiments of the 'what if?' kind or counterfactual appeals to imagined situations (like that where wanton cruelty to animals has become the ethical norm) as opposed to the 'moral approval or disapproval of actual humans'. Yet again it is hard to see how his argument can possibly work, given that *ex hypothesi* – on the rigidified-subjectivist RD account – it is human responses that 'fix the extension of "morally good" ', and thereby determine what shall count as an acceptable attitude in cases like that of wanton cruelty to animals. Moreover they must be taken to do so not only for 'actual humans' who (most of them at any rate) regard wanton cruelty as wrong by very definition but also for humans who had undergone the change from judging such behaviour wicked to judging it acceptable, or who had experienced any comparably drastic transformation in their moral sensibilities.

Thus Railton's insistence that it is 'actual' responses – in this or some other hypothetical world – that fix the extension of moral predicates goes against his equally firm declaration (in the previous sentence) that ethical properties cannot *themselves* be subject to change as a result of shifts in our moral outlook or our capacity for reaching a just evaluation of acts and their consequences. What I think emerges most strikingly here is the problem that is sure to be confronted by a moral realist – or a realist about truth-values or properties of any kind – when they attempt to formulate some version of the RD thesis which stops short of a full-scale (rigidified) account. Railton himself clearly wants to stop well short of that point since he sees such a theory as opening the way to moral emotivism, subjectivism, or relativism. 'In thinking about value,' his essay concludes,

> it is altogether too easy to project, conflating the familiar and the conventional with the natural and inevitable. One could write a pocket history of progress in moral sensibility in terms of the successive unmasking of such conflations – with respect to slavery, inherited rule, the status of women, and the borders of tribe, 'people', or nation. Objectivity about intrinsic and moral good alike calls for us to gain critical perspective on our own actual responses, not to project their objects rigidly.[42]

One could scarcely wish for a plainer, more eloquent or (to my mind) more convincing statement of the case for moral realism or – what amounts to the same thing – for a conception of ethical values that locates them in the realm of *actual* human experience rather than the realm of response-dependent attitudes, dispositions, or beliefs. Yet there is still that ambiguity about Railton's usage of the term 'actual', suggesting as it does – more in keeping with a response-dependent approach – that any 'critical perspective' thereby attained must always be subject to the ultimate tribunal of what counts *for us* or for a like-minded community of moral appraisers as an act or attitude that properly merits the description 'good' or 'bad'.

Railton is emphatic that this critical perspective cannot be had on any rigidly projectivist RD theory that equates moral value with the beliefs held by some particular ('actual') community. That is to say, its source must be a standard of 'intrinsic' moral good that inherently transcends the limiting conditions of any such *de facto* consensus and thus provides a measure of 'objectivity' against which to assess or critically evaluate our normal ('familiar and conventional') modes of response. However it is just this presumed possibility of standing somehow outside and above those value-constitutive norms that the theorists of response-dependence typically deny, or that they typically regard as an objectivist conception of truth which cannot obtain in areas of discourse (such as ethics) where truth is intrinsically a matter of conformity with the deliverance of 'best opinion'. Thus Railton may rightly protest that such claims – especially when cast in rigidified form – amount to just another more 'technical' variety of old-style ethical emotivism, or the view that moral judgements are merely expressions of approving or disapproving sentiment, and hence incapable of justification on objective or response-independent grounds. Yet of course his argument requires at least this much by way of concession to the RD case: that those judgements be conceived as involving a process of sustained reflective engagement on the valuer's part which allows us to 'gain critical perspective on our own actual moral responses'. In which case it is but a short step to the conclusion that moral properties are themselves *actualised* – acquire whatever reality they have for ethically responsive human agents – through just that appeal to our moral sensibilities which the RD theorists take as defining what *counts* as a valid, legitimate, or ethically warranted mode of response.

To put it like this is no doubt to invite the charge of patent circularity or of specifying moral attributes (such as 'goodness' or 'cruelty') wholly in terms of their significance *for us* as agents who habitually project their acculturated values and who thereby conflate, as Railton says, 'the familiar and conventional with the natural and inevitable'. His objection to this way of thinking is that it fails to explain how various communities could ever have made the kind of moral progress that has led to the abolition of slavery (at least in most parts of the world), the advancement of women's rights, or the rejection – albeit gradual and far from complete – of ethnic, tribal, or national allegiance as a cause for human antagonism. Only by upholding the realist appeal to 'objectivity about intrinsic and moral good' can we hope to maintain those progressive values and defend them as something other, and more, than a 'projection' of our own, no matter how firmly held culture-specific beliefs. For at the end of *that* road is the ground occupied by a thinker like Richard Rorty who finds no use for such high-sounding universalist talk and recommends that we adopt the more practicable task of persuading our cultural fellows (in Rorty's case, the company of fellow 'North Atlantic postmodern bourgeois-liberal pragmatist' types) to accept our views on this or that issue of shared social concern. So if we really want to get something done about homelessness or mass-unemployment then, according to Rorty, we had much better say how shocking and morally offensive it is that so many *Americans* are living on the streets and begging for food than that so many human beings should find themselves in that desperate condition.[43]

On this point Railton would no doubt agree with Norman Geras and other ethical realists who have criticised the parochialism and the strain of moral complacency in Rorty's thinking, along with its fairly blatant promotion of present-day US 'liberal' values as setting the terms for whatever counts as a morally or socio-politically persuasive case.[44] Quite the contrary, they argue: we shall do much better to consult the record of moral progress to date and acknowledge that such genuine (if partial) achievements as the widespread abolition of slavery and the greatly improved situation of women in many parts of the world have come about only through the human capacity to attain a critical-realist distance on received or acculturated habits of thought. Thus Rorty's example can be seen to backfire if one asks how far North American society has actually lived up to its own high professions of equality, liberty, social justice, and respect for basic human rights. By that standard it must be held to have fallen far short of the values supposedly enshrined in those founding documents – the US Constitution and Declaration of Independence – whose provisions have notoriously proven compatible with gross and continuing violations of justice in matters of racial discrimination, gender inequality, and massive (class-based) differentials of wealth and social opportunity. Yet this kind of critical-evaluative standpoint is simply not available to a thinker, like Rorty, who rejects the appeal to universalist (and realist) standards of moral good and who is therefore unwilling to concede that moral arguments might lay claim to an order of validity above and beyond their persuasive force within some existing community of values and beliefs. For in that case there is no way of drawing a firm or principled line between large, well-meaning though ill-defined 'liberal' communities such as those that Rorty often invokes and other, more partisan or profit-driven groups – such as slave-owners in Jefferson's time or the present-day executives of US-based multinational corporations – who possess just as strong a claim to represent a shared community of interests. Thus the shift from 'objectivity' to 'solidarity' which Rorty welcomes as a sign of our having left behind all those old universalist delusions is really more a sign of his having lost faith in the idea, as Railton expresses it, that 'progress in moral sensibility' can be achieved through the recognition of 'intrinsic moral good' and through the resultant capacity to 'gain critical perspective on our own actual moral responses'.[45]

Nevertheless, as we have seen, Railton is hard put to maintain this critical-realist perspective along with his case for the objectivity of moral values while at the same time striving to square his claims with the RD thesis on a certain, duly qualified construal. The problem emerges in sharpest relief when he cites Simon Blackburn on the limited relevance of debates about secondary qualities such as colour to debates about (purportedly) response-dependent properties such as moral goodness or badness. Blackburn explains the disanalogy as follows:

> It is not altogether simple to characterise the 'mind-dependence' of secondary qualities. But it is plausible to say that these are relative to our perception of them in this way: if we were to change so that everything in the world which had appeared blue came to appear red to us, this is what it is for the world to cease to contain blue things, and come to contain only red things. The analogue with moral qualities fails dramatically: if everyone comes to think of it as permissible to maltreat animals, this does nothing at all to make it permissible: it just means that everybody has deteriorated.[46]

Railton clearly agrees with Blackburn as concerns this crucial difference between colour-perceptions and moral judgements. After all, any argument for conflating the two instances – or for treating them as directly analogous in RD terms – must lead to a projectivist account of moral values and thence (though he doesn't say as much) to a Rortian conception of moral and social justice as quite simply what is 'good in the way of belief' among members of this or that like-minded community. Thus Railton is more drawn to the modified ('actualist') RD approach, as argued by theorists like Shoemaker, according to which grass would still be green and daffodils would still be yellow even if all perceivers were subject to 'overnight massive surgery' that produced 'intrasubjective spectrum inversion' and hence the universally agreed-upon discovery that grass had now become red and daffodils blue.[47] What this modified version involves is a re-writing of the basic RD quantified biconditional that changes it from something like: 'x is green if and only if it appears green to normal (substantially specified) human perceivers under normal (substantially specified) conditions' to something more like: 'x is green if and only if it *actually* appears that way to normal humans as they *actually* are and in just those conditions that *actually* define what counts as a "normal" (non-distorting) sensory-perceptual environment.' In the case of moral values, as indeed in the case of colour-properties, this approach would seem to have the signal advantage – from a realist viewpoint – of holding those values and properties strictly invariant despite any hypothetical change (such as that envisaged by Shoemaker) in our moral sensibilities or neurophysiological mechanisms. That is to say, it would keep them 'rigidly' fixed by reference to the way that human beings *do* in fact respond to given perceptual conditions or moral situations, as distinct from the way that they *might* (or even *would*) conceivably respond in a range of alternative counterfactual scenarios.

Thus Shoemaker's argument goes further than Blackburn's toward meeting the standard realist objection, that is, that RD approaches court the charge of epistemic and moral relativism by making physical properties dependent on the variable nature of human sensory-perceptual response and moral values dependent on the mere consensus of 'best opinion' in any given cultural context. Blackburn accepts the RD thesis with regard to colour (that spectrum-inversion would 'actually' bring it about that grass was now red, daffodils blue, etc.) but rejects any notion of extending this argument to moral values, so that wantonly maltreating animals would be perfectly acceptable if everybody suddenly came to think that there was nothing wrong in such behaviour. Shoemaker agrees absolutely on the point about moral values but sees no reason to yield crucial ground – or to make any such large concession to the RD case – on the point about colour-properties. Rather than grass becoming red and daffodils blue 'it will have become the case that green things look the way red things used to, yellow things look the way blue things used to, and so on'.[48] Nor can it be merely a developmental quirk in the nature of our various sensory faculties that colour-perceptions are so much more 'objective' – or so much better at tracking real-world properties – than other senses such as those of taste or smell. For, as we have seen, it is a main plank in Shoemaker's argument against 'strong' RD that perceptions of colour play a vital informative role in acquainting us with features of the physical world that we need to recognise or pick out with a high degree of epistemic reliability if we are to gain a basic knowledge of that world and steer ourselves successfully around it. Thus they differ from other 'secondary qualities' – perhaps to the point of not being 'secondary' at all – insofar as our sensations of taste or smell are much less involved with the cognitive tracking of objective properties and much more involved with our seeking out the kinds of experience that conduce to our better enjoyment or which maximise the preponderance of pleasant over unpleasant sensory stimuli.

In Shoemaker's words (to repeat): '[o]ur dominant interest in classifying things by flavour is our interest in having certain taste experiences and avoiding others, and not our interest in what such experiences tell us about other matters. With colour it is the other way around . . .'[49] Of course the argument would work out very differently for dogs, bats, bees, whales, migrating birds, or indeed a whole range of non-human animal species whose perceptual apparatuses differ from our own in respect of this relative weighting as between the cognitive and appetitive or the more and the less informationally oriented modes of sensory experience. However it is just the point of Shoemaker's argument that we are here considering *human* responses and, moreover, the responses of 'actual' human beings whose sensory equipment or range of perceptual modalities may be taken to fix what counts *for us* as a normal weighting. ('Normal', that is, to the extent that some people, for example, the blind or colour-blind may develop *ab*normally heightened or sharpened perceptual sensitivities in other respects which compensate for their total lack of visual information or reduced capacity for the fine discrimination of visual data.) So if indeed it is the case, as Shoemaker thinks, that an RD approach can be adapted to accommodate *both* the objectivity of colour *and* its response-dependent character as indexed to the normalised perceptual experience of 'actual' human beings then the way would appear open to a settlement on terms that should satisfy all parties. More than that, it would hold the promise of resolving a great many issues in epistemology, philosophy of mind, ethics, or even aesthetics where objectivists and subjectivists or realists and anti-realists have been slogging it out for a long time now without much hope of reaching any such settlement.

IV

However this happy solution is not to be had for reasons that Railton lays out very clearly and which I have summarised in detail above. Chief among them is the fact that Shoemaker's argument for indexing 'rigidified' colour-properties or moral values to the normative repertoire of 'actual' human response has the ultimate effect – contrary to his own realist intentions – of making those responses constitutive of what it is correctly to pick out a colour or properly to judge some action morally good or bad. Thus, as Railton says, this approach might be thought to secure 'a certain non-relativism or "objectivity" (again: independence from fluctuating attitudes or sensibilities) for moral value in a manner that closely parallels what we have said about colour'.[50] However the analogy is in fact *too* close for philosophic comfort since through 'fixing reference [to moral values] by actual human responses' it falls straight back into endorsing a form of strong or rigidified response-dependence according to which those values are determined – not tracked – by best opinion in the matter. 'As we shall see,' Railton writes, 'this alternative [i.e., rigidified RD] account may not spoil the analogy between moral value and secondary qualities, but it does suggest that the secondary qualities in questions are not those of colour, despite their paradigmatic status.'[51] What it suggests, to Railton's way of thinking, is that moral value has at least as much (perhaps more) in common with those qualities like 'sweetness' and 'bitterness' (as opposed to 'red' or 'green') that primarily have to do with our seeking out modes of experience which play a role in 'guiding choice toward the desirable and away from the undesirable'. But in that case he has pretty much abandoned the argument for moral realism – or the objectivity of ethical values – and come around to accepting the strong-RD or projectivist conception of moral 'properties' as dependent on our normative modes of response.

No doubt there is a sense in which, as he says, 'subjectivity can enter in various ways into the making and perceiving of value, some of which may have no parallel at all with the involvement of subjectivity in secondary qualities'.[52] However, as Railton also remarks, the instance of colour has acquired such a dominant role in this context – and in the way that these debates have been structured at least since Locke – that it is hard for philosophers *not* to take it as a main point of reference even when arguing for a shift of emphasis from colour to some other secondary quality, or indeed for a change in this whole line of thought about 'primary' (intrinsic) *versus* 'secondary' (i.e., response-dispositional) properties.[53] After all it was Berkeley who first showed how easily the Lockean distinction could be turned on its head so as to promote a full-scale idealist doctrine according to which *every* property must be thought of as mind-dependent and there is hence no need to entertain the metaphysically extravagant hypothesis of a reality that somehow exists outside and beyond our perceptions of it.[54] Berkeley's doctrine *esse est percipi* – 'to be is to be perceived' – is of course not the kind of conclusion that any RD theorist would willingly or explicitly embrace. Yet it often seems to beckon from the end of the road that these thinkers are travelling, not least when they deploy the example of colour as an analogue for other cognitive capacities, perceptions, or modes of judgement which are taken to involve some intrinsic appeal to the criterion of normative human response under specified (actual or optimal) conditions.

In Railton's case the suggestion is that colour-perceptions are *not* the best candidates for comparison with our moral responses since they tend to yield a 'rigidified' subjectivist conception of ethical judgement which fixes moral values entirely in accordance with the deliverance of (presumed) best opinion among those (presumptively) best qualified to judge. Thus it might be more useful, he thinks, to switch the focus to those other kinds of secondary quality – such as sweetness or bitterness – that are scarcely amenable to treatment in rigidified RD terms (since different people clearly have different responses in this regard) and which can therefore be transposed to the moral context without unduly restricting the scope for our exercise of discriminative thought or our self-education through the process of critically reflecting on accepted values and beliefs. 'To be sure,' Railton writes, 'value talk is full of visual imagery, but perceptual models of value judgement are only partly convincing, and even there gustatory imagery is also common – one is, I suppose, about as likely to say that one "savours" value as that one "sees" it.'[55] Yet one might prefer to say – above all if one endorses the realist conception of moral values that Railton wishes to defend – that *neither* kind of talk is in the least appropriate, since both involve a comparison of moral judgement with sensory-perceptual responses that simply doesn't work when its implications are more fully spelled out. Thus the analogy with visual experience breaks down on the fact that such experience is most plausibly treated as entailing a rigidified set of conditions for correct or reliably accurate perceiver-response which would make no room for the existence of differing moral attitudes and beliefs, let alone for the kinds of reflective self-critical 'distancing' that Railton thinks indispensably a part of our moral growth and development. On the other hand there is something distinctly off-key – even (one may feel) grossly inappropriate – about the notion of 'savouring' moral value or responding to instances of goodness or badness as one might to an exquisitely prepared meal or a cheap wine that had been left uncorked for a couple of months. Such gustatory metaphors may indeed capture something of our natural, instinctive reaction when confronted with an act or a situation that calls forth strong approving or disapproving attitudes. More than that, they may provide a useful corrective to the idea of moral values as rigidly fixed or determined – like colour-properties – by the response of actual human perceivers under normal conditions or circumstances. But this utility in coaxing us away from one particular inadequate conception of moral values is of course no reason to accept what amounts to just another (equally inadequate) conception, one that in effect reduces moral judgement to a matter of 'savouring' moral qualities in the manner of a culinary *bon viveur* equipped with the 'right' sorts of taste-bud. And it is all the more inappropriate, as I have said, for the fact that Railton is committed to upholding a realist philosophy of moral values and properties which would treat them as obtaining – as holding good – quite apart from our actual moral responses and even quite apart from the state of 'best opinion' among any given community of valuers.

This is not to say that Railton is stumped for any alternative suggestion as to how we might achieve a compromise settlement that successfully avoids the twin extremes of a rigidified RD account on the one hand and, on the other, a sheerly subjectivist appeal to the vagaries and nuances of moral 'taste'. It can best be had, he contends, by adopting a *relational* theory of moral value that locates the properties of goodness and badness – along with other more refined or discriminative attributes – in the *intrinsic* relationship which he takes to exist between certain kinds of action or conduct and certain kinds of apt or fitting moral response. Thus, in the case of wanton cruelty to animals, 'it is the intrinsically unliked character of the torment such conduct would cause its recipients – a torment which is unaffected by our attitude – that makes the behaviour wrong.'[56] What distinguishes a relationalist from a strong-RD (or projectivist) approach is its placing moral value firmly on the side of the consequences for others – sentient beings of whatever kind – who enjoy the benefits or who suffer the effect of our conduct toward them. What sets it apart from purely objectivist conceptions of moral value is the scope it offers for an active involvement and progressive refinement of our moral sensibilities by reflecting on those same (real or imagined) consequences and their implication for our own self-image as responsible moral agents. So there is clearly a large weight of argument resting on the phrase 'intrinsically unliked character' in the above-cited passage from Railton, a phrase that in effect has to do double duty for (1) the intrinsic character of conduct like wanton cruelty toward animals, and (2) the intrinsic character of those various responses – disapproval, repugnance, moral revulsion – which we and others do (or should properly) experience when confronted with such behaviour. No doubt it is essential to Railton's case for a relational and realist conception of moral values that the phrase should possess this ambiguous grammar or be capable of facing, so to speak, in both directions at once. What it gives us, he claims, is 'an alternative explanation of the "objectivity" – in the sense of "independence from our particular attitudes" – of our judgements about wanton cruelty or maltreating animals, a judgement that does not involve either non-relational intrinsic value (it is enough if pain is a harm to the beings experiencing it) or rigidification of our moral response to kickings and whippings'.[57] In which case moral values can be thought of as possessing just the requisite degree of objectivity to make it downright *wrong* to indulge such behaviour while also being thought of as response-dependent to just the extent that is required in order to prevent them from becoming altogether out-of-touch with our 'actual' norms of ethically evaluable conduct.

Still there is room for doubt whether this way of setting up the issue – one that is very largely forced upon Railton by his acceptance of the basic

RD terms for debate – is the only or indeed the most promising line of enquiry for anyone who seeks to defend moral realism against its various detractors. An alternative might be to shift that debate away from its current fixation on colour and other such (supposed) 'secondary properties' and more toward the other end of the scale, for example, mathematics and the physical sciences, where there is a far stronger case for conceiving of truth as *entirely independent* of whatever human beings may think or believe concerning it. Even in the case of colour, as Pettit remarks, 'a response-dependent term like "red" may refer to a perfectly mind-independent property: specifically, to the property that realises the redness role, rather than to the dispositional or role property'.[58] What this amounts to – though Pettit doesn't quite say as much – is an argument for explaining colour in terms of wavelength, reflectance, lambda, the neurophysiology of colour-perception, and so forth, rather than in terms of a formula (the standard RD quantified biconditional) which purports to establish its response-dependent character as a matter of sheerly *a priori* warrant. Of course this approach may appear to make room for such a scientific fleshing-out through its likewise standard requirement that the left-hand and right-hand sides of the equation contain a 'substantially specified' account of what constitutes a genuine instance of the property concerned and the appropriate (perceiver-normalised) response. Still there is little evidence in the RD literature that its theorists are much occupied with issues to the left of the biconditional sign, for example, property-fixing claims from physics or molecular biology, or issues to the right which bear upon aspects of response-dependence that might (in principle) be specified with reference to our best current knowledge of neurophysiology or the various cognitive processes involved. Rather, as I have said, there is a constant bias toward making those properties 'intrinsically' response-dependent in the sense that they involve some constitutive reference to the phenomenological or qualitative aspects of human perceptual experience. What is thus ruled out – or treated as irrelevant for RD purposes – is the 'realist intuition' (as Mark Powell defines it) that 'truth for the discourse in question is constituted independently of any function of human judgement'.[59]

V

Hence Pettit's worry about the way that this approach tends to generalise from the instance of 'secondary properties' like colour and use them as a means of effectively discrediting realist claims across a range of other philosophical debates where their pertinence is far from self-evident. 'The question with which we are concerned,' he writes, 'is how far realism about any area of discourse is undermined by an admission of response-dependence in this sense.'[60] One line of counter-argument is that which Pettit himself adopts by questioning whether colour is really a 'secondary quality' in the sense bequeathed by sceptical empiricists like Locke and taken over in a technically refined but otherwise very similar form by the present-day RD theorists. Another is to ask, as Pettit does, whether problematic instances like that of colour are properly analogous to or capable of generalisation over the range of 'discourses' that RD theorists tend to take as their legitimate domain. Thus a realist about mathematics would most certainly deny that the analogy worked for the basic axioms of Peano arithmetic or for statements – such as Kripke's '68 + 57 = 125' – which follow as a matter of recursive application from just those basic axioms.[61] In the same way a realist about the physical sciences would flatly deny that the truth of statements such as 'water is H_20' is in any way response-dependent or a matter of 'best-opinion' among those qualified to judge. After all, as Ralph Wedgwood pointedly remarks, the essence of H_20 'consists in its underlying nature, rather than its superficial appearances', in which case 'the nature of the concept *water* determines that the concept must stand for the natural kind, not a response-dependent property'.[62] And again:

> [c]onditions are unfavourable for perceiving water whenever there is anything superficially resembling water whose underlying structure is different from that of most samples of water; whereas conditions are unfavourable for perceiving redness only if there is some abnormality in one's perceptual function, or if the lighting and atmospheric conditions differ too much from a certain familiar paradigm.[63]

To be sure there is nothing about this statement, on the face of it, that RD theorists should find in the least objectionable. Nor would they dispute Wedgwood's proposal that any claim for the response-dependent character of properties, predicates, or judgements be restricted to just those areas of discourse where truth (or warranted assertability) is a matter of optimised human response under certain specified conditions and where the quantified biconditional is taken to hold *a priori* in virtue of just that fact. However, as we have seen, there is a marked tendency among some of those theorists to extend the scope of an RD approach well beyond the instance of (supposed) secondary qualities to other areas – including mathematics and morals – where its application is considerably more problematic.

Indeed this is hardly surprising, given the fact that response-dependence theory first took shape as an attempt to reformulate Dummett-type anti-realism in such a way as to avoid those problems while none the less holding a Dummettian line against any realist conception of truth as recognition-transcendent or epistemically unconstrained.[64] Also there is the strong Wittgensteinian influence, along with the decisive impact on thinkers like Wright of Kripke's rule-following considerations, taken as likewise blocking the appeal to truth-values that would somehow transcend our extant practices or customary ways of proceeding.[65] So one can see why the response-dependence approach is predisposed toward anti-realism – however hedged around with qualifying clauses – when it touches on those various subject-areas that might otherwise be thought to lie outside and beyond its proper domain. Wedgwood again states the issue very pointedly by asking just what *kind* of 'substantial' specification has to be provided if the standard RD formula is to serve as a means of discriminating RD from non-RD properties. Thus:

> [t]he fact that there is a biconditional conceptual truth, where the left-hand side ascribes a property to some arbitrary object, and the right-hand side speaks of some relation between the object and some type of mental response to the property, is not enough to show that the property in question is response-dependent. Otherwise, the property of being made of water would be response-dependent. We must impose a further condition: the biconditional must also be a *constitutive* account of the property in question. But we have still made no progress towards understanding what a constitutive account of a property is.[66]

Of course this account is not to be had from the RD theory itself since the biconditional is assumed to hold as a matter of *a priori* warrant – of the sheerly self-evident link between property and apt response – and can therefore provide no further ('substantial') guidance as to just what constitutes the property in question or just what qualifies the given response as a response to just that specified property. Granted there are some 'areas of discourse' (like comedy according to Wright) where it is plausible to claim that such responses go all the way down and must therefore be taken to decide what counts as a genuine instance of the kind. Granted also there are others – like colour on the RD construal – where no purely objectivist theory (such as might be provided by the physical sciences) can fully explain what it is for human beings with normal visual equipment under normal circumstances to perceive the colour 'blue' and truthfully report on what they perceive. Thus Mary the colour-blind colour-scientist must be missing out on *something* that figures in a full description of what it is to experience blueness as distinct from knowing – in some sense of 'know' – what is physically involved in that experience.[67] Then again, there is the instance of moral discourse and the need to make due allowance for the exercise of responsive (and responsible) human judgement if morality is not to be 'rigidified' in a way that lifts it entirely outside the space of reasons and justifications. Still one may doubt that these requirements can be met by an RD account which either reduces to trivial circularity ('best opinion or optimal response cannot be wrong since *by very definition* they are sure to deliver true or authoritative verdicts') or else ends up – despite protestations to the contrary – by endorsing a projectivist theory of truth and value.

Hence, as I have argued, its inbuilt bias toward an anti-realist approach, that is to say, one that sharply restricts those areas of discourse amenable to treatment in terms of objective truth-values and which thus correspondingly expands the range of those that are taken as candidates for treatment in terms of best opinion, normative response, or optimised epistemic warrant. Hence also the tendency in theorists like Wright to propose alternative, more objective-sounding criteria – such as 'superassertibility' or 'cognitive command' – while nonetheless continuing to make those criteria ultimately subject to the RD tribunal of optimised epistemic warrant. 'Where a discourse exhibits cognitive command,' Wright specifies, 'any difference of opinion will be such that there are considerations quite independent of the conflict which, if known about, would mandate withdrawal of one (or both) of the contending views.'[68] This might seem a large concession to the realist case, that is, to the argument that in certain areas of discourse truth is potentially verification- and recognition-transcendent. However there is still that saving clause – 'if known about' – which effectively proscribes the realist appeal to truth-conditions that transcend the limits of warranted assertibility. Or rather: it exploits the crucial ambiguity between a strong counterfactual reading of the clause ('cognitive command' = a feature of just those discourses that *would* be candidates for the ascription of objective truth-values from the standpoint of an omniscient knower) and a qualified verificationist reading ('cognitive command' = a feature of just those discourses that qualify for warranted assertibility according to the deliverance of attainable best opinion). On this second construal – one that jibes more readily with his whole line of approach – there is not, after all, so much difference between the criteria for cognitive command and those for superassertibility. As regards the latter, '[s]uperassertibility . . . is, in a natural sense, an *internal* property of the statements of a discourse – a projection, merely, of the standards, whatever they are, which actually inform assertions within the discourse.'[69] And again: '[i]t supplies no external norm – in a way that truth is classically supposed to do – against which the internal standards might *sub specie Dei* themselves be measured, and might rate as adequate or inadequate.'[70] But this condition must also be taken to apply to areas of discourse that are deemed fit candidates for 'cognitive command' since here likewise – on the most plausible reading of Wright's argument – there is simply no appeal beyond what is knowable *sub specie humanitatis*.

In other words the very most that Wright is prepared to grant in the way of 'objectivity' or verification-transcendence is a limit-point conception of epistemic warrant which makes only notional adjustments or concessions to the realist case. Thus the whole debate about response-dependence, and Wright's work in particular, can be seen as inheriting its main agenda from the problems bequeathed by Dummett-type anti-realism and by arguments (such as Kripke's ultra-sceptical take on the rule-following paradox) which purport to undermine any notion of objective or practice-transcendent rationality and truth. More precisely, it is the product of certain misgivings with regard to that 'strong' sceptical programme, coupled with a willingness to take it as setting the relevant terms for discussion. That those terms are such as to keep any doubts well within RD-compatible bounds is perhaps the most striking and symptomatic feature of response-dependence theory.

References

1. See for instance Philip Pettit, 'Realism and Response-Dependence', *Mind*, Vol. 100 (1991), pp. 597–626, *The Common Mind: an essay on psychology, society, and politics* (Oxford: Oxford University Press, 1992), and 'Are Manifest Qualities Response-Dependent?', *The Monist*, Vol. 81 (1998), pp. 3–43; Peter Railton, 'Red, Bitter, Good', *European Review of Philosophy*, Vol. 3 (1998), pp. 67–84; Michael Smith, *The Moral Problem* (Oxford: Blackwell, 1994); Ralph Wedgwood, 'The Essence of Response-Dependence', *European Review of Philosophy*, Vol. 3 (1998), pp. 31–54; David Wiggins, *Needs, Values, Truth* (Oxford: Blackwell, 1987); Crispin Wright, 'Moral Values, Projection, and Secondary Qualities', *Proceedings of the Aristotelian Society*, Supplementary Vol. 62 (1988), pp. 1–26 and 'Realism, Antirealism, Irrealism, Quasi-Realism', *Midwest Studies in Philosophy*, Vol. 12 (1988), pp. 25–49.
2. Crispin Wright, *Truth and Objectivity* (Cambridge, MA: Harvard University Press, 1992), p. 230; Ludwig Wittgenstein, *Philosophical Investigations*, trans. G. E. M. Anscombe (Oxford: Blackwell, 1953).
3. See especially Michael Dummett, *Truth and Other Enigmas* (London: Duckworth, 1978).
4. Wright, *Truth and Objectivity*, p. 5 (Note 2, above).
5. Ludwig Wittgenstein, *Philosophical Investigations*, Sects 201–92 *passim*; also Saul Kripke, *Wittgenstein on Rules and Private Language* (Oxford: Blackwell, 1982); Bob Hale, 'Rule-Following, Objectivity, and Meaning', in Hale and Crispin Wright (eds), *A Companion to the Philosophy of Language* (Blackwell, 1997), pp. 369–96; John McDowell, 'Wittgenstein

on Following a Rule', *Synthèse*, Vol. 58 (1984), pp. 325–63; Alexander Miller and Crispin Wright (eds), *Rule-Following and Meaning* (Teddington: Acumen, 2001).

6. See for instance Hartry Field, 'Realism and Anti-Realism About Mathematics', *Philosophical Topics*, Vol. 13 (1982), pp. 45–69.
7. Wright, *Truth and Objectivity*, p. 87 (Note 2, above).
8. See also Hartry Field, *Science without Numbers* (Princeton, NJ: Princeton University Press, 1980).
9. See Note 5, above.
10. Wright, *Truth and Objectivity*, pp. 108–9 (Note 2, above).
11. For some relevant comments and caveats in this regard, see Mark Johnston, 'Dispositional Theories of Value', *Proceedings of the Aristotelian Society*, Vol. 63 (1989), pp. 139–74 and 'Objectivity Refigured: pragmatism without verificationism', in J. Haldane and C. Wright (eds), *Realism, Representation and Projection* (Oxford: Oxford University Press, 1993), pp. 85–130; also various entries under Note 1, above.
12. Philip Pettit, 'Realism and Response-Dependence', p. 599 (Note 1, above).
13. Ibid., p. 597.
14. See Notes 1 and 11, above.
15. See Note 5, above; also John McDowell, 'Wittgenstein on Following a Rule', *Synthèse*, Vol. 58 (1984), pp. 325–63, 'Intentionality and Interiority in Wittgenstein', in K. Puhl (ed.), *Meaning Scepticism* (Berlin: de Gruyter, 1991), pp. 148–69, and 'Meaning and Intentionality in Wittgenstein's Later Philosophy', *Midwest Studies in Philosophy*, Vol. 17 (1992), pp. 40–52.
16. John McDowell, *Mind and World* (Cambridge, MA: Harvard University Press, 1994). For further discussion see also Christopher Norris, 'McDowell on Kant: redrawing the bounds of sense' and 'The Limits of Naturalism: further thoughts on McDowell's *Mind and World*', in *Minding the Gap: epistemology and philosophy of science in the two traditions* (Amherst, MA: University of Massachusetts Press, 2000), pp. 172–96 and 197–230.
17. Johann Gottlieb Fichte, *The Science of Knowledge with the First and Second Introductions*, trans. and ed. Peter Heath and John Lachs (Cambridge: Cambridge University Press, 1980); F. W. J. Schelling, *System of Transcendental Idealism*, trans. Peter Heath (Charlottesville: University of Virginia Press, 1978); also Frederick C. Beiser, *The Fate of Reason: German philosophy from Kant to Fichte* (Cambridge, MA: Harvard University Press, 1987). For Putnam's 'internal realist' approach, see especially his *Reason, Truth and History* (Cambridge: Cambridge University Press, 1981) and *Realism and Reason* (Cambridge University Press, 1983).
18. For a range of positions on this issue, see Mark Johnston, 'How to Speak of the Colours', *Philosophical Studies*, Vol. 68 (1992), pp. 221–63; Pettit, 'Realism and Response-Dependence' (Note 1, above); Mark Powell, 'Realism or Response-Dependence?', *European Review of Philosophy*, Vol. 3 (1998), pp. 1–13; and Crispin Wright, 'Euthyphronism and the Physicality of Colour', *European Review of Philosophy*, Vol. 3 (1998), pp. 15–30.
19. Wright, *Truth and Objectivity*, p. 108 (Note 2, above).
20. Ibid., p. 108.
21. Ibid., p. 82.

22. Sigmund Freud, *Jokes and their Relation to the Unconscious* (London: Hogarth Press, 1960).
23. Railton, 'Red, Bitter, Good', p. 77 (Note 1, above).
24. See also David O. Brink, *Moral Realism and the Foundations of Ethics* (Cambridge: Cambridge University Press, 1989); and Brad Hooker (ed.), *Truth in Ethics* (Oxford: Blackwell, 1996).
25. Railton, 'Red, Bitter, Good', p. 77 (Note 1, above).
26. Ibid., p. 77.
27. See for instance Michel Foucault, *The Use of Pleasure*, trans. Robert Hurley (New York: Pantheon, 1995) and *The Care of the Self*, trans. Hurley (Pantheon, 1996); Friedrich Nietzsche, *On the Genealogy of Morals*, trans. Walter Kaufmann and R. J. Hollingdale (New York: Vintage Books, 1989) and *The Will to Power*, trans. Kaufmann and Hollingdale (Vintage Books, 1968); also Richard Rorty, *Contingency, Irony, and Solidarity* (Cambridge: Cambridge University Press, 1989).
28. Railton, 'Red, Bitter, Good', p. 82 (Note 1, above).
29. Ibid., p. 83.
30. Ibid., p. 83.
31. Sidney Shoemaker, 'Self-Knowledge and "Inner Sense"', in *Philosophy and Phenomenological Research*, Vol. 54 (1994), pp. 249–314 and Jonathan Bennett, 'Substance, Reality, and Primary Qualities', in C. B. Martin and D. M. Armstrong (eds), *Locke and Berkeley* (New York: Anchor Books, 1968).
32. Shoemaker, 'Self-Knowledge and "Inner Sense" ', p. 302 (Note 31, above).
33. Ibid., pp. 302–3.
34. Railton, 'Red, Bitter, Good', p. 83 (Note 1, above).
35. Ibid., p. 83.
36. Ibid., p. 83.
37. Wright, *Truth and Objectivity*, p. 136 (Note 2, above).
38. Railton, 'Red, Bitter, Good', p. 81 (Note 1, above).
39. David Wiggins, 'A Sensible Subjectivism?', in *Needs, Values, Truth* (Oxford: Blackwell, 1987).
40. Cited by Wiggins, ibid., p. 185.
41. Railton, 'Red, Bitter, Good', p. 82 (Note 1, above).
42. Ibid., p. 84.
43. See Rorty, *Contingency, Irony, and Solidarity* (Note 27, above).
44. Norman Geras, *Solidarity in the Conversation of Mankind: the groundable liberalism of Richard Rorty* (London: Verso, 1995); also Roy Bhaskar, *Philosophy and the Idea of Freedom* (Oxford: Blackwell, 1991).
45. Railton, 'Red, Bitter, Good', p. 84 (Note 1, above).
46. Simon Blackburn, 'Errors and the Phenomenology of Value', in Ted Honderich (ed.), *Morality and Objectivity: a tribute to J. L. Mackie* (London: Routledge & Kegan Paul, 1985), p. 14.
47. Shoemaker, 'Self-Knowledge and "Inner Sense" ' (Note 31, above).
48. Ibid., p. 302.
49. Ibid., pp. 302–3.
50. Railton, 'Red, Bitter, Good', p. 70 (Note 1, above).
51. Ibid., p. 71.
52. Ibid., p. 84.

53. See especially John Locke, *An Essay Concerning Human Understanding*, ed. A. S. Pringle-Pattison (Oxford: Oxford University Press, 1969), Book II, Chap. 8, Sect. 15, p. 69; also Wright, 'Moral Values, Projection, and Secondary Qualities' (Note 1, above).
54. George Berkeley, *A Treatise Concerning the Principles of Human Knowledge*, ed. Colin M. Turbayne (New York: Liberal Arts Press, 1957); also Martin and Armstrong (eds), *Locke and Berkeley* (Note 31, above).
55. Railton, 'Red, Bitter, Good', p. 83 (Note 1, above).
56. Ibid., p. 82.
57. Ibid., pp. 82–3.
58. Philip Pettit, 'Terms, Things and Response-Dependence', *European Review of Philosophy*, Vol. 3 (1998), pp. 55–66; p. 62.
59. Powell, 'Realism Or Response-Dependence?', p. 3 (Note 1, above).
60. Pettit, 'Terms, Things and Response-Dependence', p. 4 (Note 58, above).
61. See Kripke, *Wittgenstein on Rules and Private Language* and other entries under Note 5, above.
62. Wedgwood, 'The Essence of Response-Dependence', p. 52 (Note 1, above).
63. Ibid., p. 52.
64. See Michael Dummett, *Truth and Other Enigmas* (Note 3, above) and *The Logical Basis of Metaphysics* (London: Duckworth, 1991); also Michael Luntley, *Language, Logic and Experience: the case for anti-realism* (Duckworth, 1988); Neil Tennant, *Anti-Realism and Logic* (Oxford: Clarendon Press, 1987); Crispin Wright, *Realism, Meaning and Truth*, 2nd edn (Oxford: Blackwell, 1993).
65. See Note 5, above.
66. Wedgwood, 'The Essence of Response-Dependence', p. 43 (Note 1, above).
67. See Frank Jackson, 'Epiphenomenal Qualia', *The Philosophical Quarterly*, Vol. 32 (1982), pp. 127–36 and 'What Mary Didn't Know', *The Journal of Philosophy*, Vol. 83, no. 5 (1986), pp. 291–5.
68. Wright, *Truth and Objectivity*, p. 103 (Note 2, above).
69. Ibid., p. 61.
70. Ibid., p. 61.

Chapter Four

Morals, Mathematics and Best Opinion: the Euthyphronist debate revisited

I

In Plato's *Euthyphro* the dialogue turns on some issues that have lately become central to debates in epistemology, ethics, and the philosophy of language and logic.[1] These all have to do with the topic of response-dependence (RD), or the question how far – and in what precise sense – the assessment of a given statement in terms of its truth-value must incorporate some reference to human response under certain specified (whether normal or optimal) conditions.[2] As Plato presents it, this question concerns the existence of objective moral values and the threat to morality that comes of espousing a subjectivist or response-dependent account of what constitutes the good, the virtuous, the class of genuinely pious acts, and so forth. Thus his dialogue seeks to resolve the issue as to whether the moral virtues are dependent on their being approved by the gods or whether, conversely, the gods approve moral virtues on account of their godlike capacity to know what properly (objectively) counts as virtuous conduct. Socrates takes the objectivist view that moral good is a property inherent in certain acts, dispositions, judgements, or beliefs, and hence that the gods are effectively constrained to submit their opinion to a higher tribunal of response-independent justice and truth. Euthyphro puts the opposite case, that is, that the gods are *by very definition* the ultimate arbiters of justice and truth and therefore that the gods' opinion is precisely what determines or sets the operative standard for behaviour in accordance with the moral virtues.

On the Euthyphronic account, in Crispin Wright's formulation, the gods' best judgement 'enters in some constitutive sense into the determination of which acts are pious', whereas for the Socratic realist 'gods are, by their natures, cognitively responsive to piety.'[3] Or again, as Socrates sees it, 'the piety of an act is one thing, and the gods' estimate of it another, and it is merely that the gods are so fortunately endowed that the piety of an act need never elude them if they so choose.'[4] In terms of current philosophical debate this places Socrates firmly on the side of those who insist that truth for any given (truth-apt) area of discourse is wholly independent of 'best opinion' or what counts as 'true' by the evaluative standards of those considered best qualified to judge.[5] For the Euthyphronist, on the other hand, truth in such matters *just is* what accords with the deliverance of best opinion, or with the judgement of those (gods or human beings) whose responses must be taken as defining what counts as the true, the just, or the good. 'Naturally', Wright concedes,

> it is open to each of the antagonists in this debate to acknowledge that pious acts extensionally coincide with those which, at least potentially, are loved by the gods. Socrates is contending that the piety of an action is, as it were, constituted independently of the gods' estimate of it, and Euthyphro is denying this, but each can agree that the two characteristics invariably accompany one another.[6]

All the same there is a crucial issue at stake, as Wright well knows, since on the one (Socratic) conception there are truths across a wide range of disciplines or subject-areas – mathematics, the physical sciences, history, and ethics among them – which obtain independently of best opinion while on the other (Euthyphronic) conception best opinion must be taken as the ultimate court of appeal. Nor is the position much changed when Wright introduces his idea of 'superassertibility' as a means of hopefully bringing both parties on board through his allowance that best opinion may outrun any present state of knowledge to the point where it *all but* satisfies the realist's demand by becoming something *very like* truth at the end of enquiry. For it is still the case, as Wright quickly points out, that superassertibility 'is also, in a natural sense, an *internal* property of the statements of a discourse – a projection, merely, of the standards, whatever they are, that actually inform assertions within the discourse'.[7]

Just how this is supposed to square with his apparent concession to the realist – that is, that statements are 'superassertible' only insofar as they meet a higher (even limit-point) standard of assertoric warrant – is nowhere clearly explained in Wright's presentation of the case. Rather the issue is got around somewhat shiftily by his talk of the relevant standards as involving a 'projection' from those that actually apply in some given area of discourse, and hence as remaining 'internal' to that discourse while also (somehow) making room for any future advances in knowledge that would constitute idealised 'best opinion' under optimal epistemic conditions. Nevertheless, Wright cautions, superassertibility 'supplies no external norm – in a way that truth is classically supposed to do – against which the internal standards might *sub specie Dei* themselves be measured, and might rate as adequate or inadequate'.[8] So there is not after all much in it for the realist, or nothing that would come even close to allowing for objective (that is to say, epistemically or evidentially unconstrained) standards of truth, correctness, or validity. On the contrary, Wright's caveat commits him to denying the realist's basic claim that truth must involve some correspondence-relation between a statement and its truth-maker, where the latter is 'conceptually quite independent of our standards of appraisal', or thought of as that 'on which we impinge only in an (at most) detective role'.[9]

Thus, whatever his desire to appease the opposition by finding some common ground, Wright ends up very definitely on the Euthyphronic side of this debate according which it is *not* 'because certain statements are true that they are superassertible' but rather 'it is because such statements are superassertible that they are true.'[10] In other words it is the case for human knowers – as likewise for Euthyphro's gods – that their best judgement is in some sense *constitutive* of what properly counts as piety, justice, or truth, rather than their being 'cognitively responsive' to those virtues or managing to track them with the highest degree of detective skill. No doubt, Wright concedes, there are areas of discourse where this thesis comes up against strong resistance, or where Euthyphro and his present-day disciples face considerable odds of deep-grained realist prejudice. All the same, he thinks, there is no making sense of the idea that a statement can be somehow 'undetectably true' if this entails the belief that 'the rule embodied in its content . . . can permissibly be thought of as extending, so to speak, of itself into areas where we cannot follow it and thus determining, without any contribution from ourselves or our reactive natures, that a certain state of affairs complies with it.'[11] That is to say, Euthyphro must inevitably have the last word since nothing could count as an instance of truth that transcended or eluded our best capacities for acquiring or manifesting knowledge of it. And this despite Wright's clear recognition – what sets him apart from more doctrinally committed anti-realists like Michael Dummett – that there is a strong case to be answered from the realist quarter and that it may require certain concessions to a theory that accommodates truth in the limit of idealised rational or epistemic warrant.[12]

II

Perhaps Whitehead was right in his famous claim that the entire history of Western post-Hellenic philosophy could be read as a series of footnotes to

Plato. Still there is something odd about a present-day discussion of issues in epistemology, philosophy of science, mathematics, ethics, and other fields which continues to endorse those terms for debate as if – at least for the purpose in hand – nothing much had changed in the interim. Equally odd, one might think, is the constant invocation of Locke on secondary qualities, a source that has obvious attractions in the RD context but which nonetheless lays these theorists open to the charge of pretty much ignoring what science has to say on the topic of colour and visual perception.[13] So for Locke, whereas 'the ideas of primary qualities of bodies [such as extension and shape] are resemblances of them, and their patterns do really exist in the bodies themselves . . . the ideas produced in us by the secondary qualities have no resemblance of them at all.'[14] Rather they involve – as per the RD conception – an element of perceptual or cognitive response which (with reference to a normally equipped observer under normal ambient conditions) allows us to specify what properly counts as a veridical statement or judgement.

John McDowell provides a representative update on this Lockean theme when he writes that whereas a primary quality 'would be objective in the sense that what it is for something to have it can be adequately understood otherwise than in terms of dispositions to give rise to subjective states', secondary qualities by contrast are 'not adequately conceivable except in terms of certain subjective states, and are thus subjective themselves in a sense that that characterisation defines'.[15] In other words there is a definite line to be drawn between statements whose truth is determined by the way things stand with the world quite independently of us human knowers and our various perceptual, cognitive, or epistemic powers and statements whose validity or assertoric warrant cannot be established without such reference. However – as Berkeley was quick to observe with regard to Locke's cardinal distinction – this offers the sceptic a strong hold for pushing the argument one stage further and maintaining that (so-called) 'primary' qualities are likewise nothing but 'ideas in the mind' so far as we can possibly know or perceive them.[16] And there is, I shall argue, a kindred tendency among RD theorists to start out in Lockean fashion by plainly acknowledging the crucial distinction between primary and secondary qualities – or that between objective and response-dependent areas of discourse – but then to extend the remit of an RD approach into areas such as mathematics or (arguably) morals where its application is more problematic.

This Lockean theme was taken up by Hume and transposed to the context of moral discourse in a passage from the *Treatise of Human Nature* that has become a main point of reference for RD theorists. Thus:

> when you pronounce any action or character to be vicious, you mean nothing, but that from the constitution of your nature you have a feeling or sentiment of blame from the contemplation of it. Vice and virtue, therefore, may be compared to sounds, colours, heat and cold, which, according to modern philosophy, are not qualities in objects but perceptions in the mind . . .[17]

Advocates of a response-dispositional approach are mostly keen to disavow the more subjectivist implications of Hume's 'modern philosophy' and to find some way of squaring that approach with a due regard for the truth-conditions of statements about colour and others that fall within this notional class. As Wright puts it: 'when the element of subjectivity is properly located, it poses no threat to the objectivity of secondary quality ascription, or to the idea that an object's secondary qualities constitute material for cognition, in a proper sense of that term.'[18] Still he takes it that the Lockean account of secondary qualities is a good place to start when considering these issues in epistemology and philosophy of mind. And this despite the fact that Locke's ideas on the subject are at very least open to challenge from a range of philosophical and scientific standpoints. Thus it might well be argued that they are no more definitive than his sceptical case about the impossibility of advancing from 'nominal' to 'real' definitions or essences, that is to say, his belief that science necessarily stopped short of attaining a knowledge of objectively existent microphysical structures and properties as distinct from the various attributes which figured in our best descriptions, theories, or explanatory hypotheses. Such was indeed the prevailing situation in Locke's time, most of all with respect to that particular branch of science – chemistry – in which he took a keen interest and which was yet to undergo the decisive transformation that occurred with Dalton's physics-based (atomist) conception of chemical properties. However things have moved on since then – so the realist will respond – and we now quite simply know a lot more about those structures, causal dispositions, microphysical features, and so forth, which the sceptic may still profess to doubt yet whose existence and real-world operative effects cannot be denied without completely undermining the edifice of modern science. Likewise, *pace* the RD theorists, we can nowadays claim to know a lot more about those various properties and effects of light – reflectance, refraction, wavelength distribution, impact on the retina, processing by the visual cortex, etc. – which have gone a long way toward discrediting Lockean talk of colour as a vaguely-defined 'secondary quality' dependent on vaguely-defined notions of human perceptual response. So it is hard to see what substantive *content* can be claimed for the RD thesis if it fails to admit the relevance of advances in our knowledge of the physical and physiological processes involved.

Here it is worth recalling how that thesis works out when stated in the kind of canonical notation (i.e., the logically regimented form) that RD theorists tend to favour. Such is the standard 'quantified biconditional' which sets out the terms and relevant criteria for a response-dependent account of some particular topic-domain or area of discourse. I shall take Wright's version as the most elaborately specified although it stands as a fair representative sample of kindred formulations by Johnston, Pettit, Smith, and others. Thus, according to Wright:

> For all S, P: P if and only if (if CS then RS), where 'S' is any agent, 'P' ranges over all of some wide class of judgements (judgements of colour or shape, or moral judgements, or mathematical judgements, for instance), 'RS' expresses S's having of some germane experience (judging that P, for instance, or having a visual impression of colour, or of shape, or being smitten with moral sentiments of a certain kind, or amused) and 'CS' expresses the satisfaction of certain conditions of optimality on that particular response. If the response is a judgement, then S's satisfaction of conditions C will ensure that no other circumstances could have given the judgement formed a greater credibility.[19]

In effect this amounts to a formal re-statement of the Lockean case for regarding colour – along with a range of other properties and attributes – as response-dependent *by very definition* and hence as falling within the remit of a logico-semantic analysis rather than a causal-explanatory approach that would draw on the best current knowledge of the physical sciences. Such is the result of stipulating that the biconditional holds *a priori* or in virtue of the sheerly self-evident (necessary) link between property and response. For this requirement once again rules out any claim that their covariance is primarily a matter for empirical (*a posteriori*) investigation of just what constitutes the relevant property and just what explains the pertinent response, along with those various physical conditions that define what should count as a normal, that is, non-distorting perceptual environment. In other words it makes colour and perception of colour themselves jointly dependent on a generalised theory of response-dependence which takes only token or formal account of the need to offer a 'substantive' (non-trivial) specification in each of these respects. It thus shifts the burden – or the chief focus of enquiry – from first-order questions of scientific warrant to second-order questions concerning the logical status of colour-term ascriptions, the normative criteria that govern their usage, and their role *vis-à-vis* other 'areas of discourse' where the RD thesis is taken to apply. In the process this theory acquires just the kind of *a priori*, self-validating status that it attributes to such paradigm statements as 'this is red', uttered in the presence of a red object – or one that normally elicits that response – under standard lighting and with nothing about it that would tend to produce aberrant visual/perceptual effects.[20] However it also acquires the kind of empty circularity that results from setting up the argument in such a way as to ensure that the biconditional will always obtain for any suitable (RD-qualified) statement uttered under just those thinly specified conditions. Thus any formalised rendition of the theory, like those of Johnston and Wright, will comprise a more-or-less extended sequence of interlinked tautologies since its truth-conditions are sure to be satisfied as a matter of strictly analytic (or definitional) warrant.

That the RD debate takes its bearings from two such extremely dissimilar philosophers as Plato and Locke should not perhaps be cause for surprise given this particular line of argumentative strategy. What Plato obligingly provides in the *Euthyphro* is the perfect philosophical *mise-en-scène* for a treatment of these issues which can be claimed to work out – despite Plato's (or Socrates') intention – in support of the Euthyphronic thesis as against the realist argument for truths that are thought to obtain independently of human judgement or of any evidence that we do or might possess concerning them. That is to say, it presents the issue as a straightforward choice between Socrates' version of the realist case – one that the dialogue is artfully rigged to endorse – and Euthyphro's position as elective spokesman for something very like the present-day RD approach. So if Socrates' argument shows up as committed to certain unsustainable claims – such as our somehow having *epistemic contact* with objective truths that transcend the limits of human intelligibility – then on this view the only alternative approach is one that concedes the opposing (Euthyphronic) thesis. From which it follows that truth must be subject to precisely those same limits as defined – how else? – by a response-dispositional account of their role in the deliverance of 'best opinion' under optimal conditions of human perceptual or cognitive grasp.

So the lesson of Plato's dialogue as construed by Wright is not, after all, so sharply opposed to the Lockean empiricist conception of secondary qualities in its RD-specified form. Where Euthyphro wins out against Socrates, on this construal, is in showing that a realist or Platonist argument for the existence of objective (non-response-dependent) ethical values simply cannot make sense from any humanly attainable epistemic standpoint. Thus the realist deludedly maintains that 'the piety of an act is one thing, and the gods' estimate of it another', even though 'the gods are, by their very nature, cognitively responsive to piety', and may therefore be presumed always to get things right as a result of their superior knowledge, wisdom, or acuity of moral perception.[21] For Euthyphro, on the other hand, the gods' best judgement 'enters constitutively into the determination of which acts are pious', just as, according to the RD theorist, our optimised judgements concerning colour and a range of more-or-less cognate properties must be taken as defining what normatively counts as an instance of the property in question.[22] Much the same applies to Wright's idea of 'superassertibility', offering as it does an alternative (slightly more robust) version of the RD case for regarding truth in such contexts as the deliverance of best opinion among suitably placed and qualified perceivers or judges. Thus for Socrates and his realist progeny '[i]t is because certain statements (in the discourse in question) are true that they are superassertible', whereas for Euthyphro and those who share his epistemic convictions '[i]t is because such statements are superassertible that they are true.'[23] And Euthyphro must clearly be taken to have the last word – *contra* Socrates – since there is just no way to explain how we could ever have epistemic access to truths, properties, or values that transcend the utmost powers of human perceptual, epistemic, or moral-evaluative grasp.

III

Hence the centrality of Plato and Locke to this current debate about response-dependence and its proper scope of application. The Lockean affinity is plain enough since the RD thesis has its source in the idea of secondary qualities and their intrinsic reference to duly normalised (or optimised) modes of perceiver-response. The Platonist connection is less obvious on the face of it but comes into focus as soon as one asks what it is that these theorists are seeking to present as a wrong or at any rate deeply problematic treatment of the issues concerned. Thus Platonic realism here stands in for all those subsequent (presumptively failed) attempts to secure a realm of objective truth-values that would hold good quite apart from the scope and limits of optimised human judgement. Yet there is something distinctly suspect about this way of setting up the argument, that is, a suspicion that the realist is indeed being *set up* by having her position unjustly equated with the dubious Platonist claim that we can gain access to such truths through a kind of quasi-perceptual 'contact' analogous to that of sensory acquaintance but delivering a knowledge that somehow transcends the error prone beliefs and assumptions of naive sense-certainty. This aspect of Plato's idealist metaphysics – its reliance on sublimated sensory metaphors in order to promote a doctrine of truth that should properly require no such appeal to that inferior mode of cognition – has drawn a good deal of critical attention among commentators from Aristotle down.[24] In particular it has prompted philosophers of mathematics, notably Gödel, to protest that one can indeed espouse a realist – even, in some sense, a Platonist – position on the objectivity of numbers, sets, functions, truth-values, etc., without buying into such a hopelessly confused or unworkable epistemology.[25]

Jerrold Katz puts a similar case in his book *Realistic Rationalism*, where he views this strategy for setting up the realist as a kind of guilt-by-association technique which has thoroughly skewed the recent debate in philosophy of mathematics and other fields. Thus, according to Katz:

> [t]he entire idea that our knowledge of abstract objects might be based on perceptual contact is misguided, since, even if we had contact with abstract objects, the information we could obtain from such contact wouldn't help us in trying to justify our beliefs about them. The epistemological function of perceptual contact is to provide information about which possibilities are actualities. Perceptual contact thus has a point in the case of empirical propositions. Because natural objects can be otherwise than they actually are (*non obstante* their essential properties), contact is necessary in order to discover how they actually are . . . Not so with abstract objects. They could not be otherwise than they are . . . Hence there is no question of which mathematical possibilities are actual possibilities. In virtue of being a perfect number, six must be a perfect number; in virtue of being the only even prime, two must be the only even prime. Since the epistemic role of contact is to provide us with the information needed to select among the different ways something might be, and since perceptual contact cannot provide information about how something must be, contact has no point in relation to abstract objects. It cannot ground beliefs about them.[26]

As we have seen, there are some passages in Wright – especially those having to do with issues in the philosophy of mathematics – where he appears to endorse at least a qualified version of this realist claim about abstract objects and the existence of objective (non-response-dependent) truths concerning them. Hence his suggestion that, 'in shifting to a broadly intuitionist conception of, say, number theory, we do not immediately foreclose on the idea that the series of natural numbers constitutes a real object of mathematical investigation, which it is harmless and convenient to think of the number theoretician as exploring'.[27] If we take this concession at face-value then it seems to represent a decided turn toward realism and, by the same token, a decided turn against any Dummett-type verificationist approach or indeed any Wittgensteinian appeal to communal warrant or sanction as the ultimate arbiter of correctness in rule-following (e.g., arithmetical) procedures.[28] Yet to take it at face-value is of course to ignore those various hedging clauses, as for instance that 'we do not *immediately* foreclose' on a realist conception (though we might at length be constrained to do so), or that it is 'harmless and convenient' (though perhaps illusory) to think of the number theoretician as exploring a domain of real abstract entities whose various logical entailment-relations determine the objective truth-value of our arithmetical statements. For the effect of these clauses is to qualify (even nullify) Wright's apparent 'turn' toward realism by leaving him sufficient scope to suggest that *really* they require nothing more than a due recognition of the extent to which our thinking about such matters is subject to the pull of certain residual objectivist ideas whose grip the Euthyphronist may hope to loosen but not to break altogether.

So despite his distaste for Wittgenstein's 'sneers' about 'super-rigid machinery' or the 'superlative conception' of rules – and whatever his doubts with regard to Wittgenstein's therapeutic claim that the sole aim of philosophical reflection is to 'give philosophy peace' – still Wright strongly inclines to the view that objectivist conceptions must always give rise to a vicious regress or some other kind of strictly insoluble antinomy.[29] This conviction results in turn from his failing to see how a rule could possibly be thought to lay down rules for its own correct following beyond whatever instances of practical grasp we are able to acquire or to manifest as part of our working competence. Moreover the same consideration applies to any area of discourse where the criterion for truth (or for warranted assertibility) is our possessing or at least being placed to acquire the relevant means of verification. But the realist will see absolutely no reason to go along with this prescriptive confinement of truth to just that range of candidate sentences which happen to fall within the scope of verifiability or the compass of judgements licenced by us and our reactive natures. Rather she will say that there exists a vast number of objective truths about mathematics, physics, chemistry, biology, history and other 'areas of discourse' which we don't presently know – and may indeed have no possible means of finding out – but which nonetheless determine the truth-value of any statements we make concerning them.

Scott Soames puts the realist case with respect to mathematics, physics, and other truth-apt areas of discourse in a passage that is worth quoting once again for its pinpoint clarity of thought. After all, he writes,

> a proposition can be true even if it has never been expressed by an actual utterance. It is also not absurd to suppose that it can be true even if there is no sentence that expresses it. For example, for each of the nondenumerably many real numbers, there is a proposition that it is greater than or equal to zero. If each sentence is a finite string of words drawn from a finite vocabulary, then the number of propositions outstrips the denumerable infinity of sentences available to express them – that is, there are truths with no linguistic expression.

> Moreover, if languages are man-made constructions, then propositions that are expressed by sentences could have been true even if no sentences had expressed them. For example, the proposition that the sun is a star could have been true even if no one and hence no sentence had existed to express it.[30]

For a 'strong' anti-realist like Dummett, this whole string of claims would be just another cautionary instance of the failure to heed Wittgenstein's lesson, that is, that it *cannot make sense* to postulate the existence of truths for which we possess no adequate means of ascertainment or method of proof. In his later work, Dummett sometimes tends to qualify this hardline position though without ever going so far as to concede the argument for objective or recognition-transcendent truths.[31] As regards mathematics in particular he remains firmly committed to the intuitionist claim that truth cannot conceivably outrun the best available proof-procedures that mathematicians are able to devise and which *ex hypothesi* constitute the limits of intelligibility for any mathematical statement, theorem, or well-formed conjecture.[32] In Wright's case there are signs of a greater willingness to accommodate opposing (i.e., realist) views, at least if one compares his early work where the Wittgensteinian influence is at its strongest with his more recent publications.[33] Thus he now puts forward the idea of response-dependence as a means of achieving this desired *rapprochement* between a moderate verificationist approach according to which realism figures as a 'harmless and convenient' way of treating these issues and, on the other hand, a likewise moderate realist approach which sensibly avoids placing too much stress on talk of 'objectivity' or truth beyond the limits of idealised epistemic warrant. Yet this proposed concordat works out, once again, very much in favour of the anti-realist view that in the end those limits *just are* the conditions for warranted assertibility and, moreover, that assertoric warrant *just is* what constitutes truth for any area of discourse where human judgement is in play. From which it follows, on Wright's account, that the appeal to optimised capacities of judgement under optimised epistemic conditions is one that must always lead back to some version – no matter how hedged or qualified – of the Euthyphronic thesis with respect to the role of best opinion in deciding *what counts* as an admissible, well-formed, or truth-evaluable statement. In other words it leaves no room for the basic (non-negotiable) realist claim that truth involves some determinate relation between a statement and its truth-maker, the latter 'conceptually quite independent of our standards of assessment', and taken as possessing objective truth-values on which we impinge 'only in an (at most) detective role'.[34]

Hence, I would suggest, the inbuilt tendency of an RD approach to espouse the anti-realist side of this argument – thus effectively reverting to form – whenever there is an issue that lends itself to treatment in terms of the stock Euthyphronist debate over whether best opinion necessarily tracks truth or whether truth determines best opinion. This tendency comes out most strikingly in a passage where Wright takes issue with Hilary Putnam over the latter's 'requirement of completeness' with respect to truth-apt statements at the limit of justificatory warrant. Thus, for Putnam, it is the case 'that, for each statement, *either* it *or* its rejection must be justified under epistemically ideal conditions'.[35] However, Wright responds,

> [t]here seems no good reason to impose any such completeness requirement – no particular reason why all questions which are empirical in content should become decidable under ideal conditions. Indeed, to take seriously the indeterminacies postulated by contemporary physical theory is to consider that there is reason to the contrary. We can expect that an internal realist [i.e., Putnam at this stage in his thinking] would want to suspend the principle of Bivalence for statements which would find themselves beached at the limit of ideal enquiry in this way, and ought consequently, one would imagine, to want to suspend it in any case, failing an assurance that no statements are actually in that situation.[36]

There is a certain rather piquant irony about this exchange, given that Putnam's long-haul retreat from a strong causal-realist to an 'internal'-realist position, and thence to a kind of commonsense or pragmatist 'realism' that dare not quite speak its name, was prompted very largely by his strenuous attempts to make logical sense of problems in the interpretation of quantum mechanics.[37] Those problems – for example, of wave/particle dualism, superposition, or the impossibility (according to orthodox quantum theory) of reidentifying particles from one observation/measurement to the next – were such, he thought, as to require either a change in our most basic conception of physical reality or a switch from bivalent to three-valued logic that would save quantum appearances while conserving at least the most basic components of a realist ontology or worldview.[38] I have written elsewhere about the difficulties with Putnam's proposal and the curious fact that he, like so many others, finds himself forced to pose the issue in these terms through giving short shrift to David Bohm's 'hidden-variables' theory, one that successfully accommodates the full range of predictive-observational data without any need *either* to abandon the principles of causal realism *or* to revise the ground-rules of classical (bivalent) logic.[39] However my main point here is that Wright pushes even further in an anti-realist direction by rejecting Putnam's 'completeness requirement' and maintaining that a truly consistent 'internal realist' should want to push right through with suspending bivalence not only for statements (like those of quantum mechanics) that may find themselves 'beached at the limits of ideal enquiry' but in principle for *any* statement, at least 'failing an assurance that no statements are actually in that situation'. Of course Wright is here taking issue with Putnam's particular version of the case for internal (framework-relative) realism and his particular Peircean limit-point conception of what constitutes truth 'at the end of enquiry'.[40] Still the above-cited passage shows very clearly how Wright's thinking is drawn toward an anti-realist construal of the relevant 'area of discourse' whenever the alternative is a theory that strives to conserve some realist-compatible account of truth as the deliverance of optimised epistemic warrant.

I have argued that response-dependence theory, so far from resolving the problems with Dummett-style anti-realism, in fact merely serves to displace or disguise them through its adoption of a formal device – the RD quantified biconditional – which in fact (despite its claims) does no substantive philosophical work. This is not to deny that some other, differently elaborated approach under the same generic description might produce the required result or at any rate go much further toward reconciling realism with an account of those various forms, structures, or modalities of judgement that constitute our means of perceptual and cognitive access to the world. Indeed there are some philosophers of a broadly RD persuasion – John McDowell among them – who have taken a lead from Kant's First *Critique* in attempting to do just that, that is, to explain (in McDowell's terms) how the 'receptivity' that is supposed to characterise our uptake of passively acquired perceptual data is always already structured or informed by the active 'spontaneity' which enables the mind to process and interpret those same incoming data.[41] This approach implicitly lays claim to providing much more in the way of substantive epistemological content than could ever be achieved by application of the standard RD formula. Yet it fails to live up to that high promise, chiefly because those crucial load-bearing terms – 'receptivity' and 'spontaneity' – cannot be made to shed their dualist (passive *versus* active) connotations, despite McDowell's insistent demand that we construe them rather as alternative descriptions of the selfsame jointly operative process.[42] Thus his argument amounts to just another version of the split between empirical 'data' and conceptual 'scheme' which McDowell traces through the line of descent from logical empiricism to Quine's purported demolition of that entire programme and, beyond that, to Davidson's purported demolition of Quine's residual adherence to a third 'dogma' of empiricism, namely the scheme/content dualism which still plays a role in Quine's idea of ontological relativity.[43] 'In giving up the dualism of scheme and world', Davidson writes, 'we do not give up the world, but re-establish unmediated touch with the familiar objects whose antics make our sentences and opinions true or false'.[44] Even so, as McDowell shrewdly points out, Davidson's insouciant talk of 'unmediated' contact still leaves it wholly mysterious just *how* we could ever gain acquaintance with those various supposedly 'familiar objects' that figure in our everyday commonsense knowledge of the world. 'Davidson resolves the tension he finds in Quine in the wrong direction, and the result is precisely to leave us with the philosophical problems he wants to eliminate.'[45] Thus he (Davidson) claims to diagnose the lingering dualism in Quine's argument but only at the cost of espousing a yet more radically empiricist theory, one that deprives epistemology of any normative dimension and thus lays itself open to construal – as for instance by sceptics like Rorty – as the claim that one can be as 'realist' as one likes about the impact of stimuli on our sensory receptors while still holding that truth is a product of interpretation and that interpretation goes all the way down for any practical intents and purposes.[46]

As I say, MacDowell perceives very clearly how this dualism continues to operate in thinkers such as Quine, Davidson, and Rorty who would regard themselves as having at last overcome it through a break with the tenets of old-style logical empiricism. Yet the same can be said of McDowell's proposal to shift the ground of debate by returning to those passages in Kant's First *Critique* where the talk is not so much of 'bringing intuitions under adequate concepts' – itself the source of many subsequent dualist woes – but rather of 'receptivity' and 'spontaneity', conceived as so closely bound up one with the other that the dichotomy cannot get a hold. For despite all his repeated attempts to phrase the claim in just such a way it always tends to veer back and forth between a reading that privileges spontaneity (the mind's active contribution) at the expense of receptivity or receptivity (our passive uptake of sensory information) at the expense of spontaneity. And indeed it is hard to see how things could be otherwise, given the active/passive distinction that McDowell takes over from Kant and also his strong Kantian emphasis – *contra* the empiricist notion of inert or passively acquired sense-data – on the extent to which the mind 'spontaneously' shapes and structures our knowledge of the world.

Thus: 'although experience itself is not a good fit for the idea of spontaneity, even the most immediately observational concepts are partly constituted by their role in something that is indeed appropriately conceived in terms of spontaneity.'[47] Still, he concedes, there is the equal and opposite risk of extending spontaneity so far that it comes to be thought of – in Fichtean subjective-idealist terms – as a world-constitutive power that brooks no merely empirical constraints on its sphere of operation.[48] In McDowell's words:

> [i]t can be difficult to accept that the [empiricist] Myth of the Given is a myth . . . It can seem that we are retaining a role for spontaneity but refusing to acknowledge any role for receptivity, and that is intolerable. If our activity in empirical thought and judgement is to be recognizable as bearing on reality at all, there must be external constraint. There must be a role for receptivity as well as spontaneity, for sensibility as well as understanding. Realizing this, we come under pressure to recoil back into appealing to the Given, only to see over again that it cannot help. There is a danger of falling into an interminable oscillation.[49]

However it is just this kind of oscillating movement that McDowell himself falls into when he strives to reconcile the claims of receptivity and spontaneity. Moreover, as I have argued, it is a pattern reproduced in the thinking of Wright and other response-dependence theorists, even though its effects are somewhat damped down by their adoption of a formula – the standard RD quantified biconditional – which allows them to avoid any close engagement with problems like those that McDowell confronts in his selective retrieval of Kantian epistemology.

What they share with McDowell, simply put, is the idea of giving human responses (on a suitably specified construal) more of a say in matters of epistemic warrant than could ever be allowed for by the realist conception of truth as that which obtains quite apart from 'best opinion' or the deliverance of suitably qualified subjects under ideal perceptual or cognitive conditions. Where they differ from him is in finding no use for the kind of scaled-down Strawsonian descriptivist approach *via* Kant that still takes account of epistemological issues such as those which arise in attempting to explain the mind's 'contribution' to our knowledge of 'external' (mind-independent) reality, or how precisely to characterise the relationship between 'spontaneity' and 'receptivity'. On the RD account these problems can be safely left aside once the point has been made – by way of the quantified biconditional – that the standard of correctness in perception or judgement with regard to some given area of discourse *just is* the standard reliably vouchsafed by reference to norms that must be taken to define what counts as an optimised human response. So there is no room here for the kinds of problem that McDowell inherits from Kant and which involve such an effort to explain 'how there must be a role for receptivity as well as spontaneity, for sensibility as well as understanding'.[50] However this means that there is also no room – on the RD account – for a more discriminate reckoning with issues of knowledge and truth that would go beyond laying it down as a matter of sheer self-evidence that the criteria of warranted assertibility simply *cannot be other* than those supplied by the deliverance of best opinion. So if McDowell, like Kant before him, never succeeds in squaring the claims of 'empirical realism' and 'transcendental idealism' then neither can the RD theorists succeed simply by shunting this problem aside or by defining correctness as a matter of compliance with the standard formula, that is, the requirement that properties instanced to the left of the quantified biconditional be reliably paired with perceptions or judgements instanced to the right. What this amounts to, in short, is a merely tautological truth-of-definition that avoids epistemological dilemmas of the kind confronted by McDowell but only at the cost of having nothing to say – or nothing of substantive import – as regards either the specific nature of those properties or the various cognitive and ambient physical conditions under which we are enabled to arrive at a correct judgement concerning them.

Wright effectively concedes as much when he remarks that 'no Euthyphronic concept comfortably fits the paradigm of a natural kind concept, since a priority for a suitably provisoed biconditional is inconsistent with the hostage to reference-failure which any prototypical natural kind concept must hold out.'[51] That is to say, such concepts are truth-tracking or sensitive to future discovery, as argued by causal realists like early Putnam, since they must always stand under correction through some possible future advance in our scientific knowledge of chromosomal properties, molecular structure, subatomic constitution, or whatever.[52] So plainly there is no room here for an RD approach that would treat natural kinds and their distinctive attributes as in any way dependent on the normative character of our own (however optimised or idealised) epistemic capacities. Yet it is far from clear that Wright's version of the RD argument – amounting as it does to a qualified form of Dummett-style anti-realism – can afford to make such selective concessions to the adversary case without thereby undermining its own rationale or calling the entire project into question. After all, it is just his *generalised* point with regard to the Wittgensteinian 'paradox' about rule-following that it counts decisively against the idea of any given sentence being somehow 'undetectably true', or 'extending, so to speak, of itself into areas where we cannot follow it and thus determining, without any contribution from ourselves or our reactive natures, that a certain state of affairs complies with it'.[53] The immediate context for this remark is that of mathematics – of Platonist *versus* intuitionist conceptions of mathematical truth – where Wright inclines strongly to the Wittgenstein–Dummett view that the truth-value of statements cannot be thought to transcend the scope of our best attainable proof-procedures. Yet the realist will surely want to say that the idea of mathematical truth as amenable to a response-dependent account is no less absurd than the idea that natural-kind properties or membership-conditions are somehow dependent on our perceptual capacities or state of knowledge concerning them. Where the RD approach goes wrong, she will argue, is in generalising from the standard borderline case of secondary qualities like colour to a theory which extends that approach far beyond its legitimate sphere of application. All the more so since even in the case of colour (as Philip Pettit pointedly observes) 'a response-dependent term like "red" may refer to a perfectly mind-independent property: specifically, to the property that realises the redness role, rather than to the dispositional or role property.'[54] In which case, *contra* the Euthyphronist, we must think of best opinion as tracking or detecting – rather than as fixing or determining – the extension of colour predicates.

IV

Thus anti-realism as applied to the philosophy of mathematics can be made to look plausible only through the notion that a realist approach must inherently involve some misconceived idea of our somehow having contact – quasi-perceptual or epistemic contact – with truths that are thought of as inhabiting a realm of absolute ideal objectivity.[55] However this is just another striking example of the way that such debates are shrewdly set up on anti-realist or RD terms so as to exclude any workable realist alternative. For it will otherwise seem nothing less than self-evident to competent mathematical reasoners that we *do* have a perfectly clear conception of what it means for a certain statement or theorem to be 'undetectably' true, that is to say, to possess an objective (recognition-transcendent) truth-value which happens to lie beyond our furthest powers of computation or ability to produce an adequate formal proof.

Indeed one might argue that this whole debate was sidetracked at source by Wittgenstein's somewhat simplistic idea that the standard of correctness for continuing a number-series (2, 4, 6, 8, etc.) should be taken as a paradigm case of what counts as valid or correct mathematical procedure.[56] For this is not a procedure subject to proof in the strictest mathematical terms. Rather it is an instance of inductive or iterative reasoning which the sceptic can routinely challenge on the grounds that it is always possible, with sufficient ingenuity, to devise some alternative continuation with just as good a claim to correctness by its own criteria. However the sceptic's case will appear less plausible if applied, say, to statements concerning the validity of Goldbach's Conjecture (that every even number is the sum of two primes), or to the occurrence of a hundred as yet undiscovered consecutive sevens in the decimal expansion of *pi*, or to any such well-formed but unproven (maybe unprovable) conjecture. No doubt these statements fall short of the criteria for assertoric warrant laid down by a verificationist like Dummett, or again by those, Kripke and Wright among them, who take Wittgenstein's rule-following considerations to count decisively against any claim for the existence of practice-transcendent truth values. Hence Kripke's 'sceptical solution' to the Wittgensteinian paradox, namely that communal warrant or the sanction of existing arithmetical practice is the furthest we can get toward defining what counts as a 'correct' answer in any given case.[57] Yet this verdict is not only counter-intuitive in the highest degree but apt to be taken as a *reductio ad absurdum* of the Wittgensteinian argument. That is, there is something inherently absurd about the idea that arithmetical truth can be nothing more than a product of communal opinion, so that (for instance) if a certain 'community' elected to change the operative rules and endorse some alternative to the basic axioms of Peano arithmetic then the results thus obtained (such as '68 + 57 = 5') would be perfectly valid according their own consensual standards and just as 'correct' as any other result (such as '68 + 57 = 125') delivered by our own currently favoured methods. Insofar as this conclusion can be shown to follow from the Wittgenstein–Kripke line of reasoning it surely demonstrates that the argument must rest on some faulty premise or misconception about the nature of arithmetical truth.

The premise in question is precisely that which the RD theorists take over from Kripke, albeit in a qualified and less sharply paradoxical form which tends to disguise their otherwise very marked similarity of approach. What they share with Kripke is the basic idea that truth comes down to a matter of the assertibility-conditions for any given statement and that these are intrinsically response-dependent in the sense of allowing no ultimate appeal above and beyond the deliverance of best opinion. Where they differ is in making 'best opinion' a product of optimised judgement under ideal epistemic conditions rather than referring it (as Kripke does, taking a lead from Wittgenstein) to this or that existing arithmetical practice or *de facto* range of agreed-upon methods and procedures. Thus the RD theorists, like Dummett, would mostly fight shy of Kripke's 'sceptical solution' and seek at least a measure of common ground with the realist opposition in allowing that individuals (even whole communities) should properly be counted wrong if they adopt some alternative set of axioms that ascribe the value 'false' to such statements as '68 + 57 = 125' and the value 'true' to such statements as '68 + 57 = 5'.[58] Still it is far from clear that the

RD theorists are in any strong position to adopt this line, given their basic agreement on the claim that all such ascriptions involve some strictly ineliminable reference to the nature, scope and modalities of human response.

For Kripke, the sceptical conclusion follows from the fact, as he takes it, that there is simply no way to determine what a speaker *means, intends*, or *has in mind* when she utters the statement '68 + 57 = 125'. That is, she might be working on a different (to us non-standard or 'incorrect') rule for interpreting the '+' sign, a rule that on this particular occasion just happens to produce a response in agreement with our own understanding, but which in future might produce any number of variant results. So we are unable to say for sure that her reasoning has gone off the rails – that she has failed to think consistently or apply the same rule – if she offers a different response (such as '68 + 57 = 5') the next time around, or if she regularly gets things 'wrong' when asked to perform similar kinds of calculation. On the realist (or objectivist) view this curious behaviour would clearly indicate a basic lack of arithmetical grasp, that is, an inability to take the point that addition, subtraction, and other such procedures are recursive in character and hence provide a rule – a definite standard of correctness – that cannot be subject to variation from one instance to the next. On the Kripkean view, by contrast, this argument begs the whole question as to what could possibly constitute such a standard given the familiar objections from Wittgenstein, namely (1) the lack of any 'public' criterion for determining what speakers 'inwardly' mean by their usage of expressions like the plus-sign, and (2) the vicious regress that opens up with any appeal to superordinate rules for the conduct of first-order rule-governed practice.[59] In which case we are supposedly forced back upon Kripke's sceptical solution to Wittgenstein's sceptical paradox and thus left with nothing but communal warrant as a source of the assertibility-conditions which allow us to distinguish 'correct' from 'incorrect' instances of arithmetical reasoning.

That this is in fact no solution at all – that it leaves the problem squarely in place – is the realist's likeliest (and I think fully justified) response. It has come not only, as might be expected, from outright defenders of realism in philosophy of mathematics but also from some RD theorists who have argued for a version of response-dependence that would escape the Kripkean sceptical fix without adopting a full-scale Platonist stance.[60] All the same there is room for doubt whether this can be achieved on the terms laid down by Kripke's sceptical challenge, a challenge that the theorists (or most of them) regard as simply unavoidable even while they hope to come up with some alternative RD-compatible account that might satisfy the realist. The main problem here is that this whole debate developed very largely in response to the Kripkean (or 'Kripkensteinian') challenge and has not yet managed to shake off that tutelage to the extent of posing the problem anew or envisaging a non-sceptical outcome. Thus it continues to address the rule-following paradox in much the same way that Kripke originally proposed, that is, as a matter of somehow explaining what could possibly *count* as the 'correct' application of a rule given the absence of determinate criteria for knowing what speakers have in mind when they utter some expression containing the 'plus'-sign or any other arithmetical, logical, or truth-functional term that might just be subject to variant construals.

This is why Wright sees such a problem in the notion that a sentence might be 'undetectably true' if that notion entails, as it must on the realist account, that we should think of it as somehow extending 'into areas where we cannot follow it' and thereby possessing an objective (recognition-transcendent) truth-value 'without any contribution from ourselves or our reactive natures'.[61] To be sure there are passages in Wright's later work where he seems to incline toward a non-response-dependent account of arithmetic that would place it among those areas of discourse (e.g., statements concerning shape, magnitude, or moral value) that simply don't lend themselves to treatment on RD terms, and not among those – like perceptions of colour or other secondary qualities – which on his view invite and indeed require such treatment. But here again the criteria are somewhat fuzzy since he can also be found assimilating moral judgements to comic responses, which would greatly weaken his case for objectivity with regard to morals. Thus, concerning both comedy and moral discourse: 'on a wide class of construals . . . evidence transcendence is simply not in view', while in the former case 'at first approximation . . . comic discourse is disciplined by the objective of irreproachability in the light of a community of comic sensibility'.[62] From which one might fairly conclude that Wright is less than certain – or his argument less than secure – when it comes to the issue concerning arithmetic or other such 'areas of discourse' where our standing intuitions militate strongly against any response-dependent approach. That is to say, the Kripkensteinian influence continues to loom large whenever it is a question, as it often is for Wright, of assessing some given statement, truth-claim, or area of discourse in terms of its *relative* amenability to assessment on RD terms.

One reason for this sceptical bias, I suggest, is the idea that any adequate address to the problem must always start out by explaining how standards of correctness in judgement could ever be upheld against the charge that they involve some misconceived appeal to meanings, intentions, or thoughts in the mind of this or that reasoner. Wright's great hope, in company with other RD theorists, is that it may prove possible to develop a response-dependent account of arithmetical truth that would answer the Kripkean sceptic on terms of his own choosing while not falling prey to Kripke's joint deployment of the Wittgensteinian case against 'private languages' and against any notion of correctness in rule-following that would involve such a 'private' (apodictic or inwardly self-validating) ground of appeal. Yet this very way of framing the issue is enough to give Kripkean scepticism the last word since it concedes that the truth of arithmetical statements – or the correctness of some (and not other) rule-following procedures – must always be referred to what *counts* as such among subjects who typically produce those statements or manifest those forms of rule-following behaviour. For in that case it is always open to the sceptic to rejoin that no such evidence could ever be sufficient to determine just what they meant by uttering such a statement or just which rule they had in mind when performing some arithmetical task that brought them out either in accordance or at odds with our own best opinion in the matter. Thus there is simply no squaring the RD approach with a realist account of arithmetical truth that would insist on its objective (non-response-dependent) character and would seek to head off the Kripkean challenge by asserting that such truths have nothing to do with thoughts 'in the mind' of any speaker or reasoner. Nor would the realist see much hope of strengthening the RD position by shifting the focus from that lone individual 'privately' engaged in solving some arithmetical problem to the wider community of judgement whose standards can reliably be taken to decide the issue in any given case. For this is merely Kripke's 'sceptical solution' recast in terms that go somewhat further toward meeting the realist's objection – that is, by specifying normalised or even idealised conditions of epistemic warrant – but which still refer truth to some prevailing state of best opinion among duly qualified respondents.

Where the RD theorists differ from Kripke is in holding that the relevant criteria *can* be so specified and that this can be done, moreover, without falling prey to the Wittgensteinian private-language or vicious-regress arguments. All that is needed, they propose, is some suitably provisoed version of the quantified biconditional as a means of making the case for response-dependence in a way that successfully avoids the appeal to unknowable goings-on in the mind when *le penseur* engages in the various activities of adding, subtracting, multiplying, drawing valid logical inferences, and so forth. However, as we have seen, it is precisely through the effort to avoid making any such appeal – and thereby inviting the standard range of objections – that the RD theorists are led to formulate the quantified biconditional in terms that reduce to just a kind of extended tautology or a statement of the truth-conditions for this or that area of discourse which offers no substantive specification in any given case. That is to say, the Kripkensteinian influence still shows through in their constantly adverting to the nature, scope, and modalities of human response while also manifesting an acute awareness of the problems that arise for this line of argument when construed in a more sceptical light. It is also what predisposes them against giving philosophic credence to any full-fledged realist alternative account of certain areas of discourse – such as arithmetic – that would reject the very terms and conditions on which Kripke lays down his challenge, that is, his idea that if 'there is no fact about a competent language user that constitutes her meaning addition by the sign "+" ', then there is no truth about arithmetic that can possibly amount to more than community-wide agreement or consensus. And this despite the clear signs in their work that Wright and other RD theorists have grown increasingly doubtful as to whether such an argument comes close to capturing our strong intuitions in this regard or explaining just what it is about the truths of arithmetic that makes Kripke's 'sceptical solution' so downright implausible when applied to this area of discourse. Thus Wright, in particular, can be seen to have travelled a good distance toward some kind of arithmetical realism – or at least a good distance away from any kind of anti-realist approach that might be construed as licensing the Kripkean verdict – since his earlier Wittgenstein-inspired writings on the philosophy of mathematics.[63] Still it is far from clear that his approach to these issues *via* a response-dependence theory can provide what is needed in order to block the Kripkean sceptical challenge or to meet the realist's basic requirement that the truths of arithmetic not be treated as mere facts about the way we do things in accordance with some given (however well-entrenched) arithmetical practice or set of procedural guidelines.

V

This has not prevented some RD theorists – among them John Divers and Alex Miller in a recent article – from taking a more optimistic view of the prospects for achieving both these aims.[64] Thus they think that Platonism can best be saved from the standard anti-realist objection – that is, that it places arithmetical truths beyond our utmost epistemic grasp – by bringing the Platonist to accept a duly qualified version of the RD thesis. No doubt, they concede, there are other less discriminate versions of it which would simply deny that such truths could exist in the absence of knowers or of sentient creatures (such as ourselves) suitably equipped to cognise them. Thus:

> what is unacceptable to *any* ontologist who deserves the title 'arithmetical platonist' is a conception of arithmetical truth that entails the *counterfactual* dependence of the existence of numbers on the existence of *any* minds – i.e., a conception of arithmetical truth that entails that if there had been no minds then there would have been no numbers, or that if minds had been different then numbers would have differed in their intrinsic properties.[65]

However there is no good reason, according to Divers and Miller, why the RD theorist should take this extreme view or why the Platonist should think that her position is necessarily under attack from *any* form of argument – whatever the relevant provisos attached – that maintains the response-dependent character of arithmetical truths. Thus even in the case of a paradigm secondary quality like colour it is perfectly acceptable to claim that certain objects are truly described as red – that they really do possess that quality – just so long as they *would* appear red to a normally-sighted observer under normal epistemic conditions and irrespective of whether there are, ever have been, or will ever be any such observers around. In the same way, Divers and Miller suggest, 'the judgement-dependence of arithmetical truth does not imply any commitment to the counterfactual dependence of facts about numbers on facts about minds.'[66] Rather it implies only the realist-compatible claim, as they see it, that arithmetical truth is a property of certain statements such that they *would* be recognised as true *just in case* there were competent reckoners who assigned them that value, and quite apart from the contingent fact of there happening (or not happening) to be such observers around. In effect this is another kind of counterfactual reasoning, one that derives its demonstrative force from the appeal to a hypothetical community of those best qualified to judge, and which thus comes out squarely opposed to any notion of truth-values as dependent on the actual existence of any such community.

By setting the requirement in these terms, they argue, one can head off the standard realist (or platonist) objection that arithmetical truth simply *cannot* be reduced to a matter of consensus or agreed-upon judgement amongst some 'actual' company, however well-qualified, of arithmetical reasoners. This objection has to do with the fact that there have been in the past, still are, and will no doubt continue to be certain theorems in arithmetic that cannot be proved by the best methods to hand but which are well-formed and hence perhaps amenable to proof with the advent of more powerful procedures for checking their validity. Thus, to take the stock example, it is no argument against arithmetical realism with respect to Goldbach's Conjecture that we currently possess no conclusive method for proving its validity. Rather the conjecture – that every even number is the sum of two primes – is objectively true or false *even if* the means of deciding its truth-value happens to lie beyond our present powers of computational or conceptual grasp. Thus Divers's and Miller's advice to the realist (briefly put) is that in cases of this sort she had better go along with the qualified RD approach and accept that truth must coincide with best opinion in the ideal epistemic limit or when referred to the consensus of informed judgement amongst those hypothetically best equipped to judge. All the same, they concede, there are certain problems with this account which the realist can exploit if she rejects that advice and continues to maintain that arithmetical truth is altogether recognition- or verification-transcendent. Thus 'a relevant kind of example might be that of the Goldbach constant "g" which we can take to be introduced via the description "the smallest number that is a counterexample to Goldbach's Conjecture" when we consider the judgement that g is a perfect number.'[67] The chief worry here for any RD theorist is that the non-existence of anything that corresponds to this numerical singular term is such as to threaten a damaging rift between best opinion (or optimised expert judgement) and arithmetical truth (or what should *ex hypothesi* coincide with the deliverance of best opinion). For 'since the expert's failure to identify the referent of "g" will cause her to remain agnostic concerning the truth-value of the judgement in question, we may be in a scenario in which best opinion fails to match the truth-value of the proposition in question.'[68]

Still they think that this problem can be got around on RD-acceptable terms by appealing to different 'levels of conceptual competence' or to the fact that any level so far attained by even the most expert arithmetician 'falls short of what we can properly count as informing a best judgement'.[69] That is to say, the rift can always be bridged by invoking an epistemic limit-point where truth *simply must* coincide with the deliverance of optimised human response. Thus, according to Divers and Miller:

> an ideal (i.e. maximally conceptually equipped) judge would be in a position to make a truth-value matching judgement but no actual judge, pro tem, has the conceptual equipment that qualifies her as ideal. Again, that the proposition in question is pro tem undecided, does not enforce a view of the situation in which we have a mismatch of truth-value and best judgement.[70]

In which case there is nothing – no counter-example – that could possibly defeat the RD case for best judgement (or a suitably provisoed biconditional) as the basis for defining arithmetical truth. However this should cause no worry for the realist since it leaves all her standing commitments in place, such as the *a priori* truth that 'a number is prime if and only if calculation would reveal that its only divisors are 1 and itself.'[71] All that changes with the shift from outright realism to a duly qualified (and hence, as they see it, realist-compatible) RD approach is that the *a priori* status of such truths must always *at the limit* be conceived as referring to the best judgement of those hypothetically best qualified to judge. So even the self-avowed Platonist need have no qualms about endorsing a theory which so perfectly squares with her own conviction that truth might always outrun any present-best state of arithmetical knowledge while it also gets her off the hook of explaining how we could ever gain epistemic access to truths that are taken to transcend our utmost powers of conceptual grasp. Indeed, she can wield this theory as a powerful rejoinder to sceptics or to fictionalists like Hartry Field who would press their case to the point of denying that there is *any* construal of Platonism that would save it from its own self-defeating upshot.[72] By the same token she can also outflank those other, less extreme versions of the argument – such as that put forward by Paul Benacerraf – which maintain that knowledge must stand in some causal relation to its purported object and that the Platonist conception clearly fails this test since it treats numbers as nonspatial, atemporal and mind-independent (abstract) entities that cannot possibly figure in any such account.[73] Thus the suitably provisoed RD approach should be welcomed (Divers and Miller think) by any Platonist who has taken these sceptical lessons to heart and who must therefore be in quest of an alternative theory which incorporates just that measure of response-dependence that can save her position from total collapse while maintaining the non-finality of arithmetical knowledge as we presently have it. Moreover, though they don't say as much, this line of counter-argument would also (if valid) provide a strong defence against Kripke's communitarian 'sceptical solution' and Dummett's verificationist case for warranted assertibility as the farthest we can get toward specifying truth-conditions for this and other areas of discourse.

Nevertheless, as Divers and Miller acknowledge, there are grounds on which the Platonist might yet refuse to accept these accommodating terms or to sink her difference with the RD theorist as regards the objectivity of arithmetical truth. After all, '[m]anifestly, the judgement-dependent conception is in some sense an attempt to explicate arithmetical truth as a construct out of judgements made by suitably competent individuals in epistemically privileged circumstances.'[74] And it is just this concession that the Platonist will most likely *not* be willing to make, given her commitment to the notion of truth – for this and other relevantly similar areas of discourse – as in no sense dependent on the deliverance of best opinion, optimal response, or idealised epistemic warrant. Thus she will still want to say that the RD case falls short of meeting her demand, even at the limit-point where truth is conceived (in Peircean terms) as coextensive with just that set of judgements on which best opinion is ultimately destined or fated to converge. For of course such an argument is always open to construal as a means of talking the Platonist down from her impossibly abstract heights to a sensible acceptance that truth *just is* whatever counts as such according to some given, however optimal, community of judgement. In other words, once again, the RD approach turns out to go a long way around to the conclusion (*via* various 'suitably provisoed' clauses) that in the end there is no alternative to thinking of truth as subject to the operative scope and limits of human conceptual grasp. Which is also to conclude – more in keeping with a Dummett-type anti-realist or verificationist approach – that Platonism still comes out of this encounter with its ontology in ruins and its chief contention (i.e., the objectivity of arithmetic truth) a thesis which cannot be sustained in the face of various sceptical assaults.

Other RD theorists have drawn precisely this negative conclusion, among them Jim Edwards in his essay 'Response-Dependence, Kripke and Minimal Truth'. Edwards is frankly unconvinced by the Kripkensteinian claim that truth comes down to a matter of assertibility-conditions and that these should be thought of as 'determined at bottom by a consensus in the language-using community'.[75] He also makes a clear distinction between Kripke's ultra-sceptical reading of the lesson from Wittgenstein (i.e., his denial that arithmetic statements can possess truth-conditions as well as conditions for assertoric warrant) and Dummett's more qualified version of the case which, 'although it does place some restriction upon truth conditions, allows that assertible utterance are apt for truth and falsity'.[76] Still Edwards sees great problems with the idea that a suitably provisoed response-dispositional account might capture what is valid in the realist case for the mind-independent (and to that extent 'objective') character of truth while avoiding the Platonist fix that results, so the RD theorists hold, from pushing too hard on such claims. In other words, Edwards raises serious doubts as to whether any RD approach of the kind proposed by Divers and Miller can possibly achieve its twofold aim of providing a realist-compatible alternative to Kripke's sceptical 'solution' and at the same time meeting the Kripkean challenge on terms that take sufficient account of its (presumed) philosophic force. Thus he spends the larger part of his essay running through the various RD claims with respect to favoured topics like colour-perception and enquiring just how far, and with just what kinds of result, those claims might plausibly be thought to apply in the case of arithmetical judgements. As a result of which Edwards concludes that there is simply no way of getting from the standard *a priori* quantified biconditional – with whatever built-in provisos or allowance for optimised conditions of response – to a theory that could possibly satisfy the realist unless she gives up defending her position as regards the objectivity of truth.

In short, '[a] response-dependent account of assertibility conditions cannot, it seems, sustain truth conditions. This is the challenge, as I see it, arising from Kripke's sceptical solution.'[77] And it is precisely the *a priori* character of the RD approach – its appeal to the supposed self-evident tie between valid ascriptions of colour or arithmetical truth and the deliverance of (suitably specified) best opinion – which prevents that approach from achieving the wished-for *rapprochement* with a realist argument premised on the existence of objective truth-values. After all:

> [t]he central tenet of a response-dependent account is that some judgemental response, or consensus of judgemental responses, is epistemically privileged – privileged in that this response or these responses partially determine the extension of the predicate 'red'. There is no ulterior *reason* that the judges can produce which *justify* [sic] their judgements employing 'red'. On a response-dependent account there is no logical room to question a consensus achieved by normal observers in optimal conditions.[78]

On the other hand they (the judges) might possess some kind of background theory (T) which allowed them to explain why well-placed subjects should agree, or sometimes fail to agree, in their optimised perceptual responses, and which furthermore made it possible for them (the judges) to distinguish a valid from a false or distorted consensus of opinion in the matter. After all, '[e]ven if the responses of normal observers in optimal conditions do in fact concur, it is plausible that (T) will make conceivable to them conditions under which consensus would fail – indeed, it is difficult to see how (T) could explain the de facto consensus if it did not do this.'[79] But in that case something has to give in the standard RD account since clearly the quantified biconditional can no longer be considered to hold as a matter of *a priori* warrant. Rather, it will have to be thought of as holding only on condition that it meets the requirements of (T), requirements that are *a posteriori* in the sense that they involve some appeal to a background theory which incorporates knowledge discovered through investigating just what constitutes a normal response under optimal epistemic circumstances. And of course it is always possible that such investigation may come across certain judgement-enhancing or judgement-distorting factors which find no place in the RD account since that account is limited to just those provisos which can plausibly be treated as obtaining *a priori* (perhaps more precisely: by very definition or stipulative warrant) for any candidate utterance.

Hence the real dilemma that Kripke poses for the RD theorists, according to Edwards. 'Either the users of "red" themselves have a background theory with which to explain why normal observers in optimal conditions agree in their judgements with "red" or they do not.'[80] If they do then that background theory (T) must be thought of as exerting a claim to adjudicate where differences of judgement arise or even, yet more problematically, to reject the consensus of best opinion where all respondents are perfectly agreed. If they don't, then plainly best opinion is not 'best' in any but a weak (*de facto* consensus-based) usage of the term, and the claim to apriority becomes just a piece of circular reasoning to the effect that warranted assertibility cannot be other than the deliverance of best opinion. 'Either way,' Edwards thinks, 'a response-dependent account collapses.'[81] For in so far as (T) provides the 'logical room' to question or challenge any such consensus it must thereby be taken to exert a superordinate authority which could always invalidate some (presumed) instance of *a priori* warrant. Yet insofar as the RD account is constrained to exclude that possibility – to deny the jurisdiction of (T) or (what amounts to the same thing) to stipulate that (T) must figure among the range of RD-specified provisos – its *a priori* warrant amounts to nothing more than a flat refusal to countenance the claim that there might be truth-conditions for certain areas of discourse that don't necessarily coincide with the deliverance of best opinion or optimised human response.

Of course the RD approach is most plausible – or comes up against least intuitive resistance – when applied to secondary qualities like colour, rather than to instances, like that of arithmetic, where no such account seems remotely capable of capturing what is meant or entailed by the statement '68 + 57 = 125'. Still it is precisely Edwards's point that the Kripkean case *does* purport to hold for arithmetical statements; that the alternative response-dependent approach *does* purport to answer Kripke's sceptical challenge; and – the sting in his argument – that it *cannot* effectively rise to this challenge since it is too much in hock to notions like those of conceptual apriority, epistemic (or assertoric) warrant, best opinion, or idealised consensus. For the sceptic can then come back with the standard range of counter-arguments from Kripke, among them the objection that none of these appeals – grounded as they are in the presumed regularity of optimised human response – goes any way toward answering the Kripkean point about non-projectibility.

Thus the RD theorist may produce some statement of the general form:

'A warrant to assert "68 + 57 = 125" is a warrant to assert that any further investigations as to whether "68 + 57 = 125" is assertible whose results satisfy the canonical conditions for asserting or denying "68 + 57 = 125", will also warrant the assertion of "68 + 57 = 125".'[82] But in so doing she takes it for granted – thus begging the Kripkean question – that such warrant is sustained (and strengthened) from one 'investigation' to the next, whether on the part of individual reckoners or through the existence of a stable consensus of judgement that determines what shall count as a correct rule-following procedure. And of course it is just this presumption that is challenged by Kripke's sceptical argument concerning the lack of any such sure criterion, that is to say, any 'fact' about the meaning attached to the '+' sign by a competent arithmetical reasoner that could serve to fix the conditions for correctly or consistently following a rule. Thus:

> [a]t best the earlier consensus provides evidence short of a warrant for the claim that the judgement will continue to be the consensus of the indefinitely enlarging corpus of judgements. We must recall that, according to the Sceptical Solution, there is no rational explanation of the earlier consensus. From the point of view of reasons for judgement the consensus is just a brute fact, having an unknown causal explanation. So there is nothing about that earlier consensus which itself warrants a prediction as to any future consensus.[83]

In which case there seems little hope of deliverance from Kripke's dilemma by invoking a response-dispositional account that must either entail some substantive appeal to goings-on in the minds of arithmetical reasoners (which the Kripkean argument is assumed to rule out) or else come down to a circular argument on *a priori* grounds which entails precisely nothing in the way of substantive arithmetical or philosophic import. In Edwards's words, 'we now have an argument running from the premise: "Arithmetic utterances have response-dependent assertibility conditions", to the conclusion: "Arithmetic utterances do not have truth conditions".'[84] So if an RD approach is assumed to be the only one that can possibly meet the Kripkean challenge then that challenge must itself be taken to have played all opponents clean off the field.

VI

No doubt, as Edwards readily concedes, there is something implausible – even absurd – about the claim that arithmetical utterances should be construed as having response-dependent assertibility conditions rather than truth-conditions of the kind that would render them objectively true or false quite apart from best opinion (or optimal response) amongst a given community of reasoners. Thus 'the argument might be valid and yet the conclusion false', since with *a priori* arguments of this sort validity is purely and simply a matter of complying with the dictates of logical form whereas the truth of any given conclusion depends on the truth of its premises. 'Garbage in, garbage out', as the saying more snappily goes among computer programmers and AI researchers. But then, once more, response-dependence theory must find itself impaled on the Kripkean dilemma, obliged to make a choice between specifying the conditions for assertoric warrant in strongly response-dependent terms (whereby it falls prey to Kripke's sceptical attack) or treating them rather as products of sheerly *a priori* definition (whereby it is deprived of any substantive or non-trivial content). It seems to me that Edwards is right about this and that an RD approach can offer no solution to problems such as those thrown up by Dummett-type anti-realism and by the Kripkean ultra-sceptical take on Wittgenstein's rule-following considerations. That background genealogy is most evident in Wright's case, attempting as he does to construct a duly qualified response-dependence account which explains how we can have all the objectivity we need with regard to mathematics and other such truth-apt areas of discourse while nonetheless acknowledging the force of Dummett's and Kripke's arguments. Divers and Miller put a similar case which, on the face of it, goes yet further toward assuaging the realist's doubts. But here also what emerges is a theory of arithmetical truth which yields crucial ground to the anti-realist at just the point where controversy is most often joined, that is, on the issue as to whether such truth can be conceived as potentially transcending our current best proof-procedures or even our utmost scope of conclusive verification.

The realist makes no bones about this: the correctness of the statement '68 + 57 = 125' is a matter of objective (verification-transcendent) truth and has nothing to do with the scope or the limits of best arithmetical judgement. So likewise with the truth of Pythagoras's theorem and any number of correct mathematical statements, hypotheses, or conjectures which, she will argue, possessed an objective truth-value even during the period when nobody had yet produced an adequate proof. From which it follows that in the case, say, of Fermat's Last Theorem the question of whether that theorem is true or false is a question quite distinct from the issue concerning whether or not Andrew Wiles's celebrated proof might yet turn out to contain some hidden flaw. Moreover this applies just as much to statements – such as 'Goldbach's Conjecture is true' – for which there exists no formal proof-procedure yet whose truth-value, so the realist maintains, is a matter of the way things stand with respect to an order of objective mathematical reality entirely unbeholden to our state of knowledge concerning it. The anti-realist is equally convinced that claims of this sort are strictly unintelligible and that truth must be epistemically constrained, that is to say, subject to the limits of whatever we can justifiably assert on the basis of existing or specifiable proof-procedures. In which case it makes no sense to suppose that there might (indeed must) be a vast number of to-us unknown mathematical truths for which, *ex hypothesi*, we lack the ability to recognise an adequate proof or to manifest an adequate working grasp of what their truth-conditions entail.

The only point on which both parties would surely agree is the impossibility of striking a middle-ground position such as that staked out by the current advocates of a response-dependent account. I think that they are both right about this, for reasons laid out above, but also that the failure of an RD approach is more of a problem for the anti-realist since it poses the issue of arithmetical truth in a particularly stark and unavoidable form. That is to say, it confronts us with a downright choice – *tertium non datur* – between accepting the idea that '68 + 57 = 125' is correct only by the lights of our existing (communally sanctioned) arithmetical practice and endorsing the realist (or objectivist) view that such a statement is true whatever we may happen to think or believe concerning it. In which case the clear misgivings of Wright and others with regard to Dummettian anti-realism or Kripkensteinian meaning-scepticism must be seen as reinforcing the realist argument for truths that can always potentially transcend the limits of warranted assertibility or community-wide best opinion. Thus it may turn out that the current debate concerning the scope and limits of response-dependence will result in a sharper definition of the issues and, to the extent that these problems persist, in a consequent strengthening of the realist case.

References

1. *Plato's Euthyphro, Apology of Socrates, and Crito*, ed. John Burnet (Oxford: Clarendon Press, 1977).
2. See especially Mark Johnston, 'Dispositional Theories of Value', *Proceedings of the Aristotelian Society*, Vol. 63 (1989), pp. 139–74 and 'How to Speak of the Colours', *Philosophical Studies*, Vol. 68 (1992), pp. 221–63; Philip Pettit, 'Realism and Response-Dependence', *Mind*, Vol. 100 (1991), pp. 597–626; Mark Powell, 'Realism or Response-Dependence?', *European Review of Philosophy*, Vol. 3 (1998), pp. 1–13; Peter Railton, 'Red, Bittter, Good', *European Review of Philosophy*, Vol. 3 (1998), pp. 67–84; Michael Smith,

The Moral Problem (Oxford: Blackwell, 1994); Ralph Wedgwood, 'The Essence of Response-Dependence', *European Review of Philosophy*, Vol. 3 (1998), pp. 31–54; Crispin Wright, 'Moral Values, Projection, and Secondary Qualities', *Proceedings of the Aristotelian Society*, Supplementary Vol. 62 (1988), pp. 1–26 and 'Euthyphronism and the Physicality of Colour', *European Review of Philosophy*, Vol. 3 (1998), pp. 15–30.

3. Wright, *Truth and Objectivity* (Cambridge, MA: Harvard University Press, 1992), p. 80.
4. Ibid., p. 80.
5. Among recent contributions, see especially William P. Alston, *A Realist Theory of Truth* (Ithaca, NY: Cornell University Press, 1996) and Scott Soames, *Understanding Truth* (Oxford: Oxford University Press, 1999).
6. Wright, *Truth and Objectivity*, p. 80 (Note 3, above).
7. Ibid., p. 61.
8. Ibid., p. 61.
9. Ibid., p. 80.
10. Ibid., p. 80.
11. Ibid., p. 228.
12. See Michael Dummett, *Truth and Other Enigmas* (London: Duckworth, 1978); also *The Logical Basis of Metaphysics* (Duckworth, 1991).
13. See Wright, 'Moral Values, Projection and Secondary Qualities' (Note 1, above).
14. John Locke, *An Essay Concerning Human Understanding*, ed. A. S. Pringle-Pattison (Oxford: Oxford University Press, 1969), Bk II, Chap. 8, Sect. 15; p. 69; also Johnston, 'How to Speak of the Colours' and other entries under Note 1, above.
15. John McDowell, 'Values and Secondary Qualities', in Ted Honderich (ed.), *Morality and Objectivity: a tribute to J. L. Mackie* (London: Routledge, 1985), p. 113.
16. George Berkeley, *A Treatise Concerning the Principles of Human Knowledge*, ed. Colin M. Turbayne (New York: Liberal Arts Press, 1957); also C. B. Martin and D. M. Armstrong (eds), *Locke and Berkeley* (New York: Anchor Books, 1968).
17. David Hume, *A Treatise of Human Nature* (Oxford: Clarendon Press, 1978), Bk II, Chap. I, Sect. 1; p. 469.
18. Wright, 'Moral Values, Projection, and Secondary Qualities', p. 2 (Note 1, above).
19. Wright, *Truth and Objectivity*, pp. 108–9 (Note 3, above).
20. See Johnston, 'How to Speak of the Colours' (Note 2, above).
21. Wright, *Truth and Objectivity*, p. 80 (Note 3, above).
22. Ibid., p. 80.
23. Ibid., p. 80.
24. See for instance Jerrold J. Katz, *Realistic Rationalism* (Cambridge, MA: MIT Press, 1998); also Soames, *Understanding Truth* (Note 5, above).
25. See Kurt Gödel, 'What Is Cantor's Continuum Problem?', in Paul Benacerraf and Hilary Putnam (eds), *Philosophy of Mathematics: selected readings*, 2nd edn (Cambridge: Cambridge University Press, 1983), pp. 470–85.
26. Katz, *Realistic Rationalism*, pp. 36–7 (Note 24, above).
27. Wright, *Truth and Objectivity*, p. 5 (Note 3, above).

28. See Dummett, *Truth and Other Enigmas* (Note 12, above); Ludwig Wittgenstein, *Philosophical Investigations*, trans. G. E. M. Anscombe (Oxford: Blackwell, 1953), *On Certainty*, trans. and ed. G. E. M. Anscombe and G. H. von Wright (Blackwell, 1969); and *Lectures on the Foundations of Mathematics*, ed. Cora Diamond (Chicago: University of Chicago Press, 1976).
29. Wright, *Truth and Objectivity*, pp. 228 and 230 (Note 3, above).
30. Soames, *Understanding Truth*, p. 19 (Note 5, above).
31. See Dummett, *The Logical Basis of Metaphysics* (Note 12, above).
32. See also Dummett, *Elements of Intuitionism* (Oxford: Oxford University Press, 1977).
33. See for instance Wright, *Wittgenstein on the Foundations of Mathematics* (Cambridge, MA: Harvard University Press, 1980); also *Realism, Meaning and Truth* (Oxford: Blackwell, 1987; 2nd edn 1993).
34. Wright, *Truth and Objectivity*, p. 80 (Note 3, above).
35. Cited by Wright, ibid., p. 39.
36. Ibid., p. 39.
37. The essays of Putnam's early (causal-realist) period are collected in his *Mind, Language and Reality* (Cambridge: Cambridge University Press, 1975). For his engagement with issues in quantum mechanics, see especially *Mathematics, Matter and Method* (Cambridge University Press, 1975) and *Realism and Reason* (Cambridge University Press, 1983). Putnam's acceptance of the orthodox ('Copenhagen') quantum theory and its supposed anti-realist implications can be traced through his subsequent writings, among them *The Many Faces of Realism* (La Salle: Open Court, 1987) and *Representation and Reality* (Cambridge University Press, 1988). See also Christopher Norris, 'Putnam's Progress: quantum theory and the flight from realism', in *Quantum Theory and the Flight from Realism: philosophical responses to quantum mechanics* (London: Routledge, 2000), pp. 165–93.
38. See for instance Putnam, 'How to Think Quantum-Logically', *Synthèse*, Vol. 29 (1974), pp. 55–61.
39. Norris, *Quantum Theory and the Flight from Realism* (Note 37, above).
40. See especially Putnam, *Reason, Truth and History* (Cambridge: Cambridge University Press, 1981).
41. Immanuel Kant, *Critique of Pure Reason*, trans. Norman Kemp Smith (London: Macmillan, 1964) and John McDowell, *Mind and World* (Cambridge, MA: Harvard University Press, 1994).
42. See Norris, 'McDowell on Kant: redrawing the bounds of sense' and 'The Limits of Naturalism: further thoughts on McDowell's *Mind and World*', in *Minding the Gap: epistemology and philosophy of science in the two traditions* (Amherst, MA: University of Massachusetts Press, 2000), pp. 172–96 and 197–230.
43. W. V. O. Quine, 'Two Dogmas of Empiricism', in *From a Logical Point of View*, 2nd edn (Cambridge, MA: Harvard University Press, 1961), pp. 20–46 and Donald Davidson, 'On the Very Idea of a Conceptual Scheme', in *Inquiries into Truth and Interpretation* (Oxford: Oxford University Press, 1984), pp. 183–98.
44. Davidson, ibid., p. 198.
45. McDowell, *Mind and World*, p. 138 (Note 41, above).

46. See especially Richard Rorty, 'Is Truth a Goal of Enquiry? Davidson versus Wright', *Philosophical Quarterly*, Vol. 45, No. 180 (1995), pp. 281–300; also Rorty, *Consequences of Pragmatism* (Brighton: Harvester, 1982) and *Objectivity, Relativism, and Truth* (Cambridge: Cambridge University Press, 1991).
47. McDowell, *Mind and World*, p. 13 (Note 41, above).
48. Johann Gottlieb Fichte, *The Science of Knowledge with the the First and Second Introductions*, trans. and ed. Peter Heath and John Lachs (Cambridge: Cambridge University Press, 1980)
49. McDowell, *Mind and World*, pp. 8–9 (Note 41, above).
50. Ibid., p. 9.
51. Wright, 'Euthyphronism and the Physicality of Colour', *European Review of Philosophy*, Vol. 3 (1998), pp. 15–30; p. 17.
52. Putnam, *Mind, Language and Reality* (Note 37, above); also Gregory McCulloch, *The Mind and its World* (London: Routledge, 1995).
53. Wright, *Truth and Objectivity*, p. 228 (Note 3, above); Wittgenstein, *Philosophical Investigations*, Sects 201–92 *passim* (Note 28, above); also Saul Kripke, *Wittgenstein on Rules and Private Language* (Oxford: Blackwell, 1982); Paul Boghossian, 'The Rule-Following Considerations', *Mind*, Vol. 98 (1989), pp. 507–49; Bob Hale, 'Rule-Following, Objectivity, and Meaning', in Hale and Crispin Wright (eds), *A Companion to the Philosophy of Language* (Blackwell, 1997), pp. 369–96; and John McDowell, 'Wittgenstein on Following a Rule', *Synthèse*, Vol. 58 (1984), pp. 325–63.
54. Pettit, 'Terms, Things and Response-Dependence', *European Review of Philosophy*, Vol. 3 (1998), pp. 55–66; p. 62.
55. See Notes 24 and 25, above.
56. See Note 53, above.
57. Kripke, *Wittgenstein on Rules and Private Language* (Note 53, above).
58. See for instance John Divers and Alexander Miller, 'Arithmetical Platonism: reliability and judgement-dependence', *Philosophical Studies*, Vol. 95 (1999), pp. 277–310 and Miller, 'Rule-Following, Response-Dependence, and McDowell's Debate with Anti-Realism', *European Review of Philosophy*, Vol. 3 (1998), pp. 175–97.
59. See Note 53, above.
60. See Note 58, above.
61. Wright, *Truth and Objectivity*, p. 228 (Note 3, above).
62. Ibid., pp. 82 and 106.
63. See Note 33, above.
64. Divers and Miller, 'Arithmetical Platonism' (Note 58, above).
65. Ibid., p. 303.
66. Ibid., p. 305.
67. Ibid., p. 289.
68. Ibid., p. 289.
69. Ibid., p. 290.
70. Ibid., p. 290.
71. Ibid., p. 293.
72. Hartry Field, *Realism, Mathematics and Modality* (Oxford: Blackwell, 1989).

73. Paul Benacerraf, 'What Numbers Could Not Be', in Paul Benacerraf and Hilary Putnam (eds), *The Philosophy of Mathematics: selected essays*, 2nd edn (Cambridge: Cambridge University Press, 1983), pp. 272–94.
74. Divers and Miller, 'Arithmetical Platonism', p. 305 (Note 58, above).
75. Jim Edwards, 'Response-Dependence, Kripke and Minimal Truth', *European Review of Philosophy*, Vol. 3 (1998), pp. 149–74; p. 149.
76. Ibid., p. 149.
77. Ibid., p. 173.
78. Ibid., p. 173.
79. Ibid., p. 173.
80. Ibid., p. 172.
81. Ibid., p. 173.
82. Ibid., pp. 168–9.
83. Ibid., p. 169.
84. Ibid., p. 169.

Chapter Five

Constitutional Powers: can 'best judgement' ever go wrong?

I

One claim often advanced by proponents of a response-dependent (RD) approach to issues in epistemology, ethics, and the philosophy of the social sciences is that it makes due allowance for the range of criteria – the differing standards of truth or assertoric warrant – that properly apply in our dealing with various topics or areas of discourse.[1] Thus it helps to defuse the issue between hardline realists and hardline anti-realists, or on the one hand those who steadfastly maintain that there can (indeed must) be truths that transcend our best methods of proof or verification, and on the other hand those who reject this idea since it involves our somehow (impossibly) being able to manifest a working grasp of truths that *ex hypothesi* exceed our utmost recognitional capacities.[2] What the RD approach has to offer, by contrast, is a theory that avoids this ultimate stand-off by incorporating various kinds and degrees of epistemic or evidential constraint. On Wright's account some statements are plausibly candidates for objective ('evidence-transcendent') truth, while others are subject to 'cognitive command' (where any statement might have to be withdrawn or revised in response to conflicting evidence at the limit of enquiry), and others again can be treated as 'superassertible' just so long as they meet all the relevant criteria for acceptance under optimal epistemic conditions. Therefore, so he claims, this approach has the signal virtue of not foreclosing on any conception of truth, correctness, valid judgement, or warranted assertibility which finds an appropriate application in this or that area of discourse.

From an RD standpoint the most interesting cases are those – like judgements concerning colour and other such Lockean 'secondary qualities' – where the standard of correctness necessarily involves some normative reference to human responses under certain specifiable (i.e., perceptual and ambient physical) conditions.[3] However the approach is claimed to make room for other sorts of judgement that extend all the way from mathematics, *via* morals, to comedy, or from cases where the realist would look strongly placed to maintain her evidence-transcendent conception to cases (like comic discourse) where there seems little hope of fixing normative criteria since responses may diverge so widely owing to differences of age, social class, gender, cultural background, individual temperament, etc. Still, Wright thinks, there is much to be gained by attending to such discourse-specific variations in the kinds of criteria that properly apply when assessing what counts as a correct, valid, or adequate response in any given context. Yet these distinctions are sometimes very shakily drawn, as for instance when he classes morals and comedy together as areas where 'evidence transcendence is simply not in view', yet also remarks that the normal response to comic discourse – what we properly or typically find amusing – must be thought of as 'disciplined by the objective of irreproachability in the light of a community of comic sensibility'.[4] His argument here swings right across from what sounds like a sturdily normative approach ('disciplined by the objective of irreproachability') to what can only be construed as an appeal to shared cultural habits of response ('in the light of a community of comic sensibility'). Thus the conclusion seems inescapable, on Wright's account, that moral judgements – like comic responses – are apt, fitting, or appropriate just in case they accord with some community-wide or culturally salient set of reactive dispositions. From which it follows that those dispositions cannot be subject to assessment in terms of their acknowledging (or failing to acknowledge) the claim upon our moral conscience of facts such as those of social injustice, political oppression, or wantonly inflicted suffering that might otherwise be held to justify certain responses – and disqualify others – quite apart from any merely *de facto* consensus of accredited best opinion. Hence Peter Railton's powerful objection (from a moral-realist standpoint) that the RD account fails to reckon with those various successive 'unmaskings' of communal warrant that have made up the history of moral progress 'with respect to slavery, inherited rule, the status of women, and the borders of tribe, "people", or nation'.[5] Hence also his more generalised conclusion that '[o]bjectivity about intrinsic and moral good alike calls for us to gain critical perspective on our own actual responses, not to project their objects rigidly.'[6]

So there are, as Railton says, some important issues at stake in the debate about response-dependence and its bearing on areas of discourse – such as ethics – where it may quite decisively affect our conception of what counts as a valid or legitimate exercise of judgement. This debate is often framed, by Wright and others, in terms of the contrasting views on morality presented in Plato's *Euthyphro*.[7] Thus, according to Socrates, the gods approve pious acts *just because* those acts are intrinsically pious and the gods are infallibly equipped to detect them on account of (what else?) their godlike acuity in that regard. According to Euthyphro, conversely, such acts are or should be deemed pious *just because* the gods approve them and their authoritative judgement must therefore be thought of as decisively settling the issue. This difference of views is then taken to characterise a great many other present-day debates (like those summarised above) where the realist holds that best opinion must be truth-tracking or can qualify as such only in, at most, a 'detectivist' role, while the anti-realist takes best opinion – or the deliverance of optimised human judgement – to *constitute* truth so far as we can possibly know or conceive it. Thus the question whether arithmetical truths are objective or (in some duly qualified sense) response-dependent is one that has to do not only with issues in the philosophy of mathematics – where it mostly takes rise from the challenge of Dummettian anti-realism – but also with wider aspects of our thinking about the scope and limits of human judgement.[8] Indeed it may be thought to apply across the whole range of subject-areas where an RD approach has staked its claim to resolve – or at any rate to clarify usefully – the dispute between realists and anti-realists. In the case of ethics it produces an account that makes moral 'properties' dependent on our normal responses or reactions, thereby effectively blocking any realist line of argument that would treat (say) the wanton infliction of suffering as an objective or intrinsic evil which warrants that description whether or not it happens to elicit a disapproving response.[9] Or again, if an item of US state legislature is held constitutional by the Supreme Court then, on the RD account, it *just is* constitutional owing to the Court's (constitutionally enshrined) authority to decide in such matters. For as events surrounding the 'election' of President George W. Bush have recently made all too plain there is in practice no appeal beyond or above that authority to a realist conception of natural justice that would presume to challenge or to strike down the Court's definitive ruling.

Still this example might give pause to the RD theorist who wishes to conserve a workable distinction between properties that do and properties that don't involve some essential (constitutive) relation to the kinds of judgement that properly count as possessing legitimate warrant. For there is still a strong case, so the ethical realist will argue, for holding that a decision like that of the Supreme Court – when it decreed an end to the counting of ballot-papers in a key marginal state and thereby ensured the election of Bush on a minority of the total votes cast – was wrong, unjust, politically biased, and hence *unconstitutional*. As it happens Mark

Johnston (a leading exponent of the RD approach to issues in philosophy of mind, knowledge, and perception) takes precisely this analogy as a basis for arguing that there is no legitimate ground of appeal beyond the deliverance of best judgement as referred to the highest authority in some given juridical context.[10] On this Euthyphronist conception, what the Supreme Court deems right *just is* what is right according to the verdict of a body that possesses, by very definition, the ultimate power to adjudicate in such matters. To suppose otherwise is therefore to endorse a notion of objective social, political, and moral values that would somehow transcend (and potentially invalidate) any verdict arrived at after due deliberation by the highest court in the land. Thus it is the same kind of error as that which leads the mathematical realist to suppose that there exists an order of objective truths beyond the furthest reach of our proof-procedures or which leads the realist in philosophy of science to assert the existence of objective truth-values for statements that cannot be conclusively verified or falsified.

However one could argue to converse effect that Johnston's choice of this juridical analogy to support his case is one that reflects symptomatically on the problems of response-dependence theory as applied to other (less obviously charged or controversial) areas of discourse. What it shows, again, is the inbuilt tendency of an RD approach to define truth in terms of best judgement and best judgement in terms of what normally (standardly) counts as such among well placed, authorised, or deemed-fit respondents rather than making due allowance for the standing possibility of error even on the part of those who enjoy this epistemically privileged status.[11] Thus it is not just an opportunist play on words to remark that this issue of 'constitutional' warrant is one that connects with the RD claim for the *constitutive* character of certain responses as applied to certain properties (like colour) that are taken to fall squarely within its proper scope of application. Indeed it is precisely their philosophic worry about abusive over-extensions of the RD approach that leads some theorists – Ralph Wedgwood among them – to question its general validity. 'To take another example,' he writes:

> there has been a vigorous debate in gay and lesbian studies about whether or not sexuality is "socially constructed". This may be interpreted as the question whether it is part of what it is to be, for example, a homosexual, that one identifies oneself as a homosexual, or at least as a person of the type that is actually classified in that way in one's society.[12]

Wedgwood is noncommittal about this claim which no doubt belongs to an 'area of discourse' far removed from the kinds of issue that more typically preoccupy RD theorists. All the same it does raise the question as to whether the interests of gay or lesbian individuals are best served by a constructivist view of gender 'identity' which accepts the definitions of *gay* and *lesbian* as offered (or imposed) by a prevalent discourse whose norms will inevitably tend to reinforce their marginal or deviant status. So there is a problem – albeit one largely ignored by post-structuralists and other exponents of this view – about any theory that relativises sexuality to the range of discourses, gender-roles, or subject 'positions' available at any given time.[13] Simply put it is the problem as to how such identities can be affirmed, respected, developed, or (in some sense) freely and willingly *chosen* if they are taken as belonging to 'a person of the type that is actually classified in that way in one's society'.[14] This dilemma comes out in its starkest form when thinkers like Foucault talk about an ethics of radical 'self-fashioning' – especially with regard to issues of sexual mores – while nonetheless asserting that the 'self' is nothing more than a discursive construct or a kind of transcendental illusion brought about by various quite recent (e.g., Kantian) conceptions of autonomous agency and choice.[15] It is also very evident, as Wedgwood notes, in feminist or gay–lesbian attempts to explain how a radical politics of sexual identity can somehow be promoted through the notion of gender-roles as constituted in, or constructed by, some given range of languages, discourses, or elective (how so?) modes of self-description.[16]

II

This may all seem pretty remote from the RD debate about secondary qualities such as colour and the extent to which other areas of discourse might or might not be subject to treatment in broadly analogous terms. However Wedgwood is right to make the connection since in each case discussion turns on the issue as to whether certain attributes – such as redness, moral value, social or political justice, sexual identity, or even mathematical truth – are response-dependent in the sense of allowing no appeal beyond the standards and criteria laid down by some existing normative community of judgement. He is also right to point out that if one follows the RD theorists in assuming (1) that ascriptions of colour are indeed response-dependent rather than physically specifiable in terms of wavelength, reflectance properties, neurophysiology, etc., and (2) that such cases should serve as a paradigm for epistemological debate, then the likeliest upshot is a tendency to regard many properties besides that of colour as construable along the same lines. Thus, recalling Plato's metaphor of the expert butcher, 'if redness is dependent in this way on some type of human subjective response, it would not mark any joint that the world has independently of us; this is why it is less objective than properties (such as primary qualities or natural kinds perhaps) that do mark such independent joints in the structure of the world.'[17] That Wedgwood is here so studiously noncommittal – framing his argument in subjunctive-conditional terms and entering the qualifier 'perhaps' with regard to the existence of primary qualities and the objective (i.e., response-independent) status of natural kinds – is all the more striking given his express doubts that the RD approach can make sufficient room for our realist intuitions in moral, political, and other such areas of discourse. Indeed he goes so far as to equate it with Hamlet's passing cynical reflection that '[t]here is naught good or bad but thinking makes it so', in which case clearly the Euthyphronist is endorsing a strong version of projectivism (or anti-realism) as applied to moral statements, attitudes, and beliefs. On this view, 'if I think that racism is bad, then my thought cannot be detecting any fact of the matter that is constituted independently of my thought; on the contrary, my thought is part of what makes it the case that racism is bad in the first place.'[18]

Here as so often in RD debate the crucial claim is carried – and the issue most sharply posed – by that ambiguous term 'constitute', a term whose predominant sense as implied by some particular context of usage decides how the argument will work out in any given case. Thus on the one hand it pertains to objects or properties whose nature is *constitutive* of just what it is to be such an object or possess such a property, and on the other to attributes (such as, arguably, redness or moral worth) where the criteria for valid ascription are taken to involve the *constitutive* character of our own duly normalised responses, opinions, or judgements. For the realist with respect to some particular area of discourse it is essential to maintain a firm sense of this distinction and to specify precisely where it falls between properties like shape and qualities like colour, or the statements of physics and those of ethics, or again – from the standpoint of ethical realism – the intrinsic badness of wantonly inflicting pain and the non-intrinsic (response-dependent) character of jokes or situations that we may or may not find funny. As concerns mathematics the realist will take it that the argument for drawing such a line (i.e., between objective truth-values and provability according to our present-best knowledge) is just what sets her position decisively apart from that of intuitionists or anti-realists of a Dummettian persuasion.[19] It is the same basic issue that arises in the case of disputes, like that instanced above, between upholders of the view that 'best opinion' can sometimes be at odds with natural justice and advocates of a broadly constructivist approach that allows of no appeal beyond the deliverance of those (e.g., members of the US Supreme Court) who are authorised to pronounce the final verdict in such matters. That is to say, their authority is taken to trump any notion of right practice, due procedure, or the legitimate conduct of electoral affairs that the opponent might seek to bring forward as an argument against accepting their verdict as properly ('constitutionally') valid.

That this question has aroused such partisan zeal in the context of US jurisprudential debate is scarcely surprising given the power of the Supreme Court to strike down acts of state legislature and also the fact that so much turns on its construal of a document – the US Constitution – whose precepts are themselves notoriously subject to variant (often sharply opposed) interpretations.[20] However the chief point of relevance here is the issue as to whether, or on just what grounds, a verdict at this highest constitutional level might be challenged by appealing to principles of justice that are taken to transcend and hence to invalidate the deliverance of Supreme Court opinion. After all that same document (the US Constitution) was once held by 'best opinion' to contain nothing that conflicted with antebellum beliefs about the justification of slavery or the God-given right of some human beings (in virtue of their skin-colour or ethnic origin) to dispose of others as best suited their own economic convenience. Indeed there are still those in the Supreme Court, like Justice Scalia, who consider the practice of capital punishment to possess full constitutional warrant – and hence moral legitimacy – since it clearly didn't strike the original framers as in any way a cruel, barbarous, or inhumane practice. Quite how he thinks to square this position with their likewise evident failure to perceive anything morally offensive in the practice of slavery is not, to my knowledge, a point upon which Justice Scalia has chosen to elaborate.

Such instances provide a striking test-case for the strong-RD (or Euthyphronist) claim that best opinion among those most eminently qualified or authorised to judge is not so much *responsive to* as *constitutive of* what properly counts as electoral justice, humane treatment, equality before the law, and so forth. That is to say, the chief problem with any such approach is the fact that its normative standards derive from the presumed authority of those – whether the original framers or present-day Supreme Court judges – whose deliverance is taken to define 'best opinion' not only in a certain (perhaps morally delinquent) socio-juridical context but also as regards ultimate principles of justice and truth. After all, as Peter Railton pointedly remarks, '[w]hat matters is not who is making the judgement, but *of whom* the judgement is being made, which can be constant across differences in observers'.[21] And again: 'our vocabulary of intrinsic value is . . . primarily geared to the task of asking what to seek and what to avoid, depending upon whether it would be (in some sense) a positive or negative thing to lead a given life.'[22] Thus the moral issue with regard to slavery depends not at all on the question as to whether that practice may have struck Thomas Jefferson as perfectly consistent with the principles of social and political justice set out in the American Constitution. Nor does the moral issue with respect to capital punishment depend in any way on the opinion of Justice Scalia (along with the majority of his fellow Supreme Court judges) concerning its constitutional warrant or its falling outside the accepted definition of what counts as cruel and inhumane treatment. Rather those issues have to do with the intrinsic wrongness – as abolitionists in both cases would have it – of any practice that involves the deliberate infliction of pain or humiliating torment on creatures (whether human or non-human animal) capable of feeling such things.

Thus, in Railton's words, '[h]uman approbation of its torment would not in the least improve the experience of a dog being kicked or a horse being whipped.'[23] Still less would it constitute an ethical case for the practice of slavery or the judicially approved taking of a life by 'due process' of a law that claims constitutional warrant for the practice concerned. Such was George Eliot's strong moral-realist conviction when she wrote, in *Adam Bede*, of the 'hideous symbol of a deliberately inflicted sudden death'.[24] No doubt there are those, Justice Scaglia among them, who would maintain the moral rightness of capital punishment on straightforwardly retributivist grounds or according to the principle of 'justified' suffering for wrongs that are taken to merit nothing less than repayment in kind on behalf of a duly outraged community of citizens. However this fails to acknowledge both the sheer degree of psychological torment suffered by those under sentence of death and also the larger (community-wide) effects of a juridical provision that enshrines such a violent and humanly degrading practice in the name of legality, justice and fair desert. Railton makes this point most effectively when he comments that 'the domain of what is intrinsically good for humans is not rigidly fixed by actual human responses, but reflects instead potentially changing or evolving human responses.'[25] That is to say, if we have made any kind of moral progress then it can only have come about through our improved capacity (as compared with that of our forebears) to *recognise* cases of cruel and inhumane treatment, rather than projecting moral values in a way that would give them the ultimate power to determine whether capital punishment was justified or not according to 'best opinion' as currently delivered by the highest constitutional authority.

So there is clearly something wrong with any version of the Euthyphronist case that finds no room for standards of moral judgement beyond those that happen to enjoy such last-word adjudicative warrant.

Otherwise what ethical case could there be for rejecting the moral authority of law in a system of 'justice' – such as that which prevailed under the South African apartheid regime – grounded in legally enshrined doctrines of racial discrimination?[26] At this point, so it seems, we are confronted with a choice between projectivist accounts that can find no place for moral truths that transcend the deliverance of authorised best opinion and a realist account that makes due allowance for 'potentially evolving or changing human responses' but which treats those responses as subject to assessment in terms of their promoting or demoting the values of humane and civilised ethical conduct. Thus in the case of wanton cruelty toward human or other sentient creatures 'it is the intrinsically unliked character of the torment such conduct would cause its recipients – a torment which is unaffected by our attitude – that makes the behavior wrong.'[27] And in the case of capital punishment likewise it is the intrinsically cruel and degrading character of the practice, whatever the opinion of Supreme Court judges, which entitles the ethical realist to hold that its widespread revival in the US during the past few years should be viewed as an instance of regressive rather than 'evolving' moral responses.

Hence the chief objection to any RD account of moral values that would treat them as subject to specification in terms of normative response or of best opinion among those presumptively best qualified to judge. What this approach signally fails to acknowledge is the fact that *whole communities* along with their highest tribunals, such as the US Supreme Court, might conceivably be wrong in approving certain practices (like slavery or capital punishment) or in disapproving the kinds of progressive legal or socio-political reform that would declare those practices ethically repugnant. Thus the debate between realists and RD theorists with regard to epistemological matters is closely analogous to that between different schools of thought on the nature and scope of constitutional warrant or whether any claim put forward by the highest (constitutional) authority can nonetheless be subject to legitimate challenge on grounds of natural justice.[28] In each case it turns on the issue as to just how and where the line should be drawn between properties or values that exist quite apart from any standard of best opinion and qualities or values that inherently involve such a judgement-based normative account. As concerns arithmetical statements or hypotheses in the physical sciences it is crucially a question, so the realist will argue, of not yielding vital ground to the sceptic by blurring this distinction and conceiving truth as in any way dependent on the scope or limits of human epistemic grasp. In the ethico-political sphere it is a question of maintaining that certain morally salient features of certain real-world situations are such as must properly evoke disapproval despite their endorsement or ratification by the highest sources of constitutional warrant. Among these latter (she will most likely wish to claim) are the intrinsic wickedness of slavery and apartheid as erstwhile legally sanctioned practices or again – with recent US electoral events in mind – the flagrant injustice of disenfranchising large numbers of voters through an act of politically biased judicial intervention.

III

This is why, as I have suggested, the current debate about response-dependence raises issues that extend far beyond the Locke-derived *topos* of secondary qualities while very often treating it as a paradigm case – or a standard point of reference – in ways that tend to work against any realist construal of the area of discourse in question. That tendency is most apparent when theorists such as Wright are drawn, despite their express misgivings, toward meeting the sceptic more than half-way on ground that he (the sceptic) has mapped out and mined well in advance. Thus it is far from obvious that the instance of colour provides a useful analogy for thinking about other topic-areas – among them mathematics and morals – where it is usually brought in as a means of explaining how one can still cleave to certain realist intuitions regarding (say) the truths of elementary number-theory or the quasi-objective status of certain ethical values while making due allowance for the role of best judgement in cognising or eliciting such truths. For this approach always carries the inbuilt proviso – as with the case of colour – that in some ultimate sense they cannot be conceived as existing or possessing their distinctive character apart from the deliverance of duly normalised (or optimised) human response. In other words it must be taken to imply that just as the statements 'this is blue' or 'this is red' would undergo a change of truth-value in the event of some overnight drastic change in the workings of our visual-cognitive apparatus so likewise the statements 'this act is unjust' or 'that practice is cruel and inhumane' would acquire a different truth-value in the event that there occurred some sharp degradation in our powers of moral-evaluative judgement. However, so the moral realist will argue, this is where the analogy with colour-perception breaks down since it is the intrinsic character of such acts and practices that determines their rightness or wrongness and not the mere fact of our happening to approve or disapprove them Thus a dog's being beaten, or a slave's being whipped, or a death-row prisoner's being subject to physically and psychologically tormenting treatment are practices which call for moral condemnation whatever the opinion of those who would condone them or whatever the *de facto* authoritative status of those who would declare them right and just.

Hence, as I have said, the debate taken up by RD theorists from Plato's *Euthyphro* where it is a question whether moral attributes such as virtue or justice are infallibly 'tracked' by the gods' omniscient judgement or whether, on the contrary, the gods' judgement itself determines (i.e., constitutes) what shall count as virtuous or just conduct. 'Naturally', Wright concedes:

> it is open to each of the antagonists in this debate to acknowledge that pious acts extensionally coincide with those which, at least potentially, are loved by the gods. Socrates is contending that the piety of an action is, as it were, constituted independently of the gods' estimate of it, and Euthyphro is denying this, but each can agree that the two characteristics invariably accompany one another.[29]

However the ethical realist will very likely object that this whole way of setting up the issue is one that amounts to a no-lose wager for the advocate of a response-dependence approach. Thus it either comes out in support of the strong-RD position (since the gods' judgement is taken as constitutive of moral values, in which case pious acts *just are* those acts which the gods deem pious) or else reduces to a merely tautologous truth-of-definition (since the gods unfailingly track moral virtue and can therefore *ex hypothesi* never be wrong in according or withholding divine assent). Transpose this argument to the context of debates about slavery, apartheid, or the Supreme Court's role in deciding the outcome of the 2001 US election and it becomes clear how an RD approach excludes any alternative (realist) position that would count certain practices right or wrong quite apart from 'best opinion' as brought to bear by the highest constitutional authority. This is where the ethical issue most directly links up with the issue of correctness in regard to arithmetical rule-following or the question as to what kinds of property are such as to confer an objective truth-value on our various statements or judgements concerning them. For just as it is absurd to suppose that the truth of statements such as '68 + 57 = 125' or 'the molecular structure of water is H_20' could be somehow dependent on our own or anyone's best opinion so likewise it is absurd – or an instance of fargone ethical subjectivism – to suppose that the wrongness of these practices could derive merely from our *thinking* them wrong, or again, that any verdict to contrary effect delivered by the highest juridical authority could suffice to invalidate that judgement.

Nor is it surprising that response-dependence theory should tend to shift the emphasis in this direction and thereby expand the range of

RD-specifiable properties and predicates while shrinking the range of those that fall outside its own favoured terms of approach. After all, the agenda for this debate has been set very largely by Wittgenstein's reflections on the rule-following paradox and by Kripke's subsequent sharpening of that paradox to the point where it seems to allow for no 'solution' save the sceptical-communitarian appeal to shared practices or forms of life.[30] Thus, according to Kripke, there is no 'fact' about what a competent arithmetical reckoner means by the '+'-sign that would enable us to say that she was applying the right rule in declaring '68 + 57 = 125', or misapplying 'the same' rule if she came up with a different answer the next time around, or again, that another respondent simply hadn't grasped the operative rule if he produced an answer at variance with the standard solution. For they might always be working on some different (to us plain wrong or inappropriate) rule which they could instance as mandating a different procedure from one calculation to the next or which would make deviant reckoners correct by their own arithmetical lights. Wittgenstein purports to arrive at this conclusion on various grounds, among them the vicious regress involved in appealing to rules for the application of rules for the application of rules (etc.), and the fallacy of thinking that there must exist some deep further fact about the utterer's intentions – some 'private language' of arithmetical reasoning – that would somehow serve to fix or guarantee the correctness of any such procedure. Kripke's main contribution is to bring out the close connection between these lines of argument and also to insist that the rule-following paradox cannot be resolved – or its sting removed – except through a so-called 'sceptical solution' that halts the regress by appealing to communal warrant or the shared practice of doing things this way rather than that.

RD theorists (Wright among them) have mostly been unhappy with Kripke's 'solution' since it runs up against some strong countervailing intuitions with regard to the objectivity of truth – or at any rate its non-dependence on acculturated social practice – in areas of discourse such as mathematics, logic, and the other formal sciences.[31] Thus they have attempted, here as in the moral case, to articulate some workable middle-ground position that would conserve a good measure of objectivity while not placing truth altogether beyond the compass of best human judgement and hence (as the anti-realist would have it) inviting the sceptic's standard riposte. However that position proves difficult to hold and most often gives way to an RD-specified rehearsal of the various conditions under which best judgement or optimal response can safely be assumed to coincide with truth for all relevant (humanly knowable) purposes. And from here, as we have seen, it is no great distance to the Kripkensteinian idea that what *counts* as best judgement can only be a matter of the shared standards, criteria, or practices which constitute behaviour in accordance with this or that rule in this or that community of like-minded respondents. Nor is the picture much changed if one takes Wittgenstein's point that some such practices go so deep as to make it impossible to question their validity without falling into just the kind of nonsense that the sceptic talks when he affects to doubt the reality of an 'external world' or that the solipsist talks when he purports not to believe in the existence of 'other minds'. Such practices, in his well-known metaphor, are like the bed of a river which pursues its course unaffected by the various swirls and eddies that periodically disturb its surface.[32] But of course river-beds *do* change their course over a longer period of time, just as – if one takes Wittgenstein's analogy *au pied de la lêttre* – the standards of truth in arithmetical or logical reasoning could always conceivably be subject to change through some shift in the practice-relative criteria that govern their 'correct' application. And this would also apply to those deep-laid ethical precepts which the realist regards as intrinsic to any morality that merits the name (since they have to do with objective truths about the nature of human weal or woe) but which the Wittgensteinian must think of as potentially subject to change, even if through some likewise drastic shift in our acculturated norms and practices.

As I have said, the advocates of an RD approach typically take issue with Kripke's 'sceptical conclusion' – and also with other, less extreme versions of the practice-relativist argument – since it flies so sharply in face of our standing intuitions with respect to the status of arithmetical truths or the character of moral judgement. Yet their reasoning tends constantly in that direction to the extent that it takes the instance of secondary (perceiver-dependent) qualities as a benchmark case for assessing the criteria which apply to other areas of discourse. Moreover, the response-dispositional account is one that very easily falls prey to Kripke's sceptical objection, that is, his case that no such account can provide an adequate answer to those problems from Wittgenstein (the 'vicious regress' and 'no private language' arguments) which between them purportedly block the appeal to any notion of normalised or optimal response as a basis for imputing regularities in rule-following behaviour.[33] For of course it is precisely Kripke's point that this appeal must always run up against the sceptic's line of counter-attack, that is to say, his denial that there exists (or could ever be known to exist) any deep further fact about what people mean – what they have in mind – when claiming to perform some given operation in accordance with some given rule. Thus, for instance, in the case of someone whose reckonings had so far involved no product greater than 68 it might just be that they produced all the right results up to that point but then produced a deviant result for '68 + 57' since their rule for addition was 'correct answer "5" whenever the product exceeds 68'. No doubt we might say – in puzzlement or growing irritation – 'look, you managed to get all those right answers by applying the rule correctly and consistently until now so why can't you see that the correct result ("= 125") involves nothing more than a simple recursive procedure for carrying on in the same way?' However, according to Kripke, this response simply misses the sceptic's point since it assumes that the deviant reckoner *must* have been working on the standard rule for addition (and hence grasped its recursive applicability) when producing those correct solutions in the lower number-range; also that his rule *must* be such as to incorporate those same standards of 'correctness' and 'consistency' that define what standardly counts *for us* as an instance of valid reasoning. Yet this cannot be assumed without begging the sceptic's question since it might just be, for all that we can know, that even when the answers came out right within that restricted range they did so in accordance with the non-standard (but on its own terms perfectly consistent) rule: 'follow the procedure laid down in all those elementary maths textbooks until you reach product "68" and then give the correct answer "5" whenever the text-book solution looks like exceeding that upper limit.' At least there is no appeal to any 'fact' about the reckoner's past or present meanings, intentions, or mental states that could serve to convict him of sheer inconsistency or of failing to follow 'the same' rule from one application to the next.

So we must, Kripke thinks, be ultimately stuck for an answer should he respond: 'But don't you see, the correct rule in cases like this is . . . (etc., etc.).' For if we think to come back at him with the standard argument from consistency, recursivity, the rule that decrees against 'changing the rules' at some arbitrary cut-off point, or whatever, then we are holding him accountable to just those standards that happen to inform our own (but clearly not his) rule-following procedure. More than that: we have no way of knowing that he *has* 'changed the rules' since his 'deviant' answer (along with his 'correct' responses up to that point) may well be compliant with one and the same – to him non-arbitrary – rule. Thus Kripke asks us to consider the idea that the deviant reasoner is working with concepts (call then 'quus' and 'quaddition'') which sometimes produce results in accord with those we standardly get by applying our concepts 'plus' and 'addition', but which elsewhere lead him to come up with answers wildly at odds with our own basic standards of correct rule-following. Hence the Kripkensteinian challenge: to specify in a non-circular or non-question-begging way *just what it is* about those standards that gives us this presumptive warrant for declaring that other (to us) deviant practices should be put down to some error, inconsistency, or failure of logical grasp. In other words it is the same sort of challenge that has been posed by sceptics from Hume to Nelson Goodman with regard to the validity of inductive reasoning or of any such argument that presumes to extrapolate from observed regular conjunctions of event to 'laws of nature' (such as that of causality) and our power to comprehend or explain them in accordance with the principles of rational thought.[34] What Kripke does is extend this sceptical case, *via* Wittgenstein's reflections on 'private language' and 'following a rule', to the whole range of formal disciplines – among them logic and arithmetic – where it is likewise (he argues) impossible to know when reasoners might be applying some different kind of rule and producing results that are at odds with our own but are none the less consistent and rule-compliant for that.

Goodman famously makes this point by taking the case of factitious or gerrymandered predicates, such as 'grue' (when applied to emeralds) meaning 'green if observed before a certain date and blue if observed thereafter', or 'bleen' (when applied to sapphires) meaning 'blue if observed before that date and green if observed thereafter'.[35] On his account any degree of inductive warrant for claims to the effect 'all emeralds are green' or 'all sapphires are blue' is precisely on a par with our warrant for the claims that 'all emeralds are grue' or 'all sapphires are bleen'. That is to say, the latter are no less borne out by all observations to date and are equally subject to corroboration by the evidence of future sightings or to disconfirmation by a single counter-instance should one turn up. Thus they satisfy all the standard conditions for inductive warrant – as construed by the 'naive' inductivist – while bearing out Goodman's ultra-nominalist case, that is, that we can always devise any number of artificial predicates along these lines and thereby show how induction involves a selective projection of certain 'properties' which just happen to fit with our favoured descriptions, explanatory frameworks, conceptual schemes, or whatever. It is a similar lesson that Kripke draws from the rule-following considerations, namely that any instance of 'correct' or 'deviant' reasoning in mathematics, logic, or the formal sciences will always be compatible with *some* rule or other, and that rule in turn specifiable in just such a way as to allow for its valid application according to its own standards of logic, consistency and truth.

At this stage the not-so-naive inductivist will typically retort that the Goodman-style argument can go through only if we accept the legitimacy of constructing such artificial predicates as 'grue' or 'bleen', predicates which have no place in the range of natural-kind properties or attributes, and are therefore strictly beside the point for philosophical as well as scientific purposes. Likewise, the mathematical realist will object that Kripkensteinian scepticism with regard to standards of correctness in rule-following can take hold only if one accepts the terms of Kripke's false dilemma. That is to say, his whole line of argument rests on the idea that such standards must be thought of as deriving *either* from thoughts, meanings or intentions in the mind of some individual reasoner, *or* – Kripke's preferred 'sceptical solution' – the communitarian appeal to shared practices of reasoning. However this will most likely strike the realist as a just another case of presumptive *tertium non datur* wielded as a stick to beat off alternative, better proposals. What simply drops out on this Kripkean view is the realist claim that truth-values in mathematics and certain other areas of discourse (including, arguably, that of morals) are wholly independent of whatever construal may happen to be placed upon them by individual subjects or even, at the limit, entire like-minded communities with sanction from the highest recognised authorities.

Thus it might just happen, as Hilary Putnam conjectures, that one dreamed a situation where all the most expert logicians and mathematicians (Kripke among them) had hit upon some flaw in the axioms of basic Peano arithmetic and hence concluded that the entirety of our hitherto accepted mathematical knowledge was now open to doubt.[36] But where Putnam takes this thought-experiment to show that it would then be rational for the dreamer to conclude 'yes, amazingly, we have all been wrong so far about the "truths" of elementary arithmetic' the realist will derive just the opposite conclusion, that is, that truth cannot be merely a matter of goings-on in the mind of some solitary thinker or even of accredited 'best opinion' among those judgement standardly counts as the benchmark for rational acceptability. No doubt the dreamer would 'rationally' suppose that he had much better follow the experts and not trust to his own more fallible beliefs or intuitions. Yet he would still be wrong – systematically deluded – since the dream scenario of Putnam's devising is such as to suspend all questions of objective arithmetical truth and to treat them as dependent on whatever strikes the dreamer as a 'rational' decision-procedure under these purely imaginary (unreal) circumstances. So the thought-experiment lends no support to Putnam's strong revisionist claim, that is, his idea that even the most basic axioms of elementary arithmetic or logic might just conceivably throw up some anomalous result that forced us (in deference to expert opinion) to pass every last item of our knowledge in sceptical review. What it brings out, rather, is the fallacy of thinking that truth in such matters is in any way dependent on thoughts in the mind of this or that reasoner (whether waking or dreaming) or indeed on the authoritative say-so of those who are taken to have the last word. Of course it may be said that nothing follows from this as concerns the rule-following issue since Putnam's is merely an extravagant conjecture – a latterday version of Cartesian hyperbolic doubt – which has no genuine bearing on questions in philosophy of language, logic, and mathematics. Such an argument is valid from the realist standpoint for reasons that I have offered (albeit somewhat sketchily) above. However it is not one that the Kripkean is entitled to wield with equal confidence since his own kinds of far gone sceptical conjecture (such as that we might have meant *quus* instead of *plus* in all our previous arithmetical reckonings, or have been working on the rule of *quaddition* rather than *addition*) are hardly less extravagant or downright bizarre than Putnam's dream-scenario.

My point is that the RD theorists have inherited a philosophic agenda which inclines very strongly in an anti-realist direction and which tends to endorse a Kripkensteinian 'sceptical solution' whatever the doubts on that score expressed by a thinker such as Wright. After all, Kripke spends a good deal of time arguing that no dispositionalist account of what we mean by, for example, 'addition' can possibly meet the sceptical challenge, that is, the challenge to identify some *fact* about our own previous rule-following practices that would somehow guarantee that we are now applying 'the same rule' and producing answers in accordance with it. Kripke has three main arguments here: (1) that no finite range of previous calculations could allow for the potentially infinite range of future arithmetical tasks, (2) that the dispositionalist approach fails to make due allowance for the standing possibility of error, and (3) – closely related to this – that the account is descriptive rather than normative, that is to say, confined merely to describing how we *are* in fact disposed to produce certain answers to certain arithmetical problems, rather than how we *should* respond if we are going to produce the right answer. Defenders of the dispositionalist approach have since come up with various attempts to strengthen their position against this Kripkean line of attack, as for instance by building in conditions of optimal or idealised epistemic warrant, such that the reasoner could not conceivably produce an aberrant response given her presumptively infallible grasp of the rule in question along with its full range of past, present, and future correct applications. However this strategy is open to the charge that it either reduces to an empty tautology (by invoking some kind of 'whatever-it-takes' clause) or else merely begs the sceptic's question by presupposing that we know what is meant by the idea of following 'the same' rule from one application to the next.

IV

In the face of these criticisms perhaps the best line for an RD theorist to take is that there *just are* certain dispositional responses – such as our disposition to reply '125' in answer to the query: 'What is the sum of 68 and 57?' – which possess their own kind of apodictic self-evidence and are hence in no need of further justification. However this will hardly satisfy the Kripkean sceptic who can then repeat all his well-rehearsed Wittgensteinian arguments against the idea of any such appeal to 'private' criteria of meaning and truth. For of course it is just the point of these rule-following considerations that the notion of checking our performance against some 'internal' (dispositional) standard of correctness is one that falls prey to a vicious regress, like buying a second copy of the daily newspaper so as to check the accuracy of everything reported in the first copy.[37] So there is reason to think – on the evidence of these debates so far – that a response-dependent or dispositionalist account of any given area of discourse will always give a hold for Kripkean scepticism. And this despite its attempts to avoid that undesired outcome by entering various additional clauses such as those involving 'best opinion', 'expert judgement', or – at the limit – 'optimal response under ideal epistemic conditions'. Thus the only way forward, as Kripke would have it, is one that embraces the 'sceptical solution' to Wittgenstein's rule-following paradox and which declares in favour of communal warrant – or the appeal to shared practices and forms of life – as our last, best hope in matters of epistemic warrant.

It is the same kind of argument that is standardly adduced by philosophers of the social sciences, such as Peter Winch, who have likewise claimed Wittgensteinian support for the idea that it simply *cannot make sense* to criticise such practices or life-forms from a standpoint 'external' to the values and beliefs (i.e., the judgement-constitutive criteria) that prevail among members of some given community.[38] In which case, again, there could be no legitimate moral appeal beyond or above the juridical warrant of an authorised body like the US Supreme Court, any more than one could ever be justified in declaring that certain (to us) abhorrent practices engaged in by other communities or at other times – such as slavery, apartheid, clitoridectomy, 'ethnic cleansing', or widow-burning – were objectively wrong despite enjoying widespread assent within the culture or belief-system concerned. What these examples bring home with particular force is the importance of adopting an ethical-realist approach which chiefly stresses the consequences for better or worse experienced by those on the receiving end, so to speak, or those who stand to benefit or suffer from the kinds of practice under review. To this extent it comes out sharply at odds with any approach – whether Wittgensteinian or response-dependent – that would make the 'properties' of goodness or badness contingent on whatever is taken to constitute 'best opinion' amongst arbiters of moral worth, whether denizens of a given communal life-form or Supreme Court judges with the utmost authority of constitutional warrant.

So Kripke's 'sceptical solution' to Wittgenstein's sceptical paradox is one that has a resonance beyond its application to issues in philosophy of mathematics, logic, and other formal branches of enquiry. While the ethical realist will be apt to regard it – justifiably – as a straightforward *reductio* of the sceptic's case it has more often figured in RD debate as a powerful challenge that calls for some degree of accommodating treatment, even though this concession will surely give a hold for the Kripkean to press right through and reject any kind of compromise settlement. No doubt the majority of RD theorists, Wright among them, consider their approach fully capable of saving our realist intuitions with respect to the appropriate areas of discourse and also of establishing a clear demarcation with respect to those other areas where optimised response or best opinion must be taken to play a constitutive role. Thus for instance, as Wright readily concedes, 'no Euthyphronic concept comfortably fits the paradigm of a natural kind concept, since *a priority* for a suitably provisoed biconditional is inconsistent with the hostage to reference-failure which any prototypical natural kind concept must hold out.'[39] For the well-attested fact that even 'best opinion' among experts in various scientific fields has often been wrong about certain objects and their properties is enough to show that such objects and properties cannot plausibly be treated as response-dependent but are what they are independently of our own or of anyone else's judgement. In such cases it is the physically constituent (e.g. subatomic, molecular, or chromosomal) *structure* of the various entities concerned that decides the truth-value of our statements concerning them rather than any constitutive role of best opinion or optimal response.[40] Yet as the Lockean precedent might lead us to expect, this thesis comes under strain whenever there is possible room for doubt concerning the ontological distinction between primary and secondary qualities or the grounds for maintaining such a principled separation of objective truth-values from epistemic criteria of warranted assertibility. And the doubt crops up with particular force if one begins, as the RD theorists do, from the default position 'that, for the discourse in question, optimally conceived judgement – best opinion – is the conceptual ground of truth'.[41]

Thus despite the in-principle acceptance of objective truth-values as applied (say) to natural-kind properties there is still a strong tendency to treat them as subject to revision with changes or advances in our temporally indexed state of scientific knowledge. Besides, so it is often implied, there is no good case for extending such values to other areas of discourse (such as mathematics or ethics) where the realist would consider them perfectly in order. Here again it is the Kripkensteinian paradox about rule-following that leads Wright to embrace this sceptical conclusion, or to think it an ultimate mystery how 'a sentence can be undetectably true' in the sense of 'extending, so to speak, of itself into areas where we cannot follow it and hence determining, without any contribution from ourselves or our reactive natures, that a certain state of affairs complies with it'.[42] There is no plainer statement in the RD literature of the governing premise from which these theorists start out and which constrains their approach within the terms laid down by a sceptical or anti-realist agenda. Thus Wright's various alternative proposals – such as 'superassertibility' or 'cognitive command' – are likewise specified so as to exclude any notion of truth as surpassing or transcending the scope of optimised epistemic warrant. In the first case, as he describes it, a statement is superassertible 'if and only if it is, or can be, warranted and some warrant for it would survive arbitrarily close scrutiny of its pedigree and arbitrarily extensive increments to or other forms of improvement of our information'.[43] But of course this is still to make truth dependent on *our* (no matter how optimised or counterfactually extended) means of epistemic access. In other words it is just another version of the standard RD case tuned up to the maximum possible compliance with certain stubbornly persistent and hence unignorable realist intuitions. In the latter case, 'when a discourse exhibits Cognitive Command, any difference of opinion will be such that there are considerations quite independent of the conflict which, if known about, would mandate withdrawal of one (or both) of the contending views.'[44] Comedy is Wright's highly plausible prime candidate for a 'discourse' that fails to exhibit cognitive command since any differences of opinion in what people do or don't find amusing can scarcely be thought of as subject to adjudication from some higher (objective) standpoint that would settle the issue once and for all. Yet he classifies the discourse of morals – together with that of comedy – as one for which, 'on a wide class of construals . . . evidence transcendence is simply not in view'.[45] Moreover it is clear from what Wright has to say on the rule-following considerations as applied to mathematics, logic and the formal sciences that he is still much impressed by the Dummettian anti-realist case for restricting truth-values to the compass of optimised epistemic warrant as given by our best achievable methods of proof or verification. In which case the realist can only be mistaken – in the grip of a transcendental illusion – if she ventures the (strictly) unverifiable hypothesis that there exists a vast range of mathematical truths for which we possess no adequate means of ascertainment.

V

My concern up to now has been not so much to make out a positive case for realism in moral philosophy and philosophy of mathematics but rather to show that response-dependence theory cannot, as is often claimed, deliver an account that would acknowledge the force of Dummettian anti-realism while conserving those basic realist intuitions that still carry weight with sceptically inclined philosophers like Wright. All the same this would have been a fairly pointless exercise were I not convinced that such a positive case can be, and indeed has been, made by advocates of realism in both areas of discourse.[46] That is to say, any adequate approach must allow (1) that truth is epistemically unconstrained, that is, not a matter of best opinion among those deemed fittest to judge, (2) that truth-values are in this sense objective or verification-transcendent, and (3) that any qualified RD proposal which goes some way toward acknowledging the force of arguments (1) and (2) will thereby equate best opinion with truth *sans phrase* and hence reduce to manifest circularity. In other words those RD theorists who incline toward the third option are effectively abandoning their own major thesis and embracing the realist alternative.

Wright pretty much concedes this point when he remarks – *à propos* the Euthyphronist debate – that 'it is open to each of the antagonists . . . to acknowledge that pious acts extensionally coincide with those which, at least potentially, are loved by the gods.'[47] No doubt they seem to take different views of the matter since 'Socrates is contending that the piety of an action is, as it were, constituted independently of the gods' estimate of it, and Euthyphro is denying this, but each can agree that the two characteristics invariably accompany one another.'[48] Thus, in RD terms, the choice falls out between *either* incorporating limit-point criteria of idealised epistemic warrant (such as Wright's 'superassertibility' or 'cognitive command') in order to meet the realist's objection that even 'best opinion' may sometimes get it wrong, *or* adopting the Euthyphronist stance that best opinion simply *cannot* be wrong about values like truth, virtue and justice since by very definition its verdicts must be deemed infallible. However the first line of argument will cut no ice with the realist since it still conceives truth as epistemically constrained, that is to say, as dependent – at the epistemic limit – on some duly accredited ultimate tribunal of human knowledge and judgement. Meanwhile the second option is likely to strike her as just a form of realism that dare not speak its name, or a back-door admission that the realist is right and that 'best opinion' is merely a stand-in – a face-saving RD substitute formula –

for truth conceived in objective or verification-transcendent terms. Either way, so the realist argument goes, response-dependence theory cannot do justice to our standing intuitions with regard to the truth-value of statements in areas of discourse (like mathematics and morals) where something crucial drops out if they are treated by analogy – no matter how carefully provisoed – with Lockean secondary qualities like colour and taste.

What typically results in the case of mathematics is an approach that begins with the attempt to find some workable *via media* between objectivism and Dummett-type anti-realism, but which ends up by tacitly endorsing the latter doctrine in a form (such as Alex Miller's 'Humanised Platonism') whereby truth-values must still be thought of as in some sense epistemically constrained. Thus, according to Miller:

> on the Humanised Platonist conception of tracking, we deliberately separate the idea that best opinions play an extension-determining role from the idea that they constrain rather than track the facts about the extension of the relevant predicate: in Humanised Platonism we view best beliefs as playing a constraining role with respect to the applicability of a predicate *only in virtue of the fact that they infalliblly track its extension.*[49]

So we can take the anti-realist's standard point – that 'objective' truths in mathematics or any other area of discourse must somehow (impossibly) be known to transcend our utmost powers of ascertainment – while rejecting his standard conclusion from this, i.e., that such truths can only be conceived as subject to the scope and limits of our best-available proof procedures. Instead we should see that this false dilemma comes about through a 'sublimated' conception of truth according to which any statement that is a candidate for objective mathematical truth or falsehood must have to do with 'conceptually unstructured' properties, that is to say, properties of numbers, functions, sets, logical entailment-relations, and so forth, which *in no way* partake of our conceptual activity or are *in no sense* dependent on the deliverance of best human judgement. If we can just let go of that deluded idea then the way is open to a better alternative, namely a 'Humanised Platonist' conception which 'allows us to think of ourselves as tracking or cognitively accessing the facts about the instantiation of *conceptually structured* properties'.[50] In which case, Miller argues – together with others like John McDowell and Robert Brandom – the dilemma simply falls away since there is no longer that unbridgeable gulf between objective truths and our knowledge of them.[51] Such knowledge *cannot but* conform to the way things stand with respect to (conceptually structured) mathematical truth while such truth *cannot but* fall within the compass of our best conceptual grasp.

However this solution is again one that can scarcely satisfy the realist, involving as it does the Kantian idea – most explicit in McDowell – that since objective reality (on the 'sublimated' view) is by very definition beyond our utmost powers of cognitive or epistemic grasp, therefore our knowledge can only have to do with the forms, structures, and modalities of human understanding. So if the truths of mathematics are 'conceptually structured' – like (presumably) the truths of the physical sciences and every other branch of enquiry – then we are back with the same vexing dilemma from which Miller's argument is supposed to deliver us. More precisely, his argument *appears* to dissolve it by simply denying or, one is tempted to say, sublimating the distinction between objective truth-values and those 'same' truth-values when construed as conceptually structured in accordance with (what else?) the conceptual structures of mathematically informed best judgement. But this is more like grasping one horn of the dilemma, the response-dependence horn, and then wishing the other away by extending the notion of conceptually structured properties all the way out into those various truth-domains, areas of discourse, or regions of 'reality' that happen to fall within our epistemic ken. I have written above and elsewhere about the problems that arise with McDowell's version of this Kantian argument and his curious proneness to repeat the drastically oscillating pattern of thought that marked the history of subjective and objective idealist philosophies after Kant.[52] It is the same pattern that emerges in Miller's above-quoted claim that a humanised Platonist approach to mathematics is one which 'allows us to think of ourselves as tracking or cognitively accessing the facts about the instantiation of *conceptually structured* properties'. To be sure, this allows us to 'think of ourselves' in those terms, or to think in such a way that there would seem no problem about the notion of our 'tracking' mathematical properties which are nonetheless always already 'conceptually structured' and hence – the implication can hardly be ignored – restricted to the scope and limits of humanly achievable knowledge. However the fact that we can or might be brought to accept this persuasive solution is not at all the same thing as its actually managing to resolve the standard dilemma.

Indeed Miller himself implicitly concedes as much when he writes elsewhere in his essay that '[c]onceptually structured properties thus require an epistemology couched fundamentally in terms other than those of tracking and cognitive access.'[53] For it is, he argues, just this difference of epistemological views that recommends a humanised Platonist approach as opposed to a 'sublimated' realist conception according to which 'where the property P is conceptually structured we cannot think of our judgement that a is P as tracking or accessing a fact which confers truth upon it'.[54] So there seems little prospect that the realist (or the non-'humanised' Platonist) will be won over to Miller's way of thinking, or that any limited concession to the realist along Miller's suggested lines can avoid confronting the self-same dilemma that it is meant to overcome. That is to say, what results is the usual Euthyphronist choice between building in ever more elaborate clauses that admit the limit-case argument for realism just so long as it is epistemically constrained and the alternative (tautological) RD thesis that equates truth with best judgement on purely *a priori* or definitional grounds. The first line of argument will of course strike the realist as failing utterly to meet her objection while the second will strike her as meeting it only by giving up any claim for response-dependence as other than a pointlessly roundabout endorsement of the realist case.

There is a similar problem with the RD approach to issues in moral philosophy. Here, likewise, the quest is for a middle-ground position, one that would split the difference between a realist conception of moral properties which takes them to exert an objective claim on our ethical, social, or political conscience quite apart from best opinion in the matter and a projectivist account that takes best opinion as playing an ultimate adjudicative role. Hence the idea that those properties can most aptly be thought of as analogous to Lockean 'secondary qualities' like colour, that is to say, as response-dependent in some crucial (indeed constitutive) way but only under specified normative conditions of human perceptual and epistemic grasp. However, this analogy breaks down on the fact that any such rigidified account of human moral responses is one that fails to acknowledge *either* the objective (intrinsically good or bad) character of certain acts or situations *or* the capacity of moral judgement to change and evolve – for better or worse – when confronted with the evidence in any given case. This is why, as Railton says, 'in thinking about value, it is altogether too easy to project, conflating the familiar and conventional with the natural and inevitable.'[55] And again, more pointedly in the context of RD debate:

> [o]ne could write a pocket history of progress in moral sensibility in terms of the successive unmasking of such conflations – with respect to slavery, inherited rule, the status of women, and the borders of tribe, "people", or nation. Objectivity about intrinsic and moral good alike calls for us to gain critical perspective on our own actual responses, not to project their objects rigidly.[56]

Of course it is by no means guaranteed that any critical perspective thus gained will show clear evidence of moral advancement or afford us the comforting reflection that, on balance at least, humankind is progressing toward better, more just or morally acceptable practices. Indeed one could take each of Railton's claims in the above-cited passage and point to particular well-documented cases that would constitute evidence of moral regression with respect to the basic principles involved. Thus slavery (including child slavery) is still practised in all but name throughout various parts of the 'developed' and 'underdeveloped' world, while inherited rule is still very much with us – albeit (*vide* the present-day US situation) in the form of dynastic privilege granted by inherited wealth in conjunction with the mechanisms of state and corporate power. As concerns the 'status of women' few would claim that the signs of widespread moral progress are unambiguously there to be read, while with respect to the idea that recent history witnesses a steady pushing back of the boundaries of 'tribe, "people", or nation' there is evidence from all too many quarters – the Middle East, sub-Saharan Africa, the Indian sub-continent, South-East Asia, ex-Yugoslavia, and Northern Ireland among them – that nationalist and indeed tribal animosities have lately re-emerged on a large and exceptionally violent scale. Then again, there is the case of recent US electoral politics and the way that President George W. Bush came to power through an act which disenfranchised large numbers of (mainly black) voters by the arbitrary decision – taken by his brother, the Governor of Florida – to stop counting votes at a crucial juncture in a key marginal state, a decision subsequently ratified by the Republican-dominated Supreme Court.

VI

This particular case is one that I think has a special salience in the context of RD debate. That is, it throws into sharp relief the conflict between a realist philosophy of moral values and political justice based on substantive principles above and beyond the deliverance of constitutionally warranted best opinion and a theory that takes best opinion – as represented (say) by the US Supreme Court – as rightfully (or inevitably) having the last word in such matters.[57] Thus the issue with regard to response-dependence – whether best opinion 'tracks' or 'determines' what should properly count as good or just – is one that has some large (indeed decisive) implications for our thinking about wider socio-political, juridical, and constitutional issues. For it is well within reach of the question whether George W. Bush can lay claim to a legitimate mandate for pushing through with his announced policies on 'welfare reform', healthcare cutbacks, trade deregulation, the corporate freedom to exploit natural resources without state 'interference', the redistribution of wealth through tax-breaks for the richest, the abandonment of existing arms-control treaties, the refusal to ratify international accords on environmental protection, and the adoption of a strongly isolationist policy in all matters where national self-interest might conflict with the interests of global human well-being.[58] It is also an issue that arises crucially for anyone – US citizen or not – who considers capital punishment a cruel, barbarous, and morally regressive practice whatever President Bush's well-known enthusiasm for it and whatever the juridical sanction claimed by appealing to 'best opinion' or its constitutional warrant as delivered by Supreme Court judges. Thus the moral case for abolition of capital punishment – like the moral case for abolition of slavery at an earlier period – is one that can be made to adequate effect only by appealing to principles of justice that are grounded in the facts of human suffering, victimage, and the brutalisation of moral responses in any society that condones such a practice in the name of all (presumptively assenting) citizens. That is to say, it has to find room for an ethical appeal beyond any merely *de facto* state of consensus belief amongst those citizens and even beyond the considered judgement of the highest constitutional authorities where that judgement is arguably open to challenge on humanitarian grounds.

This is where the RD-Euthyphronist case – that moral properties are 'determined', not 'tracked' by best opinion – comes up against the most powerful objection from an ethical-realist standpoint. That similar issues can be seen to arise with respect to the scope and limits of an RD approach in philosophy of mathematics is scarcely surprising given the extent to which anti-realism has dictated the agenda in these and other areas of recent philosophic debate. So there is more than a loose analogy between the claims (1) that the dispute between realists and anti-realists with regard to the truth-value of mathematical statements might be resolved by an appeal to the epistemic standard of best human judgement, and (2) that the dispute between moral realists and projectivists concerning the existence or non-existence of objective moral facts might be resolved by an appeal to best opinion among those deemed fittest to opine. What I have sought to show here is that neither claim comes close to meeting the realist's objection and that both end up – despite their professed intent – by endorsing an approach that leans strongly toward the anti-realist or projectivist position. If there is a 'third way' open to the RD theorist then it is not one that strengthens the case for epistemic warrant under optimal conditions as our best source of guidance in such matters. Rather, as I have argued, it is one that equates best judgement with truth as a matter of purely *a priori*, definitional, or stipulative warrant and which thereby reduces the RD thesis to a trivial tautology devoid of substantive philosophic content. All of which suggests that the most useful outcome of these recent debates on the topic of response-dependence may be to focus the issues more sharply and to demonstrate that no such middle-ground approach can avoid the kinds of problem that typically arise with other, more overt or doctrinaire forms of anti-realist thinking.

References

1. See for instance Bob Hale, 'Realism and its Oppositions', in Hale and Crispin Wright (eds), *A Companion to the Philosophy of Language* (Oxford: Blackwell, 1997), pp. 271–308; Philip Pettit, *The Common Mind: an essay on psychology, society, and politics* (Oxford: Oxford University Press, 1992); and Crispin Wright, *Truth and Objectivity* (Cambridge, MA: Harvard University Press, 1992).
2. See especially Crispin Wright, *Truth and Objectivity* (Note 1, above); also *Realism, Meaning and Truth*, 2nd edn (Oxford: Blackwell, 1993).
3. John Locke, *An Essay Concerning Human Understanding*, ed. A. S. Pringle-Pattison (Oxford: Oxford University Press, 1969), Book II, Chap. 8, Sect. 15, p. 69; also Mark Johnston, 'How to Speak of the Colours', *Philosophical Studies*, Vol. 68 (1992), pp. 221–63.
4. Wright, *Truth and Objectivity*, pp. 82 and 106 (Note 1, above).
5. Peter Railton, 'Red, Bittter, Good', *European Review of Philosophy*, Vol. 3 (1998), pp. 67–84; p. 84.
6. Ibid., p. 84.
7. *Plato's Euthyphro, Apology of Socrates, and Crito*, ed. John Burnet (Oxford: Clarendon Press, 1977). For further discussion of the relevant passages, see Reginald E. Allen, *Plato's Euthyphro and the Earlier Theory of Forms* (London: Routledge & Kegan Paul, 1970); also Wright, 'Moral Values, Projection, and Secondary Qualities', *Proceedings of the Aristotelian Society*, Supplementary Vol. 62 (1988), pp. 1–26; 'Realism, Antirealism, Irrealism, Quasi-Realism', *Midwest Studies in Philosophy*, Vol. 12 (1988), pp. 25–49; and 'Euthyphronism and the Physicality of Colour', *European Review of Philosophy*, Vol. 3 (1998), pp. 15–30.
8. See especially Michael Dummett, *Truth and Other Enigmas* (London: Duckworth, 1978) and *The Logical Basis of Metaphysics* (Duckworth, 1991); also Paul Benacerraf, 'What Numbers Could Not Be', in Paul Benacerraf and Hilary Putnam (eds), *The Philosophy of Mathematics: selected essays*, 2nd edn (Cambridge: Cambridge University Press, 1983), pp. 272–94; John Divers and Alexander Miller, 'Arithmetical Platonism: reliability and judgement dependence', *Philosophical Studies*, Vol. 95 (1999), pp. 277–310; Hartry Field, *Realism, Mathematics and Modality* (Oxford: Blackwell, 1989); Bob Hale, *Abstract Objects* (Blackwell, 1987) and 'Is Platonism Epistemologically Bankrupt?', *Philosophical Review*, Vol. 103 (1994), pp. 299–325; Alexander Miller, 'Rule-Following, Response-Dependence, and McDowell's Debate with Anti-Realism', *European Review of Philosophy*, Vol. 3 (1998), pp. 175–97;

and Crispin Wright, *Frege's Conception of Numbers as Objects* (Aberdeen: Aberdeen University Press, 1983).

9. See Railton, 'Red, Bitter, Good' (Note 5, above); also – for a range of views on this issue – Robert L. Arrington (ed.), *Rationalism, Realism and Relativism: perspectives in contemporary moral epistemology* (Ithaca, NY: Cornell University Press, 1989); David O. Brink, *Moral Realism and the Foundations of Ethics* (Cambridge: Cambridge University Press, 1989); Alan H. Goldman, *Moral Knowledge* (London: Routledge, 1988); Brad Hooker (ed.), *Truth in Ethics* (Oxford: Blackwell, 1996); Geoffrey Sayre-McCord (ed.), *Essays on Moral Realism* (Cornell University Press, 1988); Michael Smith, *The Moral Problem* (Oxford: Blackwell, 1994); and Wright, 'Morals, Values, Projection, and Secondary Qualities'.
10. Mark Johnston, 'Objectivity Refigured', in J. Haldane and C. Wright (eds), *Realism, Representation and Projection* (Oxford: Oxford University Press, 1993), pp. 85–130.
11. For some cogent arguments to this effect, see Ralph Wedgwood, 'The Essence of Response-Dependence', *European Review of Philosophy*, Vol. 3 (1998), pp. 31–54.
12. Ibid., pp. 34–5.
13. See for instance Judith Butler, *Bodies that Matter: on the discursive limits of 'sex'* (London: Routledge, 1993) and Linda Kauffman (ed.), *Gender and Theory: dialogues on feminist criticism* (Oxford: Blackwell, 1989).
14. Wedgwood, 'The Essence of Response-Dependence', pp. 34–5 (Note 11, above).
15. See Michel Foucault, *The Use of Pleasure*, trans. Robert Hurley (New York: Pantheon, 1985) and *The Care of the Self*, trans. Hurley (Pantheon, 1986); also *The Order of Things: an archaeology of the human sciences*, trans. Alan Sheridan-Smith (London: Tavistock, 1973).
16. See Note 13, above; also Henry Abelove, Michèle A. Barale and David M. Halperin (eds), *The Lesbian and Gay Studies Reader* (London: Routledge, 1993) and Andy Medhurst and Sally R. Munt (eds), *Lesbian and Gay Studies: a critical introduction* (London: Cassell, 1997).
17. Wedgwood, 'The Essence of Response-Dependence', p. 35 (Note 11, above).
18. Ibid., p. 34.
19. See for instance Jerrold J. Katz, *Realistic Rationalism* (Cambridge, MA: MIT Press, 1998); also Note 8, above.
20. See Charles A. Beard, *The Supreme Court and the Constitution* (Englewood Cliffs, NJ: Prentice-Hall, 1962); Philip B. Kurland (ed.), *The Supreme Court and the Constitution: essays in constitutional law from the Supreme Court Review* (Chicago: Phoenix Books, 1965); and Richard Pacelle, *The Supreme Court in American Politics* (Boulder, CO: Westview Press, 2001).
21. Railton, 'Red, Bitter, Good', p. 77 (Note 5, above).
22. Ibid., p. 77.
23. Ibid., p. 82.
24. George Eliot, *Adam Bede* (London: William Blackwood, 1875), p. 403.
25. Railton, 'Red, Bitter, Good', p. 77 (Note 5, above).
26. See especially David Dyzenhaus, *Hard Cases in Wicked Legal Systems: South African law in the perspective of legal philosophy* (Oxford: Clarendon Press, 1991) and *Judging the Judges, Judging Ourselves: truth, reconciliation and the apartheid legal order* (Oxford: Hart Publishing, 1998).

27. Railton, 'Red, Bitter, Good', p. 82 (Note 5, above).
28. See Notes 20 and 26, above.
29. Wright, *Truth and Objectivity*, p. 80 (Note 1, above).
30. See Ludwig Wittgenstein, *Philosophical Investigations*, trans. G. E. M. Anscombe (Oxford: Blackwell, 1953), Sects 201–92 *passim*; also Saul Kripke, *Wittgenstein on Rules and Private Language* (Oxford: Blackwell, 1982) and Paul Boghossian, 'The Rule-Following Considerations', *Mind*, Vol. 98 (1989), pp. 507–49.
31. See for instance Wright, *Truth and Objectivity* (Note 1, above); also Divers and Miller, 'Arithmetical Platonism' (Note 8, above); Bob Hale, 'Rule-Following, Objectivity, and Meaning', in Hale and Crispin Wright (eds), *A Companion to the Philosophy of Language* (Oxford: Blackwell, 1997), pp. 369–96.
32. Ludwig Wittgenstein, *On Certainty*, trans. G. E. M. Anscombe and G. H. von Wright (Oxford: Blackwell, 1969), Sects 95–9; also 319–21.
33. Kripke, *Wittgenstein on Rules and Private Language* (Note 30, above).
34. David Hume, *A Treatise of Human Nature* (Oxford: Clarendon Press, 1978); Nelson Goodman, *Fact, Fiction, and Forecast* (Cambridge, MA: Harvard University Press, 1955).
35. Goodman, *Fact, Fiction, and Forecast* (Note 34, above).
36. See especially Hilary Putnam, *Realism and Reason* (Cambridge: Cambridge University Press, 1983), pp. 125–6.
37. Wittgenstein, *Philosophical Investigations*, Sect. 265 (Note 30, above).
38. Peter Winch, *The Idea of a Social Science and its Relation to Philosophy* (London: Routledge & Kegan Paul, 1958).
39. Wright, 'Euthyphronism and the Physicality of Colour', p. 17 (Note 7, above).
40. See especially Hilary Putnam, *Mind, Language and Reality* (Cambridge: Cambridge University Press, 1975); also J. Aronson, R. Harré and E. Way, *Realism Rescued: how scientific progress is possible* (London: Duckworth, 1994); Michael Devitt, *Realism and Truth*, 2nd edn (Princeton, NJ: Princeton University Press, 1991); Jarrett Leplin (ed.), *Scientific Realism* (Berkeley & Los Angeles: University of California Press, 1984); Gregory McCulloch, *The Mind and Its World* (London: Routledge, 1995); Ilkka Niiniluoto, *Critical Scientific Realism* (Oxford: Oxford University Press, 1999); and Stathis Psillos, *Scientific Realism: how science tracks truth* (London: Routledge, 1999).
41. Wright, *Truth and Objectivity*, p. 111 (Note 1, above).
42. Ibid., p. 228.
43. Ibid., p. 48.
44. Ibid., p. 103.
45. Ibid., p. 82.
46. See entries under Notes 9 and 40, above, also – from a range of relevant perspectives – Katz, *Realistic Rationalism* (Note 19, above); Christopher Norris, *Resources of Realism: prospects for 'post-analytic' philosophy* (London: Macmillan, 1997) and *New Idols of the Cave: on the limits of anti-realism* (Manchester: Manchester University Press, 1997); Mark Platts (ed.), *Reference, Truth and Reality: essays on the philosophy of language* (London: Routledge & Kegan Paul, 1980); and Scott Soames, *Understanding Truth* (Oxford: Oxford University Press, 1999).

47. Wright, *Truth and Objectivity*, p. 80 (Note 1, above).
48. Ibid., p. 80.
49. Miller, 'Rule-Following, Response-Dependence, and McDowell's Debate with Anti-Realism' p. 193 (Note 8, above).
50. Ibid., p. 178.
51. See John McDowell, *Mind and World* (Cambridge, MA: Harvard University Press, 1994) and Robert Brandom, *Making It Explicit: reasoning, representing, and discursive commitment* (Harvard University Press, 1994).
52. Immanuel Kant, *Critique of Pure Reason*, trans. N. Kemp Smith (London: Macmillan, 1964); McDowell, *Mind and World* (Note 51, above). See also Ch. 4, pp. 142–4 here and Norris, 'McDowell on Kant: redrawing the bounds of sense' and 'The Limits of Naturalism: further thoughts on McDowell's *Mind and World*', in *Minding the Gap: epistemology and philosophy of science in the two traditions* (Amherst, MA: University of Massachusetts Press, 2000), pp. 172–96 and 197–230.
53. Miller, 'Rule-Following', p. 178 (Note 49, above).
54. Ibid., p. 178.
55. Railton, 'Red, Bitter, Good', p. 84 (Note 5, above).
56. Ibid., p. 84.
57. See Note 20, above.
58. The point about US isolationist policy will no doubt strike many readers as dated or irrelevant when set against the record of events since the terrorist attacks on New York and Washington of September 11th, 2001. This is not the place for a detailed reckoning with those events, their moral and political implications, or issues concerning the legitimacy of the US-led 'war' against terrorism launched by President George W. Bush with the willing or enforced support/acquiescence of various other governments. However it is worth noting that such issues cannot be held entirely separate from the question of Bush's electoral mandate – or lack of it – and hence that of whether he possessed even constitutional warrant for pursuing a campaign of retributive 'justice' against not only the (presumed) perpetrators but also the civilian population of Afghanistan, albeit accompanied by the standard expressions of regret for so-called 'collateral damage'. Indeed as I write (26th October 2001) it is becoming daily more evident that considerations of natural justice have no role to play when set against the furtherance of US global-strategic interests or the moral posturing of those among the motley 'coalition' who have caved in to pressure from the Bush administration.

    I should not wish to make a philosophical debating-point of the mass-murder of civilians, whether those in New York and Washington or those on the receiving end of US foreign policy, past and present. Still it does seem pertinent to remark that 'best opinion' in such matters can sometimes be swung so as to secure widespread endorsement and the highest 'constitutional' sanction for state-sponsored (as distinct from group-organised) acts of large-scale terrorism. Nor should it escape notice that a growing number of death-row convicts throughout the US now look set to suffer the kinds of inhumane and barbarous treatment that the Texas judiciary – with Bush's keen support – has seen fit to visit upon some of its most deprived and socially victimised citizens. I trust that these reflections will not seem off-the-point to anyone who has followed my arguments thus far.

Chapter Six

Showing you Know: on Wright's 'Manifestation Principle'

I

As mostly construed nowadays the debate between realism and anti-realism is an issue in metaphysics, philosophical semantics, and philosophy of logic rather than – or prior to – an issue in epistemology or ontology. That is, it has to do with the conditions under which we can recognise certain statements as possessing a determinate truth-value, as distinct from certain others – those belonging to the so-called 'disputed class' – which we are unable to verify or falsify by the best means at our disposal. Thus, according to Dummett, the question is whether truth can be conceived in objective (verification-transcendent) terms or whether it must always be thought of as epistemically constrained, i.e., as subject to the scope and limits of attainable human knowledge.[1] On a realist construal the truth-value of any well-formed statement in mathematics, the natural sciences, history, and other such truth-apt areas of discourse is a matter of its corresponding (or not) to the way things stand (or once stood) in reality, and depends not at all on our capacity to manifest a grasp of its operative truth-conditions.[2] From an anti-realist standpoint, conversely, there is no making sense of the idea that a statement might be undetectably true, or that we might be so placed as to know that such a statement must be either true or false despite our having no evidential grounds or adequate proof procedure by which to decide the issue.

Such is the 'manifestation principle' as specified by Crispin Wright: that 'the performance abilities that constitute an understanding of an expression do not count unless associated with the ability to *evaluate* one's own and others' performance with that expression.'[3] And since (*ex hypothesi*) the ability requires a grasp of its operative truth-conditions – that is, those that must be known to obtain if the statement is to manifest a sufficient understanding on the speaker's part – then clearly this criterion cannot be satisfied by statements of the disputed class. Thus 'understanding . . . has to be seen as a complex of *discriminatory* capacities: an overall ability to suit one's use of the expression to the obtaining of factors which can be appreciated by oneself and others to render one's use apt.'[4] In which case, it seems, there is no escaping the anti-realist conclusion that truth-values must be restricted to just that class of statements that allow for proof or verification within the limits imposed by our present-best powers of perceptual, epistemic, or evidential grasp. These passages are taken from Wright's 1989 essay 'Misconstruals Made Manifest', where he adopts an (albeit qualified) version of Dummett's anti-realist position. By 1993 – in his book *Truth and Objectivity* – Wright can be found adjusting his position so as to accommodate further objections from the realist quarter.[5] Thus he now makes room for criteria such as those of 'super-assertibility' or 'cognitive command', that is to say, limit-point standards of rational acceptability that would extend the case for idealised or optimal (rather than *de facto*) epistemic warrant when deciding which statements are properly assessable in bivalent (true-or-false) terms. All the same these concessions stop well short of allowing the realist's major premise, namely, that so long as such statements are well-formed then their truth-value can in principle transcend even the utmost scope and limits of our recognitional capacity. Thus it remains the case, now as before, that on Wright's view of the matter realism requires some viable account of 'a practical ability which stands to understanding an evidence-transcendent truth-condition as recognitional skills stand to decidable truth-conditions'.[6] And that account just as clearly cannot be had if the criterion for bivalent (truth-apt) statements is one that still involves certain epistemic constraints, even though those constraints are now envisaged as pertaining to some optimised state of knowledge when all the evidence is in.

This is why some realists – Michael Devitt among them – reject the whole idea that realism with respect to any given 'area of discourse' should be treated in logico-semantic terms as a matter of establishing the truth-conditions (or the standards of warranted assertibility) for statements of the relevant type.[7] Rather, they contend, we have much better reason for adopting an epistemological approach *via* inference to the best (most rational or causally adequate) explanation, one that is strongly borne out by the evidence of scientific progress to date. On this view, moreover – *contra* the anti-realist – truth is evidentially unconstrained in the sense that it may always transcend or surpass our utmost epistemic grasp. Of course this is just what Dummett, Wright and others of a broadly anti-realist persuasion find so puzzling about the realist case, namely that it seems to make truth unknowable or to place it forever beyond the scope of human recognition. Thus Wright again:

> [i]f truth is in general evidentially unconstrained, then – depending on its subject matter – knowing the truth-conditions of a sentence may require an understanding of how it could be undetectably true. And how could that knowledge consist – as the Manifestability Principle requires it must – in any ability whose proper exercise is tied to *appreciable* situations? How can knowing what it is for an unappreciable situation to obtain be constituted by capacities of discrimination exercised in response to appreciable ones?[8]

However this argument strikes Devitt as a case of 'putting the cart before the horse', or espousing a highly disputable theory in philosophy of language and logic in preference to a theory – that of scientific realism – which has a great deal of evidence in its favour and which cannot be disputed unless on precisely such dubious logico-semantic grounds. Nor is Devitt over-impressed by the anti-realist's standard point about the ultimate unknowability of truth if construed in accordance with the realist's claim for its objective or verification-transcendent character. On the one hand (he argues) we should not make the mistake of conflating issues about truth with issues about realism, a mistake which typically leads straight on to the anti-realist's sceptical conclusion. On the other we should recognise that science has a strong claim to have achieved significant advances in various fields through the progressive replacement of less adequate by more adequate theories, that is to say, theories which not only yield a better descriptive or causal-explanatory account of some given phenomenon but also explain why previous theories failed to deliver such results.[9]

So the realist argument for verification-transcendence is not – as the anti-realist would have it – one that creates an insuperable gulf between objective truth and the capacities of human knowledge-acquisition. Rather it is an argument that sensibly accepts the non-finality of scientific knowledge at any given stage of human enquiry but which also – just as sensibly – accepts the claim that we now know more about subatomic structures, or the properties of light, or the mechanisms of genetic inheritance than was known to anyone a century ago.[10] Yet of course such knowledge was beyond the grasp of scientists working at the time and would therefore (on a Dummett-type verificationist construal) have rendered their statements devoid of any truth value had they happened to advance some prescient theory or hypothesis which later turned out to be largely in accord with current best thinking on the matter. Nor are such instances hard to find, beginning with the speculative theories of the ancient Greek atomists and including a great number of subsequent episodes (among them the conjectures of Copernicus, Galileo, Dalton, Mendel, Rutherford, Einstein, or Crick and Watson) where theory ran ahead of verification, or where the truth-value of certain statements remained to be established through the advent of more powerful or refined investigative techniques. Yet *at the time*

– in their original context of utterance – those statements must be taken as having belonged to Dummett's 'disputed class' and hence as having lacked any truth-value by verificationist standards. In which case it cannot be rational, Devitt would maintain, to espouse a theory that produces such anomalous or counter-intuitive results merely for the sake of upholding certain theses in the philosophy of language and logic whose warrant is in any case open to question from any but a hardline or doctrinally committed anti-realist standpoint.

Wright is less committed than Dummett in this respect, mainly because he is more sensitive to the kinds of objection outlined above. Thus he goes some way toward meeting such objections by allowing for cases – such as those of mathematics and the physical sciences – where the realist would seem to have some strong arguments on her side for conceiving of truth as potentially outrunning our best available methods of proof or sources of evidence. Hence (to repeat) Wright's ideas of 'superassertibility' and 'cognitive command', the former defined as applying to a statement 'if and only if it is, or can be, warranted and some warrant for it would survive arbitrarily close scrutiny of its pedigree and arbitrarily extensive increments to or other forms of improvement of our information', while in the latter case 'any difference of opinion will be such that there are considerations quite independent of the conflict which, if known about, would mandate withdrawal of one (or both) of the contending views.'[11] However, as I have said, these concessions to the realist are sharply limited by Wright's maintaining that they must be held within a limit-point conception of epistemic warrant, one that extends just so far as allowing for some optimal 'improvement of our information' or some relevant consideration which, 'if known about', would serve to settle the dispute. Moreover this continuing bias toward an anti-realist approach comes across very strongly in Wright's discussions of the rule-following 'paradox', that is to say, the Wittgensteinian problem – taken up by Saul Kripke and others – as to what it can mean 'correctly' or 'properly' to follow a rule given the inscrutability of utterer's intent and the sheer multitude of adhoc rules that might be invoked in order to justify some non-standard, deviant, or aberrant performance.[12] Thus:

> [h]ow can a sentence be undetectably true unless the rule embodied in its content – the condition which the world has to satisfy to confer truth upon it – can permissibly be thought of as extending, so to speak, of itself into areas where we cannot follow it and thus determining, without any contribution from ourselves or our reactive natures, that a certain state of affairs complies with it?[13]

Such is the problem, according to Wright, with any realist or objectivist conception of rules that would take them to possess a truth-determining character beyond whatever we are able to establish within the limits of our current computational powers (in the case of arithmetical procedures) or the range of our current-best evidential sources (in the case of scientific hypotheses). So there is no making sense of the realist claim that truth is epistemically unconstrained or that statements can possess an objective truth-value quite apart from our capacity to acquire or to manifest a knowledge of their operative truth-conditions.

On the sceptical ('Kripkensteinian') account this issue arises with respect to all kinds of rule-following procedures, from those of elementary arithmetic to those of formal logic, inductive inference, and a whole range of kindred practices where we take it – naively – that there *must* be a correct (objectively valid) way of carrying on.[14] For such a standard would require either some superordinate rule for proper application of the first-order rule – thus engendering a vicious regress – or an appeal to some deep further fact about the follower's understanding of it which runs straight into Wittgenstein's argument against the idea of a 'private language' – a source of self-evident apodictic truth – which could somehow put a stop to that regress.[15] Thus the only solution, so Kripke maintains, is a 'sceptical solution' that locates the criteria for getting things right – for answering (say) '125' when asked 'what is the product of 68 + 57?' – in a shared practice or communal procedure where that *just is* what properly counts as a correct (acceptable) response. Wright is on occasion sharply dismissive of the Wittgensteinian 'therapeutic' idea that philosophy's sole legitimate aim is to talk us down from all these needless metaphysical perplexities and thereby (in Stanley Cavell's soothing phrase) 'lead us back, *via* the community, home'.[16] This resistance comes partly from his general sense that there are real problems about meaning, truth and objectivity which require something other than a Wittgenstein-administered course of remedial or curative treatment. However, more specifically, it also results from his attempt to do justice to widely-held realist intuitions with respect to certain areas of discourse (such as that of mathematics) while also meeting the challenges laid down by Dummettian anti-realism and Kripke's ultra-sceptical take on the rule-following paradox. How far Wright succeeds in this task and whether success can possibly be had on such terms are the main questions I wish to pursue here.

II

In a more recent article Wright works his way through various going theories or conceptions of truth and concludes that while each can be shown to give rise to certain problems with respect to certain subject-areas nevertheless there is one domain where each can most plausibly claim to capture our best working intuitions. This 'more relaxed' project of enquiry, he thinks, will 'see us trying to build an overall picture of the concept of truth – of its contents and purposes – by the assembly and integration of as wide a variety as possible of basic *a priori* principles about it – "platitudes", as I have elsewhere called them'.[17] Among those platitudes are (1) the *transparency* of truth insofar as it enters into all our propositional attitudes of believing, denying, doubting, hoping, desiring, fearing, and so forth, (2) the *opacity* of truth insofar as we know (intuitively grasp) that there must be certain truths that hold objectively even though they exceed our present-best scope of cognitive or epistemic warrant, (3) the 'conservation of truth-aptitude under embedding', that is, the fact that truth-apt propositions are subject to the various logical operators of negation, conjunction, disjunction, etc., (4) the correspondence-principle in its basic form, namely the idea that truthful propositions must in some sense match up with the way things stand in reality, (5) the distinction between (objective) truth and (epistemic) justification, (6) the strictly atemporal character of truth as holding for a given proposition at whatever time of utterance provided only that one makes certain requisite adjustments of mood or tense, and (7) the condition that truth is *absolute*, i.e., that it allows of no degrees or gradations such as might apply, epistemically speaking, to probability-weighted assessments of justification, rational belief, or assertoric warrant. All of which suggests that Wright has by now moved a long way from any lingering attachment to the tenets of Dummett-style anti-realism or the sceptical outlook supposedly entailed by Kripke's rule-following considerations.

Thus it is 'quite appealing' – Wright's phrase – to think of the 'true propositions' of basic arithmetic or number theory as 'those which sustain certain internal relations – an appropriate kind of semantic consequence – to a certain base class of propositions – the Dedekind-Peano axioms, for instance'.[18] That is to say, this is an area of discourse where we can best get along with a suitably formalised logicist concept of truth which avoids any opening for Kripkean scepticism as regards the recursive or rule-governed character of valid arithmetical procedures. Yet this option is presented as 'quite appealing' – as one that has a fair claim to acceptance on intuitive grounds – rather than as having any stronger (objective) warrant of the kind that Wright spells out in platitudes (2), (4), (5), and (7) above. Moreover, it is subject to the qualification that any necessary link between the basic axioms and the 'true propositions' of elementary arithmetic is a matter of 'internal relations' within the system, these latter construed as entailing 'an appropriate kind of semantic consequence', that is, as holding in virtue of the various definitions laid down for its operative terms and concepts. Such an account, Wright goes on to remark, 'would extend to the axioms themselves (assuming the reflexivity of the relevant internal relations)', but 'would not comfortably extend to truths of the form: *p* is a Dedekind–Peano axiom (more generally, *p* is a member of the relevant base class)'.[19] In other words it would carry no substantive implication with respect to the objective truth-value (as distinct from the intra-systemic or purely definitional necessity) of any proposition that claimed such axiomatic status. However this is to deny the chief premise of a realist approach to number-theory, namely the existence of truths and numerical entailment-relations that obtain quite apart from whether or not they receive some working definition within that system.

Scott Soames puts the case against such thinking in a passage that brings out its conflict with any objectivist conception of arithmetical truth. Thus (to repeat): 'for each of the nondenumerably many real numbers there is a proposition that it is greater than or equal to zero', from which it follows that '[i]f each sentence is a finite string of words drawn from a finite vocabulary, then the number of propositions outstrips the denumerable infinity of sentences available to express it – that is, there are truths with no linguistic expression.'[20] This point can be generalised to articulate the realist claim that in mathematics as in other truth-apt areas of discourse it is necessarily the case that truth outruns, exceeds or transcends any range of sentences that find a place within the compass of presently expressible or well-defined truth-conditions for that particular area. Thus it is a consequence of Gödel's undecidability-theorem, properly understood, that certain truths (like that of Gödel's theorem itself) can obtain as a matter of objective necessity despite our being *ex hypothesi* unable to prove them by any formal or computational means at our present-best or even our future-best disposal.[21] On the face of it this need not come into conflict with Wright's proposal that we should give up the quest for any unitary conception of truth that would apply across the board and should content ourselves rather with the sensibly scaled-down 'pluralist' idea that truth-conditions vary from one 'area of discourse' to another. This idea is philosophically attractive, he believes, 'insofar as an account which enables us to think of truth as constituted differently in different areas of thought might contribute to a sharp explanation of the differential appeal of realist and anti-realist intuitions about them'.[22] However its attractions may not be so obvious, the realist will argue, if it allows for no stronger conception of truth in arithmetic or elementary number-theory than that which renders such truth dependent on whatever is most 'appealing' in terms of intuitive preference. Nor is the case significantly strengthened, as Soames makes clear in the passage cited above, through a specification of arithmetic truth with sole reference to the formal semantics or 'internal relations' of some given definitional system.

What continues to push Wright in this markedly anti-realist direction despite his counting objectivist claims among the list of candidate 'platitudes' is his basic conviction that only a response-dependent account can hope to make sense of our actually knowing what would otherwise, by very definition, lie beyond the utmost bounds of human knowability.[23] Thus the platitudes are offered not so much as principles that *properly and correctly* apply to certain clearly-specified 'areas of discourse' but rather as various possible ways of thinking that all capture something of our working intuitions but which are otherwise up for negotiated settlement on more-or-less 'appealing' terms. This is why the idea of 'superassertibility' (i.e., of truth as what we would or should rationally accept under ideal epistemic conditions) continues to exercise the maximum appeal for Wright even though it is officially just one option among a range of hypotheses that extend all the way from correspondence to coherence or from outright objectivism to a communitarian conception of assertoric warrant. I must now quote at length since the following passage is one that goes to the heart of these issues. 'Clearly', he writes,

> a notion of this kind [i.e., that of superassertibility] must make sense wherever the corresponding notion of justification makes sense – wherever we have a concept of what it would be to justify a particular proposition, it will be intelligible to hypothesize the attainment of such a justification and its stability through arbitrarily extensive further investigation. It turns out that in any region of discourse meeting certain constraints, superassertibility will satisfy each of the platitudes listed above, so a prima facie case can be made that, with respect to those regions, the concept of superassertibility is a truth concept. In these areas it is consequently open to us to regard truth as consisting in superassertibility. In other areas, by contrast, where the relevant background conditions arguably fail – in particular, if we can see that there is no essential connection between truth and the availability of evidence – then the concept of truth will not allow of interpretation in terms of superassertibility, and the constitution of truth must accordingly be viewed differently. It is perhaps superfluous to remark that a superassertibilist conception of truth chimes very nicely with the semantic anti-realism which Michael Dummett has presented as a generalization of mathematical intuitionism, whose cardinal thesis may indeed be that truth is *everywhere* best construed in terms of superassertibility.[24]

Wright is careful to make the point that certain areas of discourse must be conceived as lying beyond the legitimate reach of any 'superassertibilist' approach, that is to say, those areas (here unspecified) where 'the relevant background conditions arguably fail' and where 'there is no essential connection between truth and the availability of evidence'. All the same it is hard to see just which areas would fall into that class, given Wright's lingering Wittgensteinian doubts as to whether an objectivist approach can be sustained even in the case of arithmetical truth where such an argument surely has the maximum degree of credibility.

Hence the very marked shift of emphasis in his final sentence, implying as it does – though without fully endorsing the claim – that Dummett's intuitionist thesis with regard to mathematics might indeed be capable of generalisation to the proposal that 'truth is *everywhere* best construed in terms of superassertibility.'[25] This suggestion is reinforced by Wright's distinctly hedgy phrasing of the objectivist case – that 'the relevant background conditions [i.e., those for superassertibility] *arguably* fail' – which in effect leaves it open to doubt whether *any* candidate 'area of discourse' should count as one where the relevant truth-conditions transcend the conditions for assertoric warrant or epistemic justification. On the face of it, as advertised, his pluralist approach is designed to accommodate this or any other such 'platitude' which strikes us as simply self-evident (or sheerly *a priori*) when applied in accordance with the governing criteria for truth-claims of just that kind. Thus 'it opens up possibilities for a principled pluralism in the following specific way: that in different regions of thought and discourse *the theory may hold good, a priori, of – may be satisfied by – different concepts*' (Wright's italics).[26] Yet this approach is less 'specific' – and to that extent less 'principled' – insofar as it constantly shifts the balance of judgement away from an objectivist conception of truth in favour of a broadly 'superassertibilist' conception. In other words, whatever his pluralist avowals, Wright is strongly drawn in the latter direction and remains sceptical of any realist approach that would regard truth-values as always potentially transcending or eluding our best means of ascertainment.

Yet it is just that claim ('platitudinous' or not) that forms the main plank of any viable realist ontology and which has been the main point at dispute between philosophers of rival (realist and anti-realist) persuasions. Thus the question is whether any *epistemic* theory of truth, however elaborately specified, can capture just what it is about certain statements (e.g., those of mathematics, logic, and the physical sciences) which confers an objective truth-value on them quite apart from any limit-point appeal to best opinion or optimised judgement. 'Surely so', a Wrightian pluralist will say, since the criteria for truth (or assertoric warrant) can always be adjusted over various areas of discourse on a principle that accommodates our standing intuitions with respect to this or that area including, as it may be, our intuitive preference for treating issues of arithmetic truth as epistemically unconstrained. 'Clearly not', the realist will say, since epistemic theories are by very definition unable to accommodate truth-values which transcend the scope of assertoric warrant under optimal epistemic conditions.[27] And she will then most likely proceed to offer a diagnostic account of the various issues that have given rise to this sceptical and anti-realist trend in present-day philosophical debate. Thus it is Wittgenstein, more than anyone, who has focused attention on a range of hypercultivated pseudo-problems – like the rule-following 'paradox' – which in turn generate pseudo-solutions (such as Kripke's) that leave those problems just as firmly in place. Yet this whole debate takes on a certain surreal aspect if one accepts that it is a matter of objective truth *sans phrase* that '68 + 57 = 125' regardless of whether that truth finds a place in the repertoire of arithmeticians or whether (perhaps through some humanity-wide epistemic catastrophe) it should suddenly exceed their utmost powers of calculative grasp. Likewise it is the case that any well-formed and adequately specified statement in the physical sciences – such as 'water has the molecular structure H_20' or 'gold is the metallic element with atomic number 79' – must be true or false (objectively so) depending on the way things stand in physical reality and quite apart from any given state of knowledge concerning it. Insofar as philosophy produces reasons for doubting or rejecting such claims, so the realist will argue, it is on a false track and in need of some (though preferably *not* Wittgensteinian) therapeutic treatment.

Moreover there is something decidedly perverse in the refusal to acknowledge that whole vast range of impressive and intricately detailed correlations between mathematics and the physical sciences which Galileo was among the first to proclaim and which can only be denied by thinkers in the grip of some preconceived sceptical doctrine. Of course it is a genuinely puzzling question, and one that philosophers cannot ignore, as to just how and why an 'abstract' discourse such as that of mathematics should possess this extraordinary power to reveal the physical constants that underwrite the laws of nature on every scale, from Planck's quantum of action to the rotation of the galaxies.[28] However this is not to say that the question should be raised to a high point of bafflement or scepticism pushed to the stage of denying both the objective (verification-transcendent) character of physical laws and the objective (recognition-transcendent) status of mathematical truths. Indeed the whole Kripkensteinian debate about rule-following – like much recent philosophy of mathematics – is marked by a curious and, one would think, a somewhat disabling lack of interest in the kinds of problem that actually preoccupy working mathematicians.[29] Thus the sceptic's case with regard to counting or simple recursive procedures like addition is not so much a problem in philosophy of *mathematics*, strictly speaking, but just another variant of the well-worn Humean puzzle about induction transposed to the context of elementary number-theory. That case would look much less plausible if applied to some genuinely complex and challenging task – such as following the stage-by-stage logical deduction of Gödel's undecidability-proof – as distinct from just accepting its upshot as a matter of taken-for-granted sceptical warrant. Hence the irony that Gödel's proof is so often instanced in support of anti-realist arguments in this and other 'areas of discourse' despite Gödel's own insistence that the proof could never have been arrived at except on a realist – indeed an avowedly Platonist – conception of mathematical truth.[30] What that proof 'indisputably established', as Penrose puts it, is that 'no *formal system* of sound mathematical rules of proof can ever suffice, even in principle, to establish all the true propositions of ordinary arithmetic.'[31] Yet insofar as the proof holds good it must be taken to show something totally at odds with the sceptic's or the anti-realist's case, namely that 'no such system of rules can ever be sufficient to prove even those propositions of arithmetic whose truth is accessible, in principle, to human intuition and insight – whence human intuition and insight cannot be reducible to any set of rules.'[32]

This is clearly *not* an intuitionist conclusion in Dummett's sense of that term, that is, an argument that mathematical truth extends just so far as the scope and limits of those theorems provable by existing formal or computational procedures. Indeed it entails just the opposite claim: that the validity of Gödel's proof is ascertainable through a process of reasoning that inherently goes beyond those limits and which thus eludes any such formalised procedure. This claim has struck some commentators (unlike Penrose) as a sad aberration on Gödel's part, a slide into Platonist (= quasi-mystical) habits of thought which require that we should somehow have epistemic contact with truths – such as those of mathematics – that are nonetheless taken to inhabit a realm of absolute ideal objectivity. However this supposedly knock-down argument against Gödelian realism can better be seen as a product of the twofold assumption (1) that standards of validity and truth can only be a matter of rule-following or formalised procedural warrant, and (2) that any realist conception such as Gödel's must necessarily involve an absurd and self-contradictory conflation of realms. Yet it is just his point – one routinely ignored by philosophers who adopt this line – that mathematical truth is *neither* coextensive with our best-available (formalised) proof-procedures *nor* the result of some mysterious quasi-epistemic 'contact' with entities (like numbers, sets, or classes) conceived as existing in a realm that Platonically transcends our mundane powers of perceptual apprehension. Jerrold Katz offers the clearest statement of just what is wrong with this way of thinking and just why the realist – or the Gödelian Platonist – should not consent to have it foisted upon her by opponents in search of a quick riposte to mathematical realism in any form. Thus (to repeat):

> [t]he entire idea that our knowledge of abstract objects might be based on perceptual contact is misguided, since, even if we had contact with abstract objects, the information we could obtain from such contact wouldn't help us in trying to justify our beliefs about them. The epistemological function of perceptual contact is to provide information about which possibilities are actualities. Perceptual contact thus has a point in the case of empirical propositions. Because natural objects can be otherwise than they actually are (*non obstante* their essential properties), contact is necessary in order to discover how they actually are . . . Not so with abstract objects. They could not be otherwise than they are . . . Hence there is no question of which mathematical possibilities are actual possibilities. In virtue of being a perfect number, six must be a perfect number; in virtue of being the only even prime, two must be the only even prime. Since the epistemic role of contact is to provide us with the information needed to select among the different ways something might be, and since perceptual contact cannot provide information about how something must be, contact has no point in relation to abstract objects. It cannot ground beliefs about them.[33]

In short, the whole debate between realists and anti-realists has been badly skewed by the dominant (anti-realist) assumption that *if* mathematical truths are objective – that is, recognition-transcendent – then necessarily they lie beyond our utmost epistemic ken and we can have no knowledge of them, whereas if we *can* lay claim to such knowledge then again necessarily those truths cannot be objective. Hence Paul Benacerraf's well-known pyrrhic conclusion, echoed in a number of essays by Hilary Putnam, that quite simply 'nothing works' in philosophy of mathematics, at least if one takes it that a viable realist account would have to satisfy the twin desiderata of (1) conserving the objectivity of mathematics, and (2) explaining how we can nonetheless acquire knowledge of truths that by very definition exceed or transcend our epistemic grasp.[34]

Dummett puts this case in terms that again present realism as faced with a strictly insoluble dilemma, one that admits of no third way between the Scylla of absolute ideal (hence unknowable) objectivity and the Charybdis of quasi-perceptual epistemic 'contact'. Thus:

> since ex hypothesi, from the supposition that the condition for the truth of a mathematical statement, as platonistically understood, obtains, it cannot in general be inferred that it is one that a human being need be supposed to be even capable of recognizing as obtaining, we cannot give substance to our conception of our having an implicit knowledge of what that condition is, since nothing that we do can amount to a manifestation of such knowledge.[35]

Dummett's criteria of 'recognition' and 'manifestation' are such as to suggest that the perceptual analogy is never far from the surface in his argument, even if they are capable of other (less obviously slanted) interpretations. Yet this is plainly to set the issue up in a way which completely misconstrues the realist (or Gödelian Platonist) position and which thereby scores what can only be seen as a false or hollow victory. Rather that position should be taken to maintain the capacity of thought to range beyond the limits of any currently-accepted formal procedure or established method of proof even though what results is a theorem (such as Gödel's) that is nonetheless subject to rigorous standards of validity and truth.

Indeed it is hard to see, on Dummett's verificationist account, how advances in mathematics, the physical sciences, or any other field of enquiry could ever come about, given his idea that their truth-conditions (or criteria of assertoric warrant) can only be a matter of their falling in with some established – recognisable and communally shared – way of proceeding. Least of all could it hope to explain how thinking is able to generate proofs – such as that which Gödel provided for his incompleteness-theorem – which constitute a massive challenge to hitherto-accepted (in this case Hilbertian) standards and norms of enquiry. That possibility is simply not in view if one adopts the Wittgensteinian approach according to which those standards and norms are such as must be taken to prevail within some given mathematical community, practice, or 'form of life'.[36] Nor is it available, as Gödel insists, if validity and truth are equated with purely formalised proof-methods or with the kinds of computational procedure that standardly figure in philosophical debates about the rule-following 'paradox'. For what the incompleteness-theorem most strikingly exhibits is the power of mathematical thought to establish certain demonstrative results which, *on its own showing*, cannot be subject to the kinds of consistent or fully axiomatised proof that had figured in Hilbert's sanguine prognosis for the advancement of mathematical knowledge.[37] Certainly it gives no reason to conclude – with Kripke – that we are bereft of criteria for 'correctly' following a rule since even elementary arithmetic contains certain axioms whose truth cannot be proved or derived as a matter of logical necessity from other axioms within the system. Rather it is to say that the Gödelian proof requires a different (though no less exacting) standard of objective warrant, one that has nothing to do with the kind of mechanical rule-following procedure that Kripke takes as the paradigm case of arithmetical reasoning. Thus Gödel showed 'that there could be no formal system F, whatever, that is both consistent . . . and complete – so long as F is taken to be powerful enough to contain a formulation of the statements of ordinary arithmetic along with standard logic'.[38] But so far from lending support to any kind of wholesale Kripkean scepticism this result can more properly be taken to show that while formal procedures undoubtedly play an indispensable role in mathematical reasoning nevertheless their limits are *not* the limits of mathematical truth or knowledge. In which case 'the insights that are available to human mathematicians – indeed, to anyone who can think logically with understanding and imagination – lie beyond anything that can be formalised as a set of rules.'[39]

III

Of course this issue of the limits of formalisation is one that has haunted philosophy ever since Russell first discovered contradictions in the logical structure of set-theory and thereby created large problems for his own (and Frege's) logicist approach to the conceptual foundations of mathematics.[40] The examples are familiar enough: 'that set whose members include all sets that are not members of themselves', 'every sentence is non-applicable', 'all Cretans are liars' [spoken by a Cretan], 'the statement contained within these quote-marks is untrue', and so forth. Russell's solution, in company with others like Tarski, was the theory of types which laid it down – as a stipulative rule – that such self-referential and paradox-creating expressions were logically illegitimate and could best be avoided by distinguishing clearly between different (i.e., object-language and metalinguistic) orders of statement.[41] In Wittgenstein's case this discovery would seem to have played a large part in prompting his shift from the austerely formal *Tractatus* position concerning language, logic, and truth to his later idea that there existed as many legitimate ways of making sense – or as many kinds of truth – as there existed diverse language-games, practices, or communal 'forms of life'. And from here it was but a short step to Wittgenstein's conception of arithmetical and other kinds of 'rule-following' procedure as grounded in nothing more objective than the fact of their playing a certain (no matter how deeply entrenched or acculturated) role in our various reckonings and reasonings.

Hence, as we have seen, Kripke's sceptical 'solution' to Wittgenstein's sceptical paradox, one that in effect merely re-states the issue in more sharply paradoxical terms and derives the same lesson concerning communal 'agreement in judgement' as the sole basis for ascriptions of truth or falsehood. Hence also the claim of Wright and others that this paradox might be deprived of its sceptical sting by adopting a response-dependence (RD) theory that equates the assertibility-conditions for certain areas of discourse with the conditions of a duly normalised, provisoed, or optimised mode of response. Thus, according to Mark Johnston:

> [i]f the concept associated with the predicate "is C" is a concept interdependent with or dependent upon concepts of certain subjects' responses under certain conditions, then something of the following form will hold *a priori*: x is C if in conditions K, Ss are disposed to produce x-directed response R (or: x is such as to produce R in Ss under conditions K).[42]

Indeed the very form of this standard RD quantified biconditional is one that clearly relates it to Tarski's disquotational formula for truth. Where Tarski offers his canonical T-sentence '"Snow is white" is true if and only if snow is white', its RD counterpart would typically run: ' "This stuff is white" can be taken as a reliable report if and only if uttered in the right circumstances by a subject with normally-functioning visual apparatus, under normal lighting conditions, with no proximal source of distorting perceptual interference', and so forth. And where Tarski supposes truth to consist – at least for all formal-definitional purposes – in the literal equivalence between any sentence named (or quoted) on the left-hand side and that self-same sentence as used (or asserted) on the right-hand side, the RD theorist will typically specify a range of epistemic or perceptual provisos which allow for the role of best opinion in securing the required degree of assertoric warrant.

Thus Tarski's purely semantic conception involves nothing more than the simple device of constructing an endlessly reiterable T-schema for each candidate sentence and then cancelling through by removing the left-hand quotation marks so as to establish that truth *just is* a matter of asserting whatever state of affairs must obtain – such as that of snow being white – in order for the sentence to be true. This is basically a version of the classical correspondence-theory which Aristotle was the first to enunciate and which Tarski accepts with minor modifications, for example, in the form 'The truth of a sentence consists in its agreement with (or correspondence to) reality', or again, 'A sentence is true if it designates an existing state of affairs.'[43] On the other hand – notoriously – it is an approach open to various alternative construals, among them minimalist conceptions of truth that treat it as a purely formal predicate with no substantive implications, deflationist accounts which push yet further in this sceptical direction, and redundancy-theories in which it figures merely as a source of added rhetorical or suasive emphasis.[44] Then again, its chief use, as some would argue, is to provide a handy means of endorsing (or denying) some open-ended range of statements, beliefs, or opinions which cannot be specified one by one. Such would be the case with generalised assertions like 'everything Tarski says in this connection is true', or 'everything that George W. Bush said during the 2000 US electoral campaign was false'. One reason for this striking lack of consensus as to the import of Tarski's theory is the fact that it can easily be viewed as reducing to a kind of all-purpose tautological 'definition' which in effect does nothing to explain or elucidate the nature and structure of truth. Tarski himself might appear to invite this charge when he describes the formal-semantic approach as a 'sober and modest discipline', one that has no pretensions of resolving 'all the ills and diseases of mankind', whether physical, social, or even philosophical.[45] His professed modesty in this regard may perhaps be taken as a gentle swipe against those among his ex-colleagues on the 'left' of the Vienna Circle – notably Neurath – who did indeed cherish such hopes for moral and socio-political improvement through the application of clear thinking to issues beyond the strict domain of epistemology and philosophy of logic.[46] Still there is a sense in which Tarski's semantic conception, whatever its formal adequacy, comes down to a purely tautological specification of 'truth' for any candidate sentence, and can therefore do nothing to adjudicate the issue between those rival (e.g., correspondence, coherence, minimalist, deflationist, or redundancy) theories that have claimed Tarskian warrant.

This is one reason why RD theorists have elected to modify Tarski's formula in such a way as to specify substantive *epistemic* criteria to the right of the quantified biconditional and thus to provide a more adequate account of what it takes for a statement to meet the conditions of warranted assertibility. Most often they have done so in response to arguments which push somewhat farther than they would want to go with the idea of 'deflating' truth to the point where it becomes just a place-holder term or a label of convenience that can well be dispensed with except for certain (rhetorical or generalising) purposes. Thus, as Wright puts it:

> [a]ccording to deflationism, there simply isn't anything which truth, in general, *is*. It's a misconstrual of the adjective 'true' to see it as expressing the concept of a substantial characteristic of which one of the traditional accounts might provide a correct analysis, or which might allow of no correct analysis. Those who think otherwise are missing the point that the role of a significant adjective doesn't have to be to ascribe a genuine property.[47]

Wright is not endorsing the deflationist account, any more than he endorses its various rivals, whether those that would affirm or those would deny the existence of any such 'correct' and 'substantial' characterisation of truth. Indeed he clearly regards that account as inadequate insofar as it fails (or refuses) to address all the issues that are sure to arise as soon as one examines the role of the truth-predicate in various specific areas of discourse, such as those of mathematics, the physical sciences, colour-perception, moral judgement, and so forth. No doubt the word 'true' is sometimes used merely as a routine 'device of endorsement', by way of superadded rhetorical emphasis, or as a means of economically quantifying over some large range of propositions. All the same this deflationist approach begs the question as to just what *kind* of commendation is involved when one uses the word in any of these ways. 'Plausibly', Wright suggests,

> if I affirm a proposition's truth, I'm commending its acceptance, commending it as meeting a certain doxastic standard, as it were. In this way, affirmations of truth – and likewise denials of truth – are normative claims. To endorse a proposition as true is to affirm that it is acceptable as a belief or statement; to deny that a proposition is true is to affirm that it's correspondingly unacceptable.[48]

This point is well taken and puts one in mind of Russell's classic riposte to William James on the sheer impossibility of devising any pragmatist criterion of truth, for example, as what is 'good in the way of belief', that would not either collapse into some kind of make-believe fantasy or else have surreptitious recourse to standards of objective (belief-independent) truth and falsehood which left no room for the pragmatist conception.[49] All the same it is an argument that perhaps cuts deeper when applied to Wright's own approach – and to that of the RD theorists generally – than he is quite willing to acknowledge. For, as we have seen, Wright's strategy in the face of these problems with defending any unitary concept of truth is to adopt an avowedly 'pluralist' approach that accepts the variety of truth-conditions (or standards of assertoric warrant) in different 'areas of discourse'. That approach in turn takes its philosophic bearings from the Wittgensteinian idea that every such discourse possesses its own criteria, that is to say, its discourse-specific standards for what properly counts as an acceptable statement or one that meets the agreed-upon (i.e., communally warranted) criteria of truth for statements of just that kind. However it is precisely by way of this criterial conception – along with the reference to plural discourses, practices, or 'forms of life' – that thinkers of a more sceptical persuasion, Kripke among them, have been able to pose their stock challenge to objectivist conceptions of truth even in areas, such as that of mathematics, where Wright would not wish to follow their lead. And this is also, I think, a chief reason for the marked ambivalence that emerges in his own work and in that of other RD theorists with regard to the status of mathematical truth, an ambivalence that emerges most often in their tendency to shift the emphasis from left to right of the quantified biconditional.[50]

IV

As it happens Russell's essay on James also contains some pointed remarks about this use of the term 'criterion', set down long before his sharp estrangement from the turn taken in Wittgenstein's later thought but still highly pertinent here. Russell's example of a valid usage of the term is one that involves consulting a library catalogue in search of some particular book and judging – on the strength of its either being listed or not listed in the catalogue – that the result of one's search provides an adequate *criterion* of whether or not it is among the library's holdings. All the same there may be books (recent publications) that are there in the library but not yet catalogued, or books that appear in the catalogue but are lost, removed from stock, or out on loan. Moreover, 'even supposing the catalogue perfect, it is obvious that when you say the book is in the library you do not *mean* that it is mentioned in the catalogue.'[51] This last point is Russell's main objection to pragmatism, namely that it involves a regular confusion between beliefs that may satisfy certain *criteria* for counting them acceptable, useful, expedient, conducive to our general well-being, etc., and truth-claims that are subject to the more stringent test of whether or not they correspond to some objective (non-belief-dependent) state of affairs. Moreover he takes issue with the pragmatist idea that the truth-conditions for any given statement can be adequately specified in terms of its meaning and its meaning in terms of those various criteria that decide what is 'good in the way of belief' for everyday practical purposes. Thus 'being mentioned in the catalogue is a *useful* criterion of being in the library, because it is easier to consult the catalogue than to hunt through the shelves.'[52] But this criterial warrant, whatever its pragmatic or time-and-labour-saving usefulness, is still nowhere near meeting the conditions for a truth-evaluable statement of fact like 'Crispin Wright's *Truth and Objectivity* is there to be found at shelf-location X.'

At this point Russell's fancy takes wing and comes up with an imaginary scenario that is maybe not quite so remote from present-day reality. Suppose, he invites us, that the British Museum catalogue had been checked and shown beyond doubt to contain a fully accurate and up-to-date record of every book that the BM library possessed. Would it then follow that the catalogue (or the library) could henceforth manage perfectly well without the books? 'We can imagine', he writes:

> some person long engaged in a comparative study of libraries and having, in the process, naturally lost all taste for reading, declaring the catalogue is the

> only important thing – as for the books, they are useless lumber; no one ever wants them, and the principle of economy should lead us to be content with the catalogue. Indeed, if you consider the matter with an open mind, you will see that the catalogue *is* the library; for it tells you everything you can possibly wish to know about the library. Let us, then, save the taxpayers' money by destroying the books; allow free access to the catalogue, but condemn the desire to read as an exploded dogmatic realism.[53]

I have quoted this passage at length not only for its prescient irony in light of current institutional trends but also, more to the point, for Russell's spot-on diagnosis of the fallacy involved in taking truth to be a matter of criterial warrant, that is to say, a matter of our having good enough reason (short of decisive evidence or proof) for affirming some given proposition. After all, as he says, 'it remains an inference from the discovery that a book is mentioned in the catalogue to the conclusion that the book is in the library.'[54] That process of inference – and others like it – may be more or less reliable depending on the kind of information at hand, the extent of our experience in assessing such data, the availability of corroborative checks, and so forth. Thus in the case of reasoning inductively from past observation of physical regularities in nature to the likelihood of their future continuance – as with Russell's well-known restatement of the problem from Hume – it is fair to claim that we possess a good *criterion* for supposing that things will carry on that way despite the standing (if remote) possibility that they might just conceivably not. So if turkeys were better at adjusting their criterial expectations to the range of circumstantial factors involved then they wouldn't be anything like so confident in predicting from the fact of their having been fed every morning for the past twelve months that food would turn up as usual on Christmas Day.[55] And of course there are other instances where this criterial warrant is a great deal stronger, as with our well-founded assurance that the sun will rise tomorrow at dawn as it has every day since the solar system was formed and with numerous predictions in the physical sciences where we possess a well-developed causal explanation of why such regularities exist. Still there is a need to distinguish between predictions of this sort that *might* just possibly go wrong (if the sun were to explode or some similar catastrophe befall our region of the universe) and those truths of physics – like the laws of subatomic structure, or chemical bonding, or celestial motion in general – that would continue to hold as a matter of objective necessity quite aside from any rational inference to the future course of events on inductive grounds. In such cases any talk of 'criteria' can only have to do with our more or less limited state of knowledge or means of ascertainment, rather than entailing – as it does very often in Wittgenstein-influenced debate – the idea that such criteria are somehow *constitutive* of the truth-conditions for some given area of discourse.

The pragmatist concept of truth as utility therefore runs up against a twofold objection: first that there are many useful (indeed well-nigh indispensable) beliefs which might not be true for all that, and second – bad news for the turkeys or inhabitants of an exploding solar system – that there might turn out to be truths which are far from 'good [or expedient] in the way of belief'. Russell makes this point in more general terms when he remarks that '[t]he arguments of pragmatists are almost always directed to proving that utility is a *criterion*; that utility is the *meaning* of truth is then supposed to follow.'[56] But this is once again to mistake the catalogue for the books, or Christmas for just another routine day in the turkey's farmyard calendar. In short, it is to reason falsely from the fact that certain kinds of inference are *criterially* warranted – that they provide a fair working basis for beliefs, hypotheses, predictions, etc. – to the pragmatist (or Wittgensteinian) claim that truth in such matters *cannot be more* than what counts as such according to those same criteria. Here again Russell's criticism is very much to the point when he comments on the typical pragmatist tendency to confuse the scientific conception of 'working hypotheses' with the idea that truth is *itself* just a working hypothesis, or, worse still, something to be judged by the pragmatist criterion of 'what works' (or fails to work) as judged by our resultant belief-state or degree of psychological well-being. Thus:

> [w]hen *science* says that a hypothesis works, it means that from this hypothesis we can deduce a number of propositions which are verifiable, i.e. obvious under suitable circumstances, and that we cannot deduce any propositions of which the contraries are verifiable. But when *pragmatism* says that a hypothesis works, it means that the effects of believing it are good, including among the effects not only the beliefs which we deduce from it, but also the emotions entailed by it, or its perceived consequences, and the actions to which we are prompted by it or its perceived consequences. This is a totally different conception of 'working', and one for which the authority of scientific procedure cannot be invoked.[57]

Russell's argument here – and his general case against the Jamesian theory of truth – will scarcely disturb neopragmatists like Richard Rorty who can see no use for such theories except (maybe) deflationist accounts on which 'truth' comes out as at most an honorific term, one that we deploy by way of 'paying compliments' to just those beliefs that we find acceptable or desirable.[58] Nor indeed would Rorty be much impressed by Russell's talk of the 'authority of scientific procedure' since in his (Rorty's) view the truth-claims of physical science are in no sense epistemically privileged but should rather be treated wholly on a par with those of other language-games such as sociology, cultural theory, fiction, or literary criticism. Still it is an argument that might give pause to those philosophers who would certainly dissociate themselves from anything like the Jamesian – let alone the Rortian – pragmatist position but who nonetheless adopt a criterial view of the truth-conditions which properly apply to this or that area of discourse. For the result of such thinking, as I have said, is to bring them out willy-nilly in accord with those aspects of Wittgenstein's later philosophy that have since given rise to some fargone, for example, Kripkean forms of sceptical doubt as concerns the objectivity of truth in mathematics and the physical sciences.

Response-dependence theory seeks to hold the line against scepticism by specifying just which areas of discourse may plausibly be held to sustain truth-conditions independent of human perceptual or conceptual grasp and just which areas – like the paradigm case of Lockean 'secondary qualities' – require due allowance for the normative appeal to such epistemic considerations.[59] Yet by adopting this criterial approach – one that makes truth *ultimately* a matter of evidential, epistemic, or assertoric warrant – the RD theorists are ineluctably drawn toward a generalised anti-realist position that blurs rather than holds the line between those areas of discourse. Here it is worth recalling Dummett's formulation of the issue on which the parties typically divide, namely that concerning statements of the 'disputed class' or hypotheses, theorems, conjectures and so forth that are well-formed and meaningful yet which cannot be proved or verified by any method at our disposal. For the realist, statements of the 'disputed class' possess an objective truth-value, quite apart from any question concerning our capacity to find it out. That is to say, they are true or false as a matter of objective (recognition-transcendent) fact, and whatever our present or even best-attainable state of knowledge concerning them.[60] Such would be the case not only with mathematical statements – like 'Goldbach's Conjecture is true' – but also with a vast (indeed innumerable) range of other statements in the physical and at least some branches of the human sciences. For the Dummettian anti-realist, conversely, such statements are intelligible only with reference to the kinds of evidential warrant that would standardly count as manifesting a grasp of the criteria for other (i.e., verifiable or non-disputed) statements. Wright takes a similar view of what is required in order for the realist case to go through: namely, some account of 'a practical ability which stands to understanding an evidence-transcendent truth condition as recognitional skills stand to decidable truth conditions'.[61] However this requirement clearly cannot be met if one adopts a criterial account of those conditions such as that proposed by Wright or if one takes it that truth is epistemically constrained, that is to say, subject to specification in terms of some (however optimised) range of knowledge-constitutive capacities. And from here it is but a short step to Dummett's stronger version of the case, one that would in principle extend to *all* statements whose meaning is taken to be given by their truth-conditions and whose truth-conditions are specified in turn by their method of proof or verification. Since this is the only criterion that counts – on Dummett's verificationist approach – it must therefore be construed as applying to every statement whatsoever, including those outside the 'disputed class' or those for which we can claim to possess sufficient evidence or an adequate proof-procedure. In which case truth can amount to no more than warranted assertibility as defined by the scope and limits of attainable knowledge.

V

Hence all the efforts of RD theorists to come up with a suitably provisoed account that avoids this strong anti-realist upshot while stopping short of a full-scale objectivist approach, one which would treat (say) the statement '68 + 57 = 125' as holding good *despite or whatever* the deliverance of best opinion among those presumptively best qualified to judge. Such is the proposal by Divers and Miller for a 'Humanised Platonist' approach that aims to conserve what is intuitively valid in the realist position – the impossibility of thinking such statements to depend entirely on best opinion for their truth-value – yet which also allows that optimised response must play some constitutive role in fixing the criteria for arithmetical truth or falsehood. Thus it is, they suggest,

> all but impossible to see how a judge could have enough in the way of conceptual competence and resources properly to identify the object of thought while also being equipped in such a way as to have the numerical properties of numbers appear to her in a systematically misleading way.[62]

However this argument is open to the charge that it either reduces to manifest circularity (by defining 'conceptual competence' in terms that simply equate best judgement with truth) or else – through the '*all but* impossible' clause – concedes that best opinion may *just possibly* diverge from truth, in which case truth must always be conceived as in principle recognition- and verification-transcendent. No doubt it is perfectly correct to claim that anyone who is well enough versed in arithmetic 'properly to identify the object of thought' – numbers and their various relationships, products, combinatorial properties, etc. – will *ipso facto* not be subject to the kind of 'systematically misleading' conception that might lead her to affirm the falsity of '68 + 57 = 125' or the truth of '68 + 57 = 29'. Thus the RD theorist is right to take issue with the Kripkean 'sceptical solution' to Wittgenstein's sceptical paradox, or the claim that any truth-value assigned to statements like these can only be a matter of communal warrant or accordance with some given arithmetical 'practice' which happens to enjoy such warrant. However his preferred alternative solution is one that can be seen to vacillate between a self-confirming *a priori* truth about the standards of correctness in judgement and a criterial approach that makes judgement (or epistemic warrant) the final arbiter of truth. On the former construal of 'Humanised Platonism' the adjective becomes pretty much redundant and the theorist might just as well be taken to endorse a Platonist, i.e., a realist and objectivist approach *sans phrase*. On the latter construal judgement – or 'conceptual competence' – regains its RD-specifiable role in matters of arithmetic truth but only at the cost of giving up any claim to deliver a solution that would adequately meet the realist challenge.

At this point the RD approach lays itself open to the standard Kripkensteinian line of attack that exploits the supposed dependence of truth on best opinion in order to insert its sceptical wedge. That is to say, it puts the case that truth (or correctness) can never be more than the upshot of certain rule-following procedures whose sole basis is the fact of their acceptance by the relevant – even if community-wide – consensus of qualified judgement. Of course the response-dependence theorist may seek to counter this sceptical move by reiterating one or other of the arguments canvassed above. Thus he can hold (1) that best opinion must by very definition be truth-tracking since it would otherwise simply not *count* as 'best opinion' but rather as an error-prone exercise of judgement that might always conceivably miss the mark. Or again, he can argue (2) that best opinion is by very definition *constitutive* of truth in the sense that we just can't conceive of truths which in principle transcend our utmost powers of epistemic or assertoric warrant. However, as I have said, version (1) comes down to a tautologous or trivially circular re-statement of the RD thesis, while version (2) effectively gives up the claim to establish some realist-compatible (Kripke-proof) conception of arithmetical truth. Hence the conflicting intuitions that surface in Wright's attempt to explain just what it is about the truths of arithmetic that seems to place them beyond the scope of a Dummett-type verificationist approach while nonetheless accepting what he takes to be the strength of Dummett's case against any realist argument that would acknowledge their objective or recognition-transcendent character.

This dilemma has been at the heart of epistemological enquiry ever since Kant first announced his 'Copernican revolution' in philosophy, one that aimed to assuage sceptical doubts by locating the grounds of veridical knowledge in human epistemic powers and capacities rather than in some unknowable realm of noumenal 'things-in-themselves'.[63] It is the same dilemma that arises when commentators strive to reconcile the claims of Kant's 'Transcendental Analytic' in the First *Critique* with the claims put forward in the 'Transcendental Aesthetic'. That is, it conspicuously fails to close the gap between a formal account of the truth-conditions that necessarily apply to all valid statements when considered from a purely analytic (definitional) standpoint and those which, according to Kant, have to do with our capacity for acquiring synthetic *a priori* knowledge through an exercise of judgement in its jointly 'receptive' and 'spontaneous' roles.[64] From the logical empiricists, via Quine and Davidson, to McDowell and the advocates of a response-dependence approach this problem has figured, explicitly or not, as a major source of unresolved tensions and conflicts.[65] Perhaps the most important (albeit negative) consequence of RD debate will be to have shown that realism with respect to any given area of discourse – such as mathematics or the physical sciences – requires an unqualified commitment to the existence of objective truth-values that cannot be sustained on any epistemic or response-dependent approach. Hence the anxiety of theorists like Wright and Miller with regard to Kripkean scepticism and the prospect that even the truths of elementary arithmetic might prove open to doubt – or capable only of a Kripkensteinian 'sceptical solution' – if that approach is pushed through to its logical endpoint.

What thus emerges most clearly from this failed attempt to hold the line against epistemological scepticism is the need to acknowledge that certain statements have truth-conditions that intrinsically transcend our present best or even our future best-possible scope of epistemic or assertoric warrant. Among them are statements concerning the truth of well-formed but unproven arithmetical conjectures, statements with respect to remote (epistemically inaccessible) regions of the universe, and statements involving the existence (or otherwise) of certain as-yet undetected microphysical entities with specified attributes of mass, charge, interaction with other particles, and so forth. They would also include a great many other candidates for Dummett's 'disputed class', such as statements that advance some definite claim with regard to historical events (like 'Neville Chamberlain twice fumbled for his handkerchief during the flight back from his final meeting with Hitler') but for which we lack – and will more than likely continue to lack – decisive evidence either way. However the most telling instances are those of mathematics and the physical sciences where this issue is posed with particular sharpness since any concession to an epistemic or non-objectivist approach must be taken as yielding crucial argumentative ground. Thus the statement 'Fermat's Last Theorem is true' was itself a true statement throughout the four centuries when mathematicians were still seeking an adequate proof, just as Newton's inverse-square law of gravitational attraction or the statement 'the charge on every electron is negative' had their truth-value fixed by the way things stood in physical reality long before they achieved articulate expression, let alone an adequate degree of scientific warrant.

That so many philosophers incline to take a different (sceptical, anti-realist, or verificationist) view is all the more curious given that progress in the natural sciences has most often come about through a willingness to break with just this kind of restrictive (ultimately anthropocentric) thinking. At any rate there seems little prospect that the issue might be resolved by adopting some RD-specified version of the Kantian idea that truth must conform to the structures and modalities of human knowledge rather than obtaining – as the realist would have it – quite apart from such (however optimised) epistemic criteria. Insofar as response-dependence theory rejects this conclusion or hedges it around with doubts and provisos there will always be room for the standard range of sceptical counter-arguments.

References

1. See especially Michael Dummett, *Truth and Other Enigmas* (London: Duckworth, 1978) and *The Logical Basis of Metaphysics* (Duckworth, 1991); Michael Luntley, *Language, Logic and Experience: the case for anti-realism* (Duckworth, 1988); N. Tennant, *Anti-Realism and Logic* (Oxford: Clarendon Press, 1987); Timothy Williamson, 'Knowability and Constructivism: the logic of anti-realism', *Philosophical Quarterly*, Vol. 38 (1988), pp. 122 32; Kenneth P. Winkler, 'Scepticism and Anti Realism', *Mind*, Vol. 94 (1985), pp. 46–52; and Crispin Wright, *Realism, Meaning and Truth*, 2nd edn (Oxford: Blackwell, 1993).
2. See for instance William P. Alston, *A Realist Theory of Truth* (Ithaca, NY: Cornell University Press, 1996) and Michael Devitt, *Realism and Truth*, 2nd edn. (Princeton, NJ: Princeton University Press, 1991).
3. Crispin Wright, 'Misconstruals Made Manifest', *Midwest Studies in Philosophy*, Vol. 14 (1989), pp. 18 67; p. 54.
4. Ibid., p. 54.
5. Wright, *Truth and Objectivity* (Cambridge, MA: Harvard University Press, 1992).
6. Wright, *Realism, Meaning and Truth*, p. 23 (Note 1, above).
7. Devitt, *Realism and Truth* (Note 2, above).
8. Wright, 'Misconstruals Made Manifest', pp. 54–5 (Note 3, above).

9. See especially Richard Boyd, 'The Current Status of Scientific Realism', in Jarrett Leplin (ed.), *Scientific Realism* (Berkeley & Los Angeles: University of California Press, 1984), pp. 41–82; also J. L. Aronson, 'Testing for Convergent Realism', *British Journal for the Philosophy of Science*, Vol. 40 (1989), pp. 255–60; J. L. Aronson, R. Harré and E. Way, *Realism Rescued: how scientific progress is possible* (London: Duckworth, 1994); Gilbert Harman, 'Inference to the Best Explanation', *Philosophical Review*, Vol. 74 (1965), pp. 88–95; Peter Lipton, *Inference to the Best Explanation* (London: Routledge, 1993); Ilkka Niiniluoto, *Critical Scientific Realism* (Oxford: Oxford University Press, 1999); Stathis Psillos, *Scientific Realism: how science tracks truth* (London: Routledge, 1999).
10. See Nicholas Rescher, *Scientific Realism: a critical reappraisal* (Dordrecht: D. Reidel, 1987).
11. Wright, *Truth and Objectivity*, pp. 48 and 103 (Note 5, above).
12. Ludwig Wittgenstein, *Philosophical Investigations*, trans. G. E. M. Anscombe (Oxford: Blackwell, 1953), Sects 201–92 *passim*; also Saul Kripke, *Wittgenstein on Rules and Private Language* (Blackwell, 1982); Paul Boghossian, 'The Rule-Following Considerations', *Mind*, Vol. 98 (1989), pp. 507–49; Bob Hale, 'Rule-Following, Objectivity, and Meaning', in Hale and Crispin Wright (eds), *A Companion to the Philosophy of Language* (Blackwell, 1997), pp. 369–96; and John McDowell, 'Wittgenstein on Following a Rule', *Synthèse*, Vol. 58 (1984), pp. 325–63.
13. Wright, *Truth and Objectivity*, p. 228 (Note 5, above).
14. Kripke, *Wittgenstein on Rules and Private Language* (Note 12, above).
15. Wittgenstein, *Philosophical Investigations* (Note 12, above), especially Sects 269–94 *passim*.
16. See Wright, *Truth and Objectivity*, p. 230 (Note 5, above) and Stanley Cavell, *Must We Mean What We Say?* (New York: Oxford University Press, 1969), p. 94.
17. Wright, 'Truth: a traditional debate reviewed', in Simon Blackburn and Keith Simmons (eds), *Truth* (Oxford: Oxford University Press, 1999), pp. 203–38; p. 226.
18. Ibid., p. 227.
19. Ibid., p. 225.
20. Scott Soames, *Understanding Truth* (Oxford: Oxford University Press, 1999), p. 19.
21. Kurt Gödel, 'On Formally Undecidable Propositions of *Principia Mathematica* and Related Systems', trans. B. Meltzer (New York: Basic Books, 1962). See also Ernest Nagel and James Newtman, *Gödel's Theorem* (London: Routledge & Kegan Paul, 1971) and S. G. Shanker (ed.), *Gödel's Theorem in Focus* (London: Routledge, 1987).
22. Wright, 'Truth: a traditional debate reviewed', p. 225 (Note 17, above).
23. See Wright, 'Moral Values, Projection, and Secondary Qualities', *Proceedings of the Aristotelian Society*, Supplementary Vol. 62 (1988), pp. 1–26, 'Realism, Antirealism, Irrealism, Quasi-Realism', *Midwest Studies in Philosophy*, Vol. 12 (1988), pp. 25–49, 'Euthyphronism and the Physicality of Colour', *European Review of Philosophy*, Vol. 3 (1998), pp. 15–30, and *Truth and Objectivity* (Note 5, above). For further discussion of response-dependence in various contexts of debate, see Jim Edwards, 'Best Opinion

and Intentional States', *Philosophical Quarterly*, Vol. 42 (1992), pp. 21–42; Bob Hale, 'Realism and its Oppositions', in Hale and Wright (eds), *The Blackwell Companion to the Philosophy of Language* (Oxford: Blackwell, 1997), pp. 271–308; Richard Holton, 'Reponse-Dependence and Infallibility', *Analysis*, Vol. 52 (1992), pp. 180–84; Mark Johnston, 'Dispositional Theories of Value', *Proceedings of the Aristotelian Society*, Vol. 63 (1989), pp. 139–74, 'How to Speak of the Colours', *Philosophical Studies*, Vol. 68 (1992), pp. 221–63, and 'Objectivity Refigured: pragmatism without verificationism', in J. Haldane and C. Wright (eds), *Realism, Representation and Projection* (Oxford: Oxford University Press, 1993), pp. 85–130; Philip Pettit, 'Realism and Response-Dependence', *Mind*, Vol. 100 (1991), pp. 597–626, *The Common Mind: an essay on psychology, society, and politics* (Oxford: Oxford University Press, 1992), 'Are Manifest Qualities Response-Dependent?', *The Monist*, Vol. 81 (1998), pp. 3–43, and 'Noumenalism and Response-Dependence', *The Monist*, Vol. 81 (1998), pp. 112–32; Mark Powell, 'Realism or Response-Dependence?', *European Review of Philosophy*, Vol. 3 (1998), pp. 1–13; Peter Railton, 'Red, Bittter, Good', *European Review of Philosophy*, Vol. 3 (1998), pp. 67–84; Michael Smith and Daniel Stoljar, 'Global Response-Dependence and Noumenal Realism', *The Monist*, Vol. 81 (1998), pp. 85–111; and Ralph Wedgwood, 'The Essence of Response-Dependence', *European Review of Philosophy*, Vol. 3 (1998), pp. 31–54.

24. Wright, 'Truth: a traditional debate reviewed', pp. 228–9 (Note 17, above).
25. See Dummett, *Truth and Other Enigmas* (Note 1, above); also *Elements of Intuitionism* (Oxford: Oxford University Press, 1977).
26. Wright, 'Truth: a traditional debate reviewed', p. 228 (Note 17, above).
27. See entries under Notes 2 and 20, above.
28. For some interesting discussion of this topic, see Martin Gardner, *The Night is Large: collected essays 1938–1995* (Harmondsworth: Penguin, 1996), especially 'How Not to Talk About Mathematics', pp. 280–93.
29. See for instance Paul Benacerraf and Hilary Putnam (eds), *The Philosophy of Mathematics: selected essays*, 2nd edn (Cambridge: Cambridge University Press, 1983).
30. See Note 21, above.
31. Roger Penrose, *Shadows of the Mind: a search for the missing science of consciousness* (London: Vintage Books, 1995), pp. 64–5.
32. Ibid., p. 65.
33. Jerrold J. Katz, *Realistic Rationalism* (Cambridge, MA: MIT Press, 1998), pp. 36–7.
34. See Benacerraf, 'What Numbers Could Not Be', in Benacerraf and Putnam (eds), *The Philosophy of Mathematics*, pp. 272–94 (Note 29, above); also Hartry Field, *Realism, Mathematics and Modality* (Oxford: Blackwell, 1989); Bob Hale, *Abstract Objects* (Blackwell, 1987) and 'Is Platonism Epistemologically Bankrupt?', *Philosophical Review*, Vol. 103 (1994), pp. 299–325; Putnam, *Mathematics, Matter and Method* (Cambridge: Cambridge University Press, 1975); Soames, *Understanding Truth* (Note 20, above); and Wright, *Frege's Conception of Numbers as Objects* (Aberdeen: Aberdeen University Press, 1983).
35. Dummett, *The Logical Basis of Metaphysics*, p. 375 (Note 1, above).

36. Wittgenstein, *Philosophical Investigations* (Note 12, above); also *On Certainty*, ed. G. E. M. Anscombe and G. H. von Wright (Oxford: Blackwell, 1969) and *Lectures on the Foundations of Mathematics*, ed. Cora Diamond (Chicago: University of Chicago Press, 1976); Crispin Wright, *Wittgenstein on the Foundations of Mathematics* (Cambridge, MA: Harvard University Press, 1980).
37. See W. B. Ewald (ed.), *From Kant to Hilbert: a source book in the foundations of mathematics* (Oxford: Clarendon Press, 1996).
38. Penrose, *Shadows of the Mind*, p. 90 (Note 31, above).
39. Ibid., p. 72.
40. For detailed discussion of these set-theoretical paradoxes, see E. W. Beth, *The Foundations of Mathematics* (Amsterdam: North-Holland, 1966); also A. A. Fraenkel, Y. Bar-Hillel and A. Levy, *Foundations of Set Theory* (North-Holland, 1973).
41. Alfred Tarski, 'The Concept of Truth in Formalized Languages', in *Logic, Semantics and Metamathematics*, trans. J. H. Woodger (Oxford: Oxford University Press, 1956), pp. 152–278.
42. Johnston, 'Dispositional Theories of Value', p. 141 (Note 23, above).
43. Tarski, 'The Semantic Conception of Truth and the Foundations of Semantics', in Wright and Simmons (eds), *Truth*, pp. 115–43; p. 118 (Note 17, above).
44. See for instance – from a range of viewpoints – Donald Davidson, 'The Folly of Trying to Define Truth', in Blackburn and Simmons (eds), *Truth*, pp. 308–22 (Note 17, above); Dorothy Grover, *A Prosentential Theory of Truth* (Princeton, NJ: Princeton University Press, 1992); Anil Gupta, 'A Critique of Deflationism', in Blackburn and Simmons (eds), *Truth*, pp. 282–307 (note 17, above); Hartry Field, 'Deflationist Views of Meaning and Content', *Mind*, Vol. 103 (July 1994), pp. 249–84; Paul Horwich, *Truth* (Oxford: Blackwell, 1990) and 'The Minimalist Conception of Truth', in Blackburn and Simmons (eds), *Truth*, pp. 239–63 (Note 17, above); Richard L. Kirkham, *Theories of Truth* (Cambridge, MA: MIT Press, 1992); and Frank P. Ramsey, 'The Nature of Truth', *Episteme*, Vol. 16 (1991), pp. 6–16.
45. Tarski, 'The Semantic Conception of Truth', p. 121 (Note 43, above).
46. See Nancy Cartwright, Thomas Uebel, *et al.*, *Between Science and Politics: the philosophy of Otto Neurath* (Cambridge: Cambridge University Press, 1995).
47. Wright, 'Truth: a traditional debate reviewed', p. 205 (Note 17, above).
48. Ibid., p. 211.
49. Bertrand Russell, 'William James's Conception of Truth', in Blackburn and Simmons (eds), *Truth*, pp. 69–82 (Note 17, above) and William James, *Pragmatism: a new name for some old ways of thinking* (New York: Longmans, 1907). James's response to Russell may be found in his *The Meaning of Truth* (Longmans, 1909).
50. See for instance John Divers and Alexander Miller, 'Arithmetical Platonism: reliability and judgement-dependence', *Philosophical Studies*, Vol. 95 (1999), pp. 277–310 and Miller, 'Rule-Following, Response-Dependence, and McDowell's Debate with Anti-Realism', *European Review of Philosophy*, Vol. 3 (1998), pp. 175–97.
51. Russell, 'William James's Conception of Truth', p. 75 (Note 49, above).

52. Ibid., p. 75.
53. Ibid., pp. 75–6.
54. Ibid., p. 75.
55. See Russell, *The Problems of Philosophy* (London: Oxford University Press, 1912).
56. Russell, 'William James's Conception of Truth', p. 75 (Note 49, above).
57. Ibid., p. 81.
58. See for instance Richard Rorty, *Consequences of Pragmatism* (Brighton: Harvester, 1982) and *Objectivity, Relativism, and Truth* (Cambridge: Cambridge University Press, 1991).
59. See entries under Note 23, above.
60. Dummett, *Truth and Other Enigmas* (Note 1, above).
61. Wright, 'Misconstruals Made Manifest', p. 23 (Note 3, above).
62. Divers and Miller, 'Arithmetical Platonism: reliability and judgement-dependence', pp. 277–310; p. 293 (Note 50, above). See also Miller, 'Rule-Following, Response-Dependence, and McDowell's Debate with Anti-Realism' (Note 50, above).
63. Immanuel Kant, *Critique of Pure Reason*, trans. Norman Kemp Smith (London: Macmillan, 1964).
64. For a recent attempt to retrieve and vindicate this Kantian theory of judgement, see John McDowell, *Mind and World* (Cambridge, MA: Harvard University Press, 1994).
65. See also Christopher Norris, 'McDowell on Kant: redrawing the bounds of sense' and 'The Limits of Naturalism: further thoughts on McDowell's *Mind and World*', in *Minding the Gap: epistemology and philosophy of science in the two traditions* (Amherst, MA: University of Massachusetts Press, 2000), pp. 172–96 and 197–230.

Index of Names

Note: This is a 'names-only' index since the topics covered are all within a fairly circumscribed area of philosophical debate and the reader will most likely be quick to identify the various positions concerned. Thus – for instance – it would not have served any useful purpose to index 'anti-realism' for the sections discussing Michael Dummett's canonical statements in this regard, or to flag all references to the RD (response-dispositional/response-dependence) approach along with those various theorists who have offered some particular line of argument for or against that approach. I have therefore chosen to provide detailed annotation for each chapter rather than a topic-index that would offer less in the way of informative guidance. There is a name-entry for bibliographical (i.e., chapter endnote) references only where these indicate the first mention of a major source, where they amplify some pertinent point of discussion, or where they give details of work not discussed in the main text. The most compendious listing of RD-related books and articles may be found at pp. 93–4, Note 1.